PARENTS AND YOUNG MENTALLY HANDICAPPED CHILDREN:
A Review of Research Issues

PARENTS & YOUNG MENTALLY HANDICAPPED CHILDREN

A REVIEW OF RESEARCH ISSUES

HELEN McCONACHIE

CROOM HELM
London & Sydney

BROOKLINE BOOKS
Cambridge, Massachusetts

Croom Helm Ltd, Provident House, Burrell Row,
Beckenham, Kent, BR3 1AT

Croom Helm Australia Pty Ltd, Suite 4, 6th Floor,
64-76 Kippax Street, Surry Hills, NSW 2010, Australia

British Library Cataloguing in Publication Data

McConachie, Helen
Parents and young mentally handicapped
children: a review of research issues.
1. Mentally handicapped children —
Education 2. Parent and child
3. Education, Preschool
I. Title
371.92'8 LC4602.5
ISBN 0-7099-4608-2

Brookline Books, PO Box 1046,
Cambridge, MA 02238

Library of Congress Cataloging-in-Publication Data

McConachie, Helen.
Parents and young mentally handicapped children.

Bibliography: p.
Includes index.
1. Mentally handicapped children – Education – United States. 2. Mentally handicapped children – United States – Family relationships. 3. Special education literature. I. Title. [DNLM: 1. Education of Mentally Retarded. 2. Family. 3. Mental Retardation. WS107.5.R5 M478p]
LC4631.M33 1986 371.92'8 86-13383
ISBN 0-914797-28-X (Brookline Books)

Printed and bound in Great Britain by
Biddles Ltd, Guildford and King's Lynn

CONTENTS

For Ian

ACKNOWLEDGEMENTS

Peter Mittler, Professor of Special Education at Manchester University, read the versions of this book when it still formed part of a Ph.D. thesis. His advice and enthusiasm were invaluable to me.

Peggy Jones is much more than an extraordinarily skilled typist. Her commitment and personal friendship to me made the book possible.

The review of literature was undertaken while I was Research Fellow at the Hester Adrian Research Centre, Manchester University, and Senior Lecturer in Psychology in the Speech Pathology and Therapy Section, Manchester Polytechnic. To my colleagues in those departments who gave encouragement and help I offer my belated thanks.

Chapter One

INTRODUCTION

Background

Over the past fifteen years or so, increased awareness of the difficulties facing families of young mentally handicapped children has been coupled with the creation of more coherent services for families. The philosophy behind these service developments has reflected a trend toward 'normalisation', that is promoting conditions which will allow mentally handicapped people to live as ordinary a life as possible. It also implies a realisation of mentally handicapped people's capacity for developing skills, given appropriate conditions. The role of parents in fostering their children's early development has obviously been seen as of central importance.

One approach which has received considerable attention has been the involvement of parents in teaching their young mentally handicapped children. Its rapid development was boosted by the view that parents of handicapped children had been underestimated by professionals in the past, and that increased consideration should be given to practical rather than to therapy-oriented intervention (Wolfensberger, 1967). Published studies soon showed that parents could learn the principles and techniques of behaviour modification, and successfully change problem behaviour in their children and teach them new skills (e.g. as reviewed by Berkowitz and Graziano, 1972; Johnson and Katz, 1973; and O'Dell, 1974). More recent and more comprehensive programmes for young handicapped children have been constructed around the sequences of normal development (e.g. Bricker and Bricker, 1976; Shearer and Shearer, 1976). Renewed impetus came from the collective findings of early intervention programmes for handicapped and disadvantaged children in the USA (Bronfenbrenner, 1976; Lazar and Darlington, 1979). Parent involvement was found to be an essential catalyst for maintaining the effects of educational programmes; the setting of programme goals for or with parents was strongly related to positive outcomes for children even several years later.

Recent research in parent involvement has explored many different issues; for example, programme characteristics such as how much intervention is necessary (e.g. Heifetz, 1977a,b; Sandow and Clarke, 1978; Cheseldine and McConkey, 1979), the problems posed by children of differing levels of severity of handicap (e.g. Wishart, Bidder and Gray, 1980) and follow-up of the maintenance and generalization of learning (e.g. Baker, 1977; Gardner, 1983). Service philosophies are undergoing change in response to parents' demands, from 'parent training' to 'partnership' (Mittler and McConachie, 1983) and thus are being challenged to develop flexibility and responsiveness to individual differences amongst parents and families.

Scope of the book

The primary aim of the book is to draw together a coherent conceptual framework for the involvement of parents in teaching their young mentally handicapped children. The strategy adopted is to review and analyse available literature about the families of handicapped children, covering a wide sweep of issues and ideas. As described above, parental involvement in teaching has become an apparently successful and widely-supported intervention strategy in helping families. However, very many questions remain to be answered about its appropriate future development. Which parents respond most enthusiastically to involvement in teaching, and which do not? How does it affect other family members? Is there time in the day for teaching? Are parents not 'teachers' already? How may parents' feelings about their handicapped child be affected?

These questions touch on many aspects of family living with a handicapped child. The literature reviewed necessarily is drawn from a wide field, and thus the research and practice issues considered may inform the structuring of a variety of approaches to service provision for families of young mentally handicapped children, not solely parental involvement in teaching. However, the book is not intended to provide practical guidelines for services; it remains essentially a review of research literature.

The development of services for families generally proceeds in an erratic manner, tied as much to personalities, pressures and funding as to carefully thought-out principles. A review of research provides an opportunity for a long, balanced look at how services have developed, and what their fundamental aims are. There is available a large literature about mental handicap, but in many ways it has remained parcelled-up into separate topics, and research is too often not translated into practice. The book is an attempt to present issues and conclusions from research literature in a way which will readily suggest lessons for how professionals may understand families more fully and how they may proceed in helping families to bring up their mentally handicapped children.

The remainder of this chapter begins the task of outlining a conceptual framework for teaching interventions, and introduces some of the issues which will be developed further in later chapters.

An ecological framework

The rationale for involving parents in teaching their handicapped children has frequently hinged on practical factors: parents ask for advice on how best to help their child; early intervention is important and there are too few trained professionals to carry it out; mentally handicapped children need planned generalization of their learning; and so on (e.g. Yule, 1975). However, consideration of current theory and conclusions in child development research suggests that a strategy of working with parents (or parent-substitutes) is more than practical: it is fundamental.

Ecological principles are increasingly recognised as important in the framing and conducting of child development research, and of services to children (Bronfenbrenner, 1977). The development of individual children can only be understood in relation to the various environments in which they live, and to the complex and continuous interactions which occur between them and the environment. Parents too do not feel and act in a vacuum. They are affected on the one hand by the value systems of society as regards mental handicap, and on the other hand by their continuing changing interaction with their child.

Thus children's development and the environment are interdependent, and any study or intervention requires to take account of the different nested levels of environmental systems in which the child is a participant - parent-child interaction, the home, the extended family, the community, the culture of the child's society - as these change over time. Recognition of this complexity is essential in order to minimise the occurrence of unwanted and unforeseen effects of intervention (Willems, 1977). For example, a planned and (short-term) beneficial modification of a child's behaviour may have longer-term negative consequences for the parents such as a loss of confidence in their autonomous skills as parents, or may be short-lived because controlling contingencies within the sibling group (e.g. preferring to have a scapegoat) have not been taken into account. Recent research in child development provides several examples of studies undertaken within an ecological framework, including exploration of the reciprocal influence of infants and fathers (e.g. Lamb, 1981a; Beail and McGuire, 1982), research into three-way interaction systems such as child-father-mother, or child-mother-new baby, within a family context (e.g. Clarke-Stewart, 1978; Pedersen, Anderson and Cain, 1980; Dunn and Kendrick, 1982), and the introduction of the study of family structures, functions and processes into mental handicap research (e.g. Beckman, 1984; Blacher, 1984a; Turnbull and Winton, 1984).

The use of an ecological framework also requires making explicit the role of the observer or intervener. Not only is the observer part of the social system at the time of observation, but the full meaning of the events can be grasped only by pooling the knowledge, and acknowledging the value systems and perceptions, of all the participants. Thus, the ecological approach calls into question the tenets of 'value-free' 'objective' scientific method. One example is the choice of categories for observation or analysis which, it can be argued (e.g. Cooper, Costello, Douglas, Ingleby and Turner, 1974), are inevitably framed by the observer's assumptions. Some parent-child interaction researchers have attempted to tackle this problem by adopting the strategy of asking the parents themselves to describe the units of the interaction (Elkins, 1981). This issue will not be addressed further here but is mentioned because of its relevance in interpreting research conclusions, and in questioning the traditional role definitions of parent and professional. It implies the need to reframe intervention strategies on a basis of equal partnership.

The most salient figure in the child's immediate environment is likely to be a parent. Research into child development has now generally moved on from unidirectional models, such as studying the effect of the parent's attitudes and actions upon the child (e.g. Becker and Krug, 1965), to a recognition of the reciprocal nature of the interaction between parent and child, and the study of patterns of individual differences. Instead of considering quantity of parental attention, or of child utterances, strategies are being developed which take account of synchrony and responsiveness. Children are recognised as active participants in interaction. Further than this, 'development' itself is redefined, and is not seen simply as a maturational process. The interactive view of development stresses the growth of intentional activity, and the ability of children to reflect upon the adequacy and relevance of their own performance (Shotter, 1974). The recognition of the social context, and foundation, for development implies the importance of the role of parents who are able to reflect back to children the consequences of their actions and to structure the perceptual features of objects and events by communicating their significance (Mogford, 1973).

Early on, each parent and child will develop a consistent and individual style of interaction (e.g. Escalona, 1973). Babies bring to their earliest social interactions individual characteristics which will affect the behaviour of others towards them (Schaffer, 1977a; Thomas and Chess, 1977). Equally, parents (or rather, mothers, who have almost exclusively been the focus of such research) evidence an individual blend of differing styles at different periods in the child's infancy. At times, they will maintain interaction through carefully phasing their activity to the baby's, at times facilitating the child's activity through helping when necessary, at times initiating a new activity by redirecting the child's attention, and at times controlling the child by specific demands attuned to the child's interest and level of comprehension (Schaffer, 1977b).

As well as charting differences in interaction style, research has inevitably also concerned itself with elucidating potential problems in interaction. For example, there are indications that a substantial proportion of young working-class mothers suffer from depression and that this depression is associated with emotional and learning problems in their children (e.g. Richman, 1974; Pound, Cox, Puckering and Mills, 1985). In a recent study comparing depressed mothers of two year olds with a control group, the two groups did not differ on a variety of indices, for example, in the amount of warmth or negative comments mothers expressed nor in the amount of time they were fully involved with the child. However, depressed mothers generally spent more time unoccupied, more time in physically active play with their children, made fewer suggestions of activities to the child, and the children were less likely to respond to mothers' 'link' statements, i.e. verbal or non-verbal additions to the interaction which are clearly linked to the content of the child's activity (Puckering and Mills, 1982; Mills, Puckering, Pound and Cox, 1985). The researchers focus on the subtle differences in quality of 'meshing' of interaction which distinguish the depressed from the control mothers. Smooth meshing seems essentially to be a matter of anticipation by each partner to the interaction, and each being able to predict the perspective and behaviour of the other. Reduced interactive responsiveness may deprive children of opportunities for practice of focussed attention and concept formation, and increase their experience of conflict.

Research in the USA in particular has been aimed at defining which parental strategies have maximal potential for enhancing children's cognitive and emotional development (e.g. Clarke-Stewart's (1977) summary of research and propositions of policy for the Carnegie Council on Children). The theory that differences in child attainments were linked to early comparative deprivation had previously led to the setting up of the enormous Head Start programme. It must be noted, however, that the translation of research findings into policy recommendations is often of dubious validity (Lamb, 1980). For example, much of the research is correlational, and begs the question of direction of effects; 'responsive' parents may become so because of particular child characteristics. To extract from the research a recommendation that all parents should adopt particular 'beneficial' parenting styles not only violates the research intention, but may ignore many factors such as the cultural relativity of definitions of child competence (e.g. Gray and Wandersman, 1980; Ogbu, 1981), and thus of 'parental competence' (Belsky, Robins and Gamble, 1984) (see Chapter 2).

Research into the effects of parental handling strategies and children's cognitive development at first emphasised relationships with various demographic variables. But more recently, higher predictive accuracy has been found in finer-grained analyses of interaction variables. For example, children's cognitive development has repeatedly been shown to be positively related to parents' provision of play materials, warmth and non-restrictiveness, responsiveness to child initiations, and language stimulation (Clarke-Stewart, VanderStoep and Killian, 1979). Rutter's (1985) summary emphasises in addition the importance of avoiding noise-confusion (i.e. a background of high intensity sound which is not discriminable nor meaningful to the child), and also "teaching of specific skills and opportunities for the child to explore and to try out new skills and activities" (p.686). White and Watts (1973) have noted that the amount of time mothers spend in directly instructing their children is surprisingly small. Instead, the mothers they define as 'effective' tend to employ various 'low-keyed facilitative techniques'. "They get an enormous amount (in terms of frequency) of teaching in 'on the fly', and usually at the child's instigation." (p.243)

Thus, whether research is primarily descriptive, or on the other hand, influenced by deprivation theory and thus looking to define 'good' patterns of parental handling, a key factor to emerge is interactive responsiveness, both of the parent and of the child. In many ways, the parent's responses to the child will be unselfconscious and unplanned - however, recently research has also considered the mediating role of the parent's perceptions of the child and of their joint activity (e.g. Parke, 1978; McGillicuddy-DeLisi, 1982; Olson, Bates and Bayles, 1982). Parents' perceptions can also be seen as part of the ecological framework surrounding the child.

Parents and handicapped children

When the child has been identified as 'handicapped', differences might be expected in interaction with parents from the patterns which are observed between parents and non-handicapped children. For example, the child may be less predictably responsive, and parents' perceptions of the child's behaviour may be affected by their assumptions about the child's capacities, or by loss of confidence in their ability to handle a child who is 'different'. The child may also be directly hindered in experience and learning about the world by impaired sensory channels or limited motor action.

Recent research into the interaction between parents and handicapped children does suggest differences in pattern from comparable groups of parents and non-handicapped children. For example, Berger and Cunningham (1983) observed mothers and children from one to six months of age and found less successful mutual adaptation of responses between mothers and their Down's syndrome children. Jones (1977) studied slightly older children and found fewer initiations by Down's syndrome children, less feedback by the mothers and less successful turn-taking than in a control group matched on developmental age. However, some comparable studies have found greater group similarity in interaction (e.g. Buckhalt, Rutherford and Goldberg, 1978; Vietze, Abernathy, Ashe and Faulstitch, 1978).

Observed differences seem to be mainly of two kinds - the number and clarity of cues given by the child, and the success of meshing of the interaction. These suggest a need for early intervention, in order to encourage maximally rewarding patterns of interaction for both partners. The role of a parent in making clear to the child boundaries and associations of objects and events is likely to be even more essential for a mentally handicapped child. Research evidence as to the nature of the cognitive deficits implicated in mental handicap has been summarised by O'Connor and Hermelin (1974) as "a failure of categorizing or coding following immediate perception or short term storage" (p. 224). The parent thus may need to structure more clearly or more repetitively his or her responses to the child's cues, and also to work harder in the first place to elicit behaviour from the handicapped child (Walker, 1982).

Parents as teachers

In a sense, when professionals seek to involve parents in teaching their mentally handicapped children, they have missed a basic point - the parents are already teachers. The interactive view of cognitive and emotional development overtakes cost-effectiveness arguments for working through parents, and underlines its psychological necessity, i.e. that parents are the most salient 'others' in the child's world (Mogford, 1976). Also the parent is likely to know the child best, and to be aware of the subtlety of the cues from the child. For example, it is very often the parents who notice first that 'something is wrong' with the child, and who wait for months before their observations are validated by professional opinion.

However, given the evidence referred to above of less successful mutual adaptation in parent-handicapped child interaction, it seems vital that any intervention be shown to enhance rather than to distort further the child's experience. There is little discussion of possible ill-effects of intervention - indeed it seems more often to have been assumed that parent involvement projects can at the least not do any harm to children or to parents. Yet an early study of intervention with disadvantaged children found that children who took part in preschool provision in fact gained more than children who received not only the preschool provision but whose mothers also attended group meetings and had home visits from staff (Karnes, Hodgins and Teska, 1969). The authors interpreted the findings in terms of disruption of the mother-child relationship through unintentionally devaluing the existing mother-child interaction. Mogford (1979a) has shown that clashes in turn-taking in interaction occur particularly when mothers of handicapped children attempt to initiate activity directed toward chosen therapeutic goals. And many instances can be found of parents reporting feeling under too-great pressure from an intervention programme (e.g. Gregory, 1976; Buckley, 1981; Turnbull and Turnbull, 1982).

An emphasis on enhancing the structure of the child's experience through increased responsiveness of the parent would seem to require to take account of the dyad's well-established style of interaction. For example, Beveridge (1982) has explored individual differences in parent interaction style along a dimension of directiveness, and has found evidence of greater effectiveness of intervention when it is individually tailored to parents. To take account of individual differences would also call into question the relevance of 'packaged' approaches to working with parents. On the one hand, handicapped children tend to have uneven profiles of development, so that their strengths and weaknesses will have to be planned for individually. The 'normal' sequence of development may not always be the appropriate strategy to follow. In addition, each parent is also an individual. For example, some families may be under too great an economic or emotional strain to sustain consistent teaching. Working with parents must thus also imply recognising parents as partners in the enterprise, respecting their individual values and strengths on a par with professionals', and mutually admitting weaknesses.

Structure of the book

Within the conceptual structure outlined above, a number of areas of enquiry seem likely to be of relevance in informing the development of appropriate, flexible intervention with parents and young mentally handicapped children.

In Chapter 2, the research evidence concerning the family life of mentally handicapped children will be reviewed. The development of a coherent, conceptual framework is taken further in Chapter 3, through analysis of the limitations of past research on families. The second main theme of the review, parents' reactions to a handicapped child, is explored in Chapters 4 and 5, with the latter chapter concentrating on the methods by which attitudes and feelings may be measured. In Chapter 6, the topic of 'stress' is analysed, as it has been applied in research on families of mentally handicapped children.

The third major theme of the review is the study of interaction between parents and children. How interaction contributes to development is explored in Chapter 7. As differences in parental characteristics are of major interest in the review, comparison of mothers and fathers in interaction with their (non-handicapped) children is made in Chapter 8, and this topic is carried over also into Chapter 9, where research on parents' interaction with handicapped children is reviewed. Finally, the rapidly-increasing literature on parents as teachers of their young handicapped children is reviewed in Chapters 10 and 11, the latter concentrating on the interaction between different characteristics of programme design and differing characteristics of parents.

Thus, the research reviewed touches on a number of different levels of the ecological framework within which it is argued that intervention must be conceived. The review of literature provides background and analysis for a conceptual framework for future intervention and research, and its implications are drawn out and speculated upon in the final chapter.

Chapter Two

FAMILY LIFE OF HANDICAPPED CHILDREN

INTRODUCTION

The underlying theme of the introductory chapter, and of this book is the potentially beneficial outcome for a mentally handicapped child of parental involvement in teaching. Until recently there seems to have been a division of concern in the literature between research focussing on the development of the handicapped child, and research looking at families (for example, at the difficulties of everyday living, stress reactions, parents' attitudes). Yet part of the initial impetus for the development of practically-based services involving parents was to relieve some of the burden of care upon families, by providing accurate information about normal and abnormal child development, and passing on effective teaching strategies to help make the child easier to manage. The ultimate goal was to enable families, through these and other services such as earlier school placement, respite care, toy libraries, etc., to continue to care for the mentally handicapped child in the community, a principle enshrined in the 1971 Government White Paper 'Better Services for the Mentally Handicapped'.

Some researchers have shown awareness of this interrelationship of themes, by suggesting that adequate evaluation of early intervention with handicapped children requires broader outcome measures (Stedman, Anastasiow, Dokecki, Gordon and Parker, 1972; Burden, 1978) including

> "...things such as increased family comfort and decrease in divorce rate, a lower incidence of behavior problems in the siblings, increased opportunities for self-expression by mothers, among others. These, perhaps, are pretty soft

> signs, but they may be a lot more important as measures of the effectiveness of intervention than is a rise in IQ or increased motor capacity on the part of the child." (Brazelton, 1976, p.329)

Current developments in service philosophy go further and suggest that maximum benefit for the child will be achieved only when the family's home situation and system of values are fully incorporated into the initial stages of decision-making about the nature and timing of intervention.

> "Partnership can take many forms but it must be on a basis of equality, in which each side has areas of knowledge and skill that it contributes to the joint task of working with the child.... Partnership calls for an exploration of the needs of the families, of their perceptions of the child's abilities to respond, of their feelings about their own competence and their own emotional and social resources as a family." (Mittler, 1978, p.247)

The first half of this literature review will examine two aspects of the child's ecology: firstly, what is known about daily living with a handicapped child, and secondly, attitudes and reactions of family members to the handicapped child. Privations both practical and emotional may be expected to result from the child's handicap, and seem key areas to consider in the design and evaluation of service intervention.

PRACTICAL PROBLEMS

Caring for a mentally handicapped child poses many practical problems, and exacerbates others not directly caused by the child. These include financial strains, housing problems, prolonged dependency in basic care, continuous attention and supervision, travel problems, etc. These will be reviewed briefly, as a background to succeeding discussion of models of family roles and interaction.

Finance

Mentally handicapped children may directly impose

extra financial burdens upon families in various ways: incontinence leading to laundry expenses, replacement bedding, extra nappies or pads; replacements for destroyed clothes, from frequent washing or prolonged crawling; extra heating; special foods; extra toys and games; travelling to clinics. Such expenses continue to be catalogued in surveys of families' needs, despite improved services (in Britain) such as the Attendance Allowance, Health Service provision of disposable nappies, and grants from the Family Fund for items such as a car, a washing machine or a tumble dryer (e.g. compare Tizard and Grad, 1961, and Glendinning, 1983). Financial difficulties contribute to stress on parents. Chetwynd (1985) showed that large heating bills were highly predictive of stress in mothers of mentally handicapped children. Lonsdale (1978) interviewed 60 families of developmentally delayed children and found that 1 in 6 reported having a hard struggle financially. Of those who described their situation as adequate, some commented that it would not be so without state financial help. However, lack of control groups in such survey research means that the greater financial burdens on families are in fact asserted rather than thoroughly demonstrated. As severely mentally handicapped children are distributed across all social classes, lower income in comparison with the general population is not an explanation of the families' financial burdens.

<u>Housing</u>

Poor housing has frequently been cited as a major problem for families with severely handicapped children, e.g. overcrowding, damp (for children prone to chest infections), stairs (for children who cannot walk), shared or outside toilets (for children who are not toilet trained) (e.g. Tizard and Grad, 1961; Carnegie United Kingdom Trust, 1964; McMichael, 1971; Butler, Gill, Pomeroy and Fewtrell, 1978). The extent of housing problems varies with the part of the country surveyed, and has improved markedly over time. But Wilkin (1979) still found that ten per cent of families he interviewed, with a severely mentally handicapped child living at home, had no inside toilet (in Greater Manchester in 1975). A national study, following up children identified as having health problems or disability in the 1970 birth cohort of 14,000 children (Osborn, Butler and Morris, 1984), was less gloomy about the picture in 1980-81. All except one family had a bath and inside toilet. However, they were more crowded than control families and less likely to have central heating (Cooke and Lawton, 1985). Even where the house seems convenient for the family's needs, lack of a good garden fence, for example, may create problems in supervision of the child. Housing problems have been shown to be associated with families' applications for admission to long-term care of their mentally handicapped child (Tizard and Grad, 1961; Jaehnig, 1974). Poor housing has direct effects in increasing the difficulties inherent in child-rearing; it also has indirect results in terms of child behaviour problems and of maternal ill-health (Carnegie United Kingdom Trust, 1964; Richman, 1974).

Child care

Mentally handicapped children often make heavy demands on the family's time and energy through needing supervision to keep them out of danger, and stimulation where they have limited ability to occupy themselves. In one study of six to 14 years old severely handicapped children, mothers recorded an average of over seven hours spent every day on care, supervision, occupation and training of children (Dupont, 1980). Many children also need increased attention at night (Holt, 1958; Wishart et al., 1980; Gallagher, 1982; Glendinning, 1983; Dixon and Flanagan, 1984; Wastberg, 1985), beyond the age where it would be expected for a non-handicapped child. Glendinning (1983) concludes that:

> "In contrast to the rearing of most children, a disabled child's prolonged dependency gives rise to an essentially repetitive set of servicing functions, which can be physically taxing, mentally exhausting, and dispiritingly monotonous." (p.41)

Thus, for some parents at least, the child's handicap takes away from child-care much of the enjoyment of change and progress toward independence.

In the daily routine, the essential tasks of housework are added to physical care and supervision of the child. However, this point has frequently been overlooked in surveys of the care of children in the family, despite the fact that the children may, for example, produce greatly increased laundry demands through incontinence (Wilkin, 1979; Dupont, 1980; Ayer and Alaszewski, 1984).

Fathers

Given the increased workload outlined above, one might expect fathers to be more involved than usual. Over 50 per cent of fathers of young Down's syndrome children (Carr, 1975), hearing-impaired children (Gregory, 1976) and physically handicapped children (Hewett, 1970) have been reported to have a 'high' level of participation in child-care. However this is very similar to levels for fathers of non-handicapped four year olds (using the same interview technique, Newson and Newson, 1968). Markova, Macdonald and Forbes (1980) did suggest that their small sample of fathers of haemophiliac children participated more than control fathers.

The level of fathers' participation has been linked to a number of additional variables. For example, Hewett (1972) and Jaehnig (1974) found that fathers of handicapped children admitted to care were significantly more likely to be described as non-participant in child-care and housework than fathers of children at home. Wilkin (1979) did not find such a difference. There are also conflicting suggestions as to whether the level of fathers' participation is related to the degree of the child's handicap or 'difficultness': Carr (1975) found no relationship, Markova et al. (1980) found fathers participated less the more severe the haemophilia, and Wilkin (1979) and Ayer and Alaszewski (1984) found fathers of profoundly mentally and physically handicapped children participated more in physical child-care. All three findings seem plausible - Down's syndrome children when young are often slow in their development but not qualitatively different from the usual pattern; if specialist nursing is required, then fathers may tend to be excluded; but a child's needing to be lifted and carried might necessitate father's participation. As with many studies of the families of non-handicapped children (e.g. Newson and Newson, 1968; Oakley, 1974), middle-class fathers of handicapped children are generally found to participate more highly in child-care and in housework than working-class fathers, but Cooke and Lawton (1984) found the opposite pattern. The factor of social class may have little predictive power for individuals; studies of the general population have noted how some working-class patterns (e.g. mother working, or father unemployed) may increase paternal participation (Maxwell-West and Konner, 1976), and some middle-class patterns (e.g. managerial and traditional professional occupations) may necessitate concentration on career and curtailment of time and energy for home life (Barnett and Baruch, 1978; Elliot, 1978).

An immediate problem in evaluating such descriptions of involvement in child-care lies in how to interpret the level of participation described as 'high'. Firstly, as the surveys described above usually rely on mothers' reports, 'mothers' participation' is taken for granted, and 'fathers' participation' is assessed through answers to imprecise questions about how much the father would do of various child-care tasks. Secondly, levels of 'high', 'medium' and 'low' participation have generally been related just to the population interviewed, and therefore are difficult to interpret. Recent general population studies, which have asked more carefully what actually happens, have concluded that father participation is generally low. For example, Oakley (1974) found only 15 per cent of fathers had a high level of participation in housework, and 25 per cent in child-care. And this study still did not establish who was responsible for a particular task, rather than who helped. The picture is similar as regards fathers of mentally handicapped children. Wilkin (1979) asked who usually did various child-care and household tasks, and rated all the family members as participants or helpers or giving no support. He set as 'high participation' a level which could have been achieved by the vast majority of fathers, even allowing for their time outside the home working (i.e. providing help with most tasks and participating equally in one or two). He suggested virtually all fathers could share equally in minding children at weekends, baby-sitting, cleaning the house, washing dishes and shopping. However, less than a quarter of fathers were actually participating highly, and they were far more involved in child-care than in housework. Only twelve per cent of fathers provided any help at all with washing clothes. There were only two tasks in which more than half of fathers participated equally with mothers, lifting the child and baby-sitting. Neither necessarily reflects willingness to participate, in that lifting and carrying is a practical necessity, and mothers were usually at home too when baby-sitting was rated.

> "The inescapable conclusion is that most could have and should have done more to ease the burden on their wives. They were not very different from most ordinary fathers in the extent of their contribution, but the difficulties faced by their wives were much worse than those faced by most other mothers." (Wilkin, 1979, p.133)

Most fathers and mothers perceive father's role in child-care as beginning after the baby stage, and being concerned primarily with discipline, play and spending time outside the home (Russell, 1979a). One of the factors inhibiting participation of fathers of mentally handicapped children may be that many have little experience in appropriate activities for very young children, and that mentally handicapped children stay longer at this developmental level. A study of two to 15 years old mentally handicapped children in Dublin found that only half of fathers were reported by mothers to have a daily play session with their child, although more did so at weekends. The sessions with fathers were almost entirely restricted to outings, watching television and rough and tumble play (McEvoy and McConkey, 1983).

Thus, research into the daily tasks of living with a mentally handicapped child suggests that family patterns are similar to those found in families of non-handicapped children, and therefore that in most cases the mother is under greater pressure. Mothers' ability to carry on coping seems to be more strongly related to resources in the family, particularly fathers' participation, than to the severity of the child's handicap (Bristol, 1982). Relationships of fathers' participation with other indices (such as the child's handicap) tend to be contradictory: however, clearer associations might emerge from a study of the content as well as the quantity of parental involvement with the child. In addition, the contribution of other members of the family would need to be included in a total study of child-care and housework tasks.

Siblings

In studies of the family life of mentally handicapped children, siblings have usually attracted only passing mention, perhaps because they are not centrally involved in making decisions in relation to the handicapped child (Kew, 1975). The feelings and attitudes of siblings will be discussed in Chapter 4; their role in child-care and housework will be reviewed briefly here.

It has been reported in a number of studies that siblings may resent the direct or indirect demands of living with a handicapped child, i.e. having to do more child-care and housework themselves, and/or lacking attention from their parents because the parents are too busy (e.g. Holt, 1958; Farber, 1959; Lloyd-Bostock, 1976; Butler et al, 1978; Simeonsson and McHale, 1981). However, reported percentages are generally small and control groups are not used. Other similar studies have found that siblings helped at home, but did not regard it as a particular burden (e.g. Graliker, Fishler and Koch, 1962; Cleveland and Miller, 1977). The studies which stress a lack of problems tend to be those in which siblings were interviewed directly, rather than their reactions being filtered through parental report. However, these are also usually studies where the siblings are now young adults or where the handicapped child is considerably younger than the sibling. Such factors may act to reduce the actual or reported impact of the handicapped child on the sibling's daily life.

Several studies report the siblings enjoying taking a large role in playing with the handicapped child, and even trying to teach the child (e.g. Grossmann, 1972; Fuchs, 1974; McConachie and Domb, 1983; Stoneman and Brody, 1984). (Also see Chapter 10.) Wilkin's (1979) study of 120 families found that slightly over half of the siblings in the eight to eleven year age range made some contribution to the domestic routine, and three quarters in the twelve to sixteen year age group. Almost a third of these (i.e. 38 siblings) had a relatively high level of participation, and 31 out of the 38 were girls. This finding of family reliance on older girls is one supported by several studies (e.g. Farber, 1959; Cleveland and Miller, 1977; Vadasy, Fewell, Meyer and Schell, 1984), and Gath (1974) showed a relationship with a raised incidence of behaviour problems and educational difficulties.

Thus, generally siblings do not seem to be adversely affected by the increased tasks involved in caring for a mentally handicapped child, and report positive effects such as a greater maturity and thoughtfulness about others. However, some individuals undoubtedly are burdened, perhaps most usually older female siblings. Research so far has not enabled clear identification of those siblings who are most likely to be at risk. One suggestion was raised by Fuchs (1974) who noted that in 19 out of the 25 families she studied, a deliberate degree of organisation was introduced at critical points of the family routine, designed to reduce any adverse impact on siblings. That is, parents tried to arrange extra activities just with the non-handicapped children, to ensure peace and quiet while siblings did homework, and adjusted the handicapped child's bedtime. This type of organising was absent in six families, and in five of these tension was noted between siblings and handicapped child.

Grandparents

Even less attention has been paid to grandparents of handicapped children, in both descriptive and research literature. Yet recent theorising about family life has emphasised that families generally have extensive contact with their close relations, even though they may live in a nuclear family structure. Shanas (1973) surveyed six industrialised societies and found that 80 per cent of elderly people had contact at least once per week with their adult children. The majority of these elderly people are likely to be grandparents. A survey of 117 American three year old children in middle-class families found that 59 per cent had at least weekly contact with maternal grandparents, and 42 per cent with paternal grandparents (Lewis, Feiring and Kotsonis, 1984). (Contact included phone as well as face to face contact.) A British study of three year olds found that over 60 per cent of mothers saw their own mothers at least once a week (Richman, Stevenson and Graham, 1982).

Such evidence as exists suggests that grandparents of handicapped children have similarly high levels of contact. Wilkin (1979) found that around two-thirds of close relatives (grandparents, aunts and uncles of the handicapped child) living in the same large town were seen at least once a week. In an interview study of eight grandmothers of handicapped children aged five years and under, Ellington (1984) noted that all had contact at least once a week. (As her study was explicitly focussed on grandparents, the sample may well be biased toward greater contact.) Harris, Handleman and Palmer (1985) found that maternal grandparents of autistic children visited significantly more often than paternal grandparents.

However, it is not possible to predict level of support from a knowledge of frequency of contact. In Wilkin's study, of all relatives in regular contact, only four per cent helped with school-holiday minding of the child, three per cent helped with shopping, and ten per cent did some baby-sitting. However, in Ellington's study, half of the grandmothers did baby-sit, and two did not only because they were themselves rather frail, being over 70 years of age.

Various factors affect the amount and nature of the support received. Firstly, mothers may not expect much practical help, especially with older children. Instead, they may value the knowledge that help will be there in a crisis, and that they have social contact with other adults (Farber, 1959; Wilkin, 1979). The practical help given may be less obvious than joining in daily chores, for example, making available financial support for a holiday or making clothes for the child (Hewett, 1970). Secondly, the age of the grandparents may be significant: if they are working or have young children themselves they may not be able to offer much practical support; and elderly grandparents may depend on their son or daughter, rather than vice versa. Thirdly, a number of studies suggest that a middle range of frequency of contact with grandparents may be more helpful than very frequent or infrequent contact (Tinsley and Parke, 1984), particularly in the case of the father's parents (Farber, 1959). Though contact with the mother's parents may be a more usual source of support, at least two studies have emphasised the important potential contribution of the father's parents in supporting the family. Both Lonsdale (1978) and Waisbren (1980) found an association between perceived supportiveness of paternal grandparents, and fathers' positive motivation toward the handicapped child and greater activity with the child.

Transport

Going out with the child can pose major difficulties if the child is not fully independently mobile, has poor health, incontinence or behaviour problems. However, having their own car makes the major difference as to whether the family can take the child out (Hewett, 1970). As well as the usual travelling for shopping, outings, social contacts, etc., families will have the additional pressure of visits to hospital clinics, or visiting the child if taken into hospital, perhaps at a centralised specialist facility some distance away. If the ambulance service is used, it entails earlier starts to journeys, and longer visits (McMichael, 1971; Glendinning, 1983). In Britain, the Mobility Allowance is not available to children under 5 years of age.

Parental employment

Given the additional tasks involved in caring for a mentally handicapped child, and the current emphasis upon early service intervention and involvement of parents in teaching their children, some effect might be expected on parental employment patterns.

Wilkin (1979) found that 18 per cent of fathers of his research sample were unemployed, which was high for the area and for the time. He suggested that long-term paternal unemployment may be one coping strategy adopted by some families. In a study of 263 applicants to the Family Fund, one quarter reported effects on fathers' employment such as restriction on choice of work or promotion opportunities, or pressure to increase their earnings (Glendinning, 1983). Wastberg (1985) reported that in a Swedish study of mentally handicapped children and their families, 16 per cent of fathers said they had made some adjustment of their working arrangements or hours because of the child. These effects would be difficult to measure objectively. Hewett (1970) found no evidence that fathers altered their working hours in order to spend more time with their handicapped child: the same proportion did shift work as in a comparable general population sample.

The pressures are more obvious on mothers' employment. It is "now normal for women to work, and withdrawal from the labour market and return to it is the general pattern" (Department of Employment, 1975, p.3). Employment has also been shown to be an important factor for women in the maintenance of good mental health (Brown and Harris, 1978). Care of a handicapped child may increase mothers' need for employment, because of the family's extra expenses, and for relief from the isolation felt by many mothers of handicapped children. Yet a reduced proportion work outside the home, especially full time, in comparison with the general population (Baldwin, 1977; Watson and Midlarsky, 1979; Hunter, 1980; Eheart and Ciccone, 1982; Glendinning, 1983; Carr, 1985; Wastberg, 1985), one reason being greater difficulty in arranging child-care.

Evidence about mothers' employment experiences and aspirations is scanty perhaps because a traditional role-division, father employed and mother at home with children, is assumed by researchers (or their sample may contain only such families if investigations are conducted during the weekday (Russell, 1979a)). It is also assumed by services: "The expectation that a woman will provide the necessary care within the family, whatever the costs to herself, still underpins the reality of community care" (Equal Opportunities Commission, 1982, p.40). Thus, the pressure of others' expectations is added to the various practical difficulties women encounter in finding satisfactory employment.

CONCLUSIONS

This brief review of some aspects of family life with a handicapped child leads to a number of conclusions with implications for services and for research.

Firstly, the majority of studies, particularly the recent ones, emphasize

> "...that in most respects these families resemble others in the society. Most of their roles and values are drawn from and are sustained in a flow of events similar to that experienced by other families." (Farber, 1975, p.247)

This conclusion is voiced both by researchers and by parents, with reference to many different kinds of handicap, whether all ages of children are considered or solely preschool children (e.g. Hewett, 1970; Roskies, 1972; Wishart, Bidder and Gray, 1981). Thus, a research or service strategy which assumes a perspective of family deviance would be seriously distorted.

Secondly, 'community care' in practice is largely care by mothers; family role divisions are little altered despite increased tasks in bringing up the child. Farber (1975) has described how, if a problematic situation hits at what is defined as one person's area of responsibility, less affected members of the family will tend to adapt as little as possible, i.e. the "chauvinism of the powerful". Yet, in a time of great questioning of traditional family role divisions, parents of handicapped children may both wish the father to participate more, particularly in child-care, though this may seem hard to achieve (Gallagher, 1982).

Thirdly, much of the stressful impact of demands created by the child's handicap is not inevitable, and can be much ameliorated by appropriate service provision (Pilling, 1973; Burden, 1980). When parents are asked what services they feel they need or which are essential to them, the majority agree on playgroups (Lonsdale, 1978), minding the child in the school holidays and at weekends, help with transport, and baby-sitting in the evenings (Wilkin, 1979; Dupont, 1980). These are in theory needs which are not difficult to meet, but as yet they are patchily provided for and then often by voluntary rather than statutory services.

Fourthly, families' responses to the stresses of daily living are essentially individual and not easily predictable (Bradshaw and Lawton, 1978; Crnic, Friedrich and Greenberg, 1983). The existing research studies have many shortcomings in terms of ecological validity which have limited their usefulness. In summary, they adopt a clinical focus, assume a static research model, make assumptions about cultural norms and are generally unidimensional, unidirectional and unimodal. These conceptual and research problems will be discussed in more detail in the following chapter.

Chapter Three

FAMILY LIFE: RESEARCH STRATEGY, AND METHODS

ANALYSIS OF CURRENT RESEARCH STRATEGY

Clinical focus

The point was made at the end of Chapter 2 that some studies of families assume detrimental effects of living with a handicapped child from the start, even describing them as "handicapped families" (Kew, 1975), without defining what 'normality' might be. There is a danger that the behaviour of families may be interpreted as abnormal whatever they do, and distinctions blurred between 'psychological' and practical problems.

But further than this, the research is clinically based, i.e. focussed on a group of children defined loosely as similar on diagnostic grounds such as 'mental handicap' and thus as 'different' from other children, despite the obvious characteristics which each shares with all children, and others which he or she does not share with any other mentally handicapped child. Research on the parents focusses on changing reactions to various stages of development and characteristics of the child, rather than on individual motherhood or fatherhood per se. Just as research on sex 'differences' has obscured individual differences and ways in which males and females are alike (Chetwynd and Hartnett, 1978), so a clinical focus on handicap may have retarded the development of more adequate models for understanding family functioning in families of mentally handicapped children.

Static models

Many studies have observed or interviewed families

once, and have failed to reflect changes in perspective and functioning over time. For example, the difficulties posed by a three year old may be very different from when that child is fifteen (Suelzle and Keenan, 1981). Also parents' developing understanding of their situation may be reflected in changing reactions to professionals. Schwartz (1970) has described how parents' initial strategy may be to accept what professionals suggest, as they sort out the confusion of what the child's handicap may mean to the family's routines. Later they are more likely to become sceptical, and either withdraw or actively question what is offered. As these strategies are responses to the combination of their experiences in receiving services, their relationship with the handicapped child and their view of their family life as a whole, they necessarily change over time.

A few studies have followed families through the mentally handicapped child's preschool years and beyond: Carr (1975, 1985), Gath (1978), Gath and Gumley (1984), and Cunningham (1983a) all studied Down's syndrome children, who are usually identified soon after birth (though n.b. several will continue to have a Developmental Quotient within normal limits (e.g. Connolly, 1978; Rynders, Spiker and Horrobin, 1978)). Specific events such as entering school can be evaluated in a longitudinal study, in order to see what problems they create, and also which families perceive these events as stressful. Wikler, Wasow and Hatfield (1981) have suggested that periodic crises rather than chronic stresses are the ones which families find most difficult, and these may be missed by a 'one-off' study.

<u>Other systems in the child's ecology</u>

As has been implied above, contexts other than the home may have a major effect upon parents and children, and have not been adequately considered in research on families (Roskies, 1972; Bronfenbrenner, 1977). For example, at the level of the community, a child's entering a nursery for handicapped children will give the mother some much-needed time to herself, but will also signal publicly his or her 'differentness' to a degree which may not have occurred since the original diagnosis was made. At the broadest level of an ecological analysis, the values and assumptions which govern service developments impinge upon parents, who may or may not share them. For example, mentally handicapped children are normally now offered a school place before three years of age, but parents may not share the assumption of early and special schooling being automatically 'a good thing', if they see their child primarily as a child and only secondarily as handicapped, and if their own schooling evokes bad memories. Early services to families - extended health visitor services, mothers' groups, visits from a home teacher - all tend to assume a mother available at any time at home.

Thus parent-child interaction in the home is affected both by the practical features and by the ideological frameworks of a network of settings and social structures, including those shared with the rest of the community and those specific to 'handicap'. The aspects mentioned above are obvious sources of discussion by parents. However they are affected also by overarching cultural expectations which are not so easily identified. For example, the public face of British and American society places great emphasis on parent-child contact in the first few years, and on the teaching of children by adults through play. Yet these values regarding parenting are certainly culturally relative, within as well as between cultures (Ogbu, 1981), and determined by economic, historical and political forces. The pattern described above aims to foster children who are self-confident achievers. Other patterns of parent-child interaction are assumed to be deficient in terms of promoting the child's 'competence'. However, Levine (1980) has analysed the possible detrimental effects of the geographical 'exporting' of such child-rearing values to different economic and social contexts, within which alternative priorities and definitions of competence may be accepted, such as being a sharing member of a social group, and not relying on praise or other external indicators of success (Dixon, LeVine, Richman and Brazelton, 1984).

Parents of handicapped children have great responsibilities laid on them when in fact they may feel relatively powerless (Graham, 1982). The cultural assumption that parents (mothers) are responsible for fostering their children's development through interaction would seem to have potentially harmful effects on parents whose children are not going to quickly achieve self-sufficiency and compete with others, i.e. mentally handicapped children. That is, there paradoxically is a pressure for mothers to redouble their efforts along the usual lines. This pressure would seem to detract from other individual family goals, and to ignore other subcultural values of child-rearing.

The family as a system

Research strategies have frequently concentrated only on one family member (e.g. the child or the mother) and on one-way effects (e.g. the handicapped child's effects on his or her siblings). The family as a system or functional unit, within which individuals exert reciprocal influences on each other, has rarely been studied (Crnic, Friedrich and Greenberg, 1983). More adequate frameworks for conceptual analysis are required, if research is to inform the prediction (and avoidance) of detrimental effects of intervention in the family system.

Much American research of the 1950's and 1960's was influenced by the theoretical perspective of Talcott Parsons. He analysed the nuclear family in terms of well-defined role relationships which promote stability and balance, where parents are more powerful than children, and fathers exercise 'instrumental' leadership and mothers 'expressive' leadership (Parsons and Bales, 1955). Tallman (1965) suggested that in a family with a severely mentally handicapped child the parental role differentiation would be heightened, with greater adjustment difficulties for fathers as they would be unable to fulfill their role in socialising the child to meet the achievement demands of the outside world. His research on parents' adaptability (assessed from parental reactions to hypothetical situations) provided evidence in support of various propositions about fathers' reactions derived from the theory. He also suggested ways in which, and points in the child's life when, fathers might be sensitively helped. However, this type of research does not look at what actually takes place in a family day to day, and ignores ways in which parents do not conform to the theoretical roles. Greater detail of family organisation was studied by Farber (1960), who then distinguished different ways in which families responded to the discovery that their child was handicapped (e.g. as a 'role organisation crisis' or a 'tragic crisis'). Individual differences in reaction and organisation were recognised, but lack of control groups and reliance on parent reports still limited understanding of how perceived patterns of change and development are different from what would be expected with any child. The emphasis is on how the child affects the family, and not vice versa.

The assumptions underlying this type of structural analysis of family functioning have come under severe criticism, and more recent research has been influenced by evidence about cultural diversity, and by ideas about change in family role structures (Rapoport, Rapoport and Strelitz, 1977). For example, there has been much questioning of, and a recent rapid growth of research into, the role of fathers in child development (Lamb, 1976a, 1981a), though very little on fathers of handicapped children (McConachie, 1982). Old models have been found wanting, and have "constrained research efforts regarding the child's relationship not only to the father but also to peers, grandparents, uncles, aunts, friends, and others" (Lewis and Weinraub, 1976, p.179). For example, it had been assumed that fathers had no role to play with young children, except as a support to mothers (Bowlby, 1951), even though Schaffer and Emerson (1964) had shown that many infants formed their primary attachment with their fathers, despite spending much less time with them than with their mothers.

As far back as 1943, Gardner suggested that fathers (American) had ample time for fathering, but did not use their opportunities. Current ideology suggests that since then fathers have become more and more involved with their children, and that role-relations in families are more 'symmetrical'. Neither of these claims stands up to inspection. Recent studies have shown consistently that fathers of young children on average spend around two hours per week on basic child-care tasks (feeding, nappy-changing, etc.) (reviewed in Russell and Radin, 1983) in contrast with mothers who may spend 18 hours (Russell, 1979b). Russell also showed that when parents were both at home, mothers still did much more than fathers of basic child-care. The discrepancy is repeated, but to a lesser extent, in the case of playing with the child (Kotelchuk, 1976; Russell, 1979b). In over 90 per cent of the families in Russell's study both mothers and fathers said that mothers had the major responsibility for child-care, and this picture applied even when both parents had paid employment. In the total sample, 60 per cent of fathers were not spending any time taking complete care of their children. Both mothers and fathers believe that things have changed since their own parents' day. But Lewis (1984) has shown that there is almost no difference between answers to questions about how much fathers do of nappy-changing, putting children to bed and bathing them between 1960 and 1980. (In each case around 40 per cent of fathers almost never changed a nappy.) Thus despite much discussion of change, the actual extent of fathers' participation in child-care has generally been much overestimated.

In researching the carrying out of household tasks, it is now recognised that to ask 'who helps?' assumes the mother's ultimate responsibility for organisation in the home. Thus in studying families, research strategy has begun to question previous assumptions, and to look beyond verbal reports of family life to what actually happens, at how decisions are made which perpetuate inequities (Pleck, 1985) and at how conflicting ideologies in the same individual or family can create tension (e.g. 'sharing' versus 'motherhood is natural') (Holly, 1982).

Very recently, literature reports have begun again to discuss the use of comprehensive models for understanding families of handicapped children (e.g. Nihira, Meyers and Mink, 1980; Foster, Berger and McLean, 1981; Simeonsson and McHale, 1981; Crnic, Friedrich and Greenberg, 1983; Mink, Nihira and Meyers, 1983; Turnbull, Summers and Brotherson, 1983; Belsky, Robins and Gamble, 1984; Bubolz and Whiren, 1984; Nihira, Mink and Meyers, 1984; Stoneman and Brody, 1984). For example, Turnbull et al. suggest that families can be described under four headings - the process of interaction, structures (e.g. number of people, religion, role assignment), functions (e.g. degree of stress on economic, affectional, educational etc.) and developmental stages.

> "No family can adequately attend to all functions. The issue is one of setting priorities for parents' attention and finding resources to assist the family with others. Every family should not emphasize the educational function - perhaps their time would be far more effective in areas such as guidance, religion and affection. Intervention programs should be sensitive to the natural rhythms and preferences of each family." (Turnbull, Brotherson and Summers, 1982, p.8)

Likewise, siblings see their relationship with the handicapped child against the background of such family expectations, and feel successful or unsuccessful in the relationship in individual ways (Featherstone, 1980). Other authors use slightly different conceptual headings, but all stress the need to tie together multiple variables of the home environment with analysis of the development of the mentally handicapped child. Nihira and Mink and co-workers (see above) have conducted a large, four year longitudinal research study aiming to integrate measures of child and family with details of interactional patterns within the family system. Using cluster analysis and various instruments describing the home environment and interactions, they have identified five distinctive types of families with a mentally handicapped child living at home (total sample 115). This taxonomy includes families described as 'cohesive, harmonious', 'control-oriented, somewhat non-harmonious','low disclosure, unharmonious', 'child-oriented, expressive' and 'disadvantaged, low morale'. These groupings have then been shown to differ significantly in terms of various parent and child characteristics, and also in terms of the child's adaptive skills and self-esteem at school (Mink et al., 1983).

The strengths of such attempts at models of family functioning are the implications they have for intervention. Firstly, many points of intervention are possible, because the influences on parents are multiple. Secondly, they suggest that intervention which strengthens as many of the subsystems as possible will be most efficacious, and that positive interventions in one subsystem (e.g. increasing a mother's social support) are likely to enhance functioning in other subsystems.

The design and implementation of research of this scope and complexity are prohibitively difficult. But the elements of the research strategy can be traced in other contemporary developments; i.e. looking beyond unidirectional questions of effects to description of interaction in dyads, triads, etc.; recognising dimensions in the family other than mother and child; and using longitudinal and multimodal designs (Crnic, Friedrich and Greenberg, 1983).

Multimodal designs

Studies of families of handicapped children have usually been unimodal: either questionnaires about attitudes, or interviewing parents (usually mothers) about stresses of daily living. Even behavioural studies of mother-child interaction have largely failed to take into account other possibly contributory variables. There are difficulties and advantages to each single type of approach in descriptive research, depending also upon the questions asked and thus the theoretical background. For example, attitude research developed largely from psychoanalytic theory about the birth of a handicapped child, and consequent 'loss' of an expected non-handicapped child; the British tradition has largely been more pragmatic and perhaps aimed at political and social reform.

However, the present shift toward multimodal research strategies represents more than simply adding data from two or three methods together as cross validation (Lytton, 1973). It is as mentioned above derived partly from reevaluation of theory about child socialisation - including recognition of the roles of all family members, and also that the child's environment is more sensitively described in terms of interactional processes than in terms of crude variables such as social class (Bradley and Caldwell, 1979; Nihira et al., 1980). Partly, it is also derived from theoretical analysis of the importance of cognitive variables in interaction, i.e. that family members' knowledge and viewpoints influence their behaviour toward each other and their perceptions of others' behaviour. Parke (1978) has noted

> "... the failure to adequately distinguish between parental reports as objective measures of parental behavior and parental reports as indices of parental knowledge, attitudes, stereotypes and perceptions. These latter classes of variables are legitimate and important sources of data and are not easily derived from observation alone. These types of parental reports provide information about ways in which parents perceive, organize, and understand both their infants and their roles as parents." (p.76)

Thus, it can be concluded that future study of the family life of handicapped children requires, at the least, discussion of the limitations of the data collection method adopted, and at best a pooling of data from different angles of focus and levels of conceptual complexity. A number of methods used to study families of handicapped children will be reviewed below in terms of their potential to describe individual differences, environmental process, the roles of various family members and the separation of behaviour from attitudes.

DAILY LIFE

Parents' books

There are a very large number of books and pamphlets available, written by mothers and fathers of mentally handicapped children, which include descriptions of the ordinary events of everyday life, as well as opinions and feelings about the overall question of the child's handicap. Some include comparisons with other families (e.g. Featherstone, 1980; Hannam, 1980) and comments on published research. By definition, they are a source of information on individual differences, and changes over time. They give insight into the roles of various family members, but less so than might be expected. Very often either a parent writes in the first person singular and hardly mentions their partner (e.g. Murray, 1967; Van der Houten, 1968; Brown, 1974; Smith, 1975; Kaufman, 1976; Schaefer, 1979; Boston, 1981) or the parent writes 'we' and rarely distinguishes mother's and father's feelings and contributions (e.g. Wilks and Wilks, 1974; Collins and Collins, 1976). This might reflect a close sharing of ideas and work, but seems more likely to represent a blindness to actual role divisions and a joint perspective adopted for the process of presenting the family's story publicly. The relation of the family to its environment and the cultural values it holds can be interpreted from the story; however, parents who write are a restricted and self-selected group, able to articulate ideas and fight for what they need, therefore the range of the analysis is very restricted. No separation of behaviour and attitudes is possible from the writing, and would in any case undermine the power and importance of such books.

Interview surveys

Interviews about daily living have been mentioned in Chapter 2, and some problems in method already outlined. For example, when mothers are asked about fathers, siblings, etc., their answers are likely to reflect their expectations as much as what actually happens. There is also a filtering process dependent on how they see the interviewer in relation to themselves, for example, as someone who seems to assume that the central business of life is bringing up children, and who is interested in them solely as members of a deviant group, i.e. 'parents of handicapped children'. An unspoken negotiation takes place around the official morality of child-rearing and of family life, and the parents' own ideas about how to make sense of their situation (e.g. 'coping splendidly', 'self-sacrificing', 'changing society's attitudes', 'just as normal', etc.) (Voysey, 1975). It is therefore difficult to separate reports of behaviour from attitudes, quite apart from the fact that questions are often imprecise. Brown and Rutter (1966) have shown that reliability of information about family life is greatly enhanced when questions are asked about the performance of specific tasks over a particular time period. They also use information from tone of voice and critical versus positive statements to define levels of 'expressed emotion' in the interview, i.e. using the interview to collect two quite separate types of information.

The roles of separate family members are liable to be obscured, unless each is interviewed separately. However, few researchers have interviewed fathers of handicapped children on their own (Farber, 1959; Cain and Levine, 1963; McConachie, 1979; Markova et al., 1980). Grandparents are sometimes cited as important, either as a help or as a hindrance, yet there seems to be no published study in which grandparents have been interviewed directly about their role with their handicapped grandchild (see Chapter 4). The questions asked about family members are largely repetitions of these asked about mothers, i.e. they are not founded in theoretical expectations about family role structures (Oeser and Hammond, 1954), they look only at 'substitute mothering'. For example, questions are usually asked about 'who helps?'. Yet there are a number of possible divisions of roles, e.g. into 'helper', 'participant', 'the one responsible', 'never involved', all of which might be built up into a profile of each family member's activity, and each family's role structure.

Results are usually presented as differences between group means, though enhanced by individual quotes from parents to indicate the range and diversity of reports. However, from group associations it is largely impossible to link one piece of information about a family to another, to see how couple cooperation and other patterns might build up. Interview studies with large, satisfactorily representative populations do however allow for the tracing of associations with demographic variables, and for comparisons with control groups, to check the 'ordinariness' of reported events.

Questionnaires

Questionnaires have been used to cover some of the same ground with families of mentally handicapped children as semi-structured interviews (e.g. Wishart et al., 1981). In this case, family members' answers are constrained by predetermined categories, for example, of frequency of particular activities, but usually individuals answer separately where more than one family member is asked.

Other questionnaires in this area are more focussed, to reduce problems of interpretation. For example the Gallagher-Cross Family Role Scale (Gallagher, Cross and Scharfman, 1981; Gallagher, Bristol, Cross and Scharfman, 1983) looks at which parent takes major responsibilities as food shopper, cook, nurse, buyer of clothes, child teacher, child discipliner, etc. and which are shared. Here the emphasis is explicitly on values, which can then be compared with actual behaviour. A second example is the Family Routines Inventory (Jensen, James, Boyce and Hartnett, 1983) (though not yet used with handicapped children). This measures 28 positive, strength-promoting family routines, i.e. observable repetitive behaviours which involve two or more family members and which occur with predictable regularity (e.g. 'children do regular household chores', 'family eats at the same time each night', 'parent(s) have some time each day for just talking with the children'). The Inventory was developed from intensive observational studies of families (Boyce, Jensen, James and Peacock, 1983), and is completed by parents' indicating both the frequency with which a particular routine occurs, and its importance to their family life. Previous research had suggested that family routines can "'protect' against ill health by providing stability and continuity during periods of stress" (Jensen et al., 1983, p.201). A similar Family Task Interview has been used in studies of obese children to reveal characteristic patterns of interaction (Loader and

Kinston, 1984).

These research tools allow for the description of individual differences in family organisation, though they do not indicate how or why these 'make sense' for the family in their present circumstances and how they have developed. Distinguishing the roles of various family members clearly (i.e. not simply the parents), and distinguishing actual behaviour from attitudes are two functions not adequately achieved by these tools.

Observation

There appear to be no studies of intensive direct observation of daily living in families with handicapped children partly because of the intrusion this would represent, and partly because of (probably insurmountable) methodological difficulties in data-collection (see discussion in Chapter 7). There do exist anthropological studies, such as Henry (1967) who lived with families of autistic children in order to describe processes of family cohesion, but provides no quantitative data. Studies of children in hospital are rather more easily undertaken. Oswin (1971, 1978) has studied handicapped children living in long-stay hospitals through observing whole days at a time, and she noted particularly the emptiness of the children's lives (on average, no interactions for 92 per cent of the time (1978)). One small study of profoundly handicapped children living at home included observation of interaction with family members for one hour a day after school, and made comparisons with matched children living in hospital. Children at home received four times as much attention as those in hospital, and the interaction was generally contingent and appropriate (Beail, 1985). However, a focussed study of this nature does not reflect the totality of the children's activities, and family organisation throughout the day.

With non-handicapped children, attempts have been made to provide a detailed picture of the experiences to which preschool children of varying British social and economic backgrounds are normally exposed at home (Davie, Hutt, Vincent and Mason, 1984). However, this stretched only to six observations of one hour on different days, limiting drastically information on contact with different family members. The study did give a comprehensive picture of children's varying activities (52 codes used). A systematic difference was found between mothers' and fathers' interaction depending on the family position of the child. That is, fathers would spend much more time in interaction with eldest or only children than they did with children who were the youngest in the family; mothers' interaction did not vary in this way.

In the USA, Caldwell has supplemented similar direct observations with an attempt to measure the potential of the young child's home as a stimulating educational environment, the Home Observation for Measurement of the Environment (HOME) Inventory (Bradley and Caldwell, 1979). The Inventory is scored both from observation and from interview, and the rater records the number and type of the child's toys, the educational potential of the parent's play with the child, amount of physical punishment, degree of choice the child is allowed, etc. The Inventory has been shown to predict cognitive ability in young children, with sufficient accuracy to be used as a screening measure (Adams, Campbell and Ramey, 1984). It has been used with at risk and handicapped children, for example, in helping the family to increase the educational potential of the home environment (Bradley and Caldwell, 1978; Piper and Ramsay, 1980). It has also been shown that characteristics of developmentally disabled children, such as frequency of crying, predict home environment scores, as do parental perceptions of the child's activity (Affleck, Allen, McGrade and McQueeney, 1982). Thus a number of variables covering children's characteristics, parents' perceptions, the marital relationship and the home environment are inextricably linked in understanding the 'transaction' between child and family (Nihira et al., 1980; Mink et al., 1983).

Depending on how the data are presented, the observational strategies described above can offer detailed information on the range of individual differences, and of the interaction between the child and the environment. Behaviour is separated from attitudes of family respondents, though of course not from the value judgements and observational set of the researchers. Generally, the method concentrates study on one family member (mother) and the child.

Structured reporting

Structured diaries of family life and the child's activities, filled in by parents (e.g. Hetherington, Cox and Cox, 1976) have generally been found too great an undertaking to be pursued by many parents of handicapped children or for many days (Sloper, 1983). Where the information to be recorded is restricted to frequency of physical care interactions (Johnson and Deitz, 1985) or duration of time spent in basic care or play (Dupont, 1980), parents of handicapped children can carry out such structured reporting reliably for a seven day period (or even 14 days (Joosten, 1979)). Such information can then guide intervention so that it does not increase the parents' burdens of care rather than lightening them. McHale and Huston (1984) did not ask parents to write information down, but instead telephoned them on nine separate occasions to check off a listing of which household and child-care tasks and leisure activities had occurred, and which parent (of non-handicapped children) had been involved in the preceding day.

A more complex method which overcomes some of the time and reactivity problems of direct observation, which enables the inclusion of all family members and others, which can reflect individual differences in family organisation, and which minimizes the effect of the interviewee's attitudes and perceptions on data collection is the 'standard day' interview (Douglas, Lawson, Cooper and Cooper, 1968). The interview covers the previous twenty-four hours in terms of the child's activities, and also the levels of interaction with others. Coding is in ten-minute units, with shorter events described separately. The method allows description of a wide range of differences between families, but it has also been shown that there are few differences between days of the week (bar Sundays), and individual families show consistency over time. Mothers have been shown to recall events reliably (in a study comparing interview and observation). Hoffman (1967) described a very similar method and suggested that it overcame 'good impression' errors in the data through the effort to recall details. The method has been shown to distinguish between excessively 'house-proud' mothers and controls, for example, in terms of time spent in concentrated interaction, and in amount of physical restriction placed on the child (Cooper and McNeil, 1968). Light (1979) found a relationship between a high proportion of time spent in concentrated interaction with adults, and mutual responsivity and sensitivity of observed interaction between four year old non-handicapped children and their mothers.

Two studies with handicapped children have utilised the standard day interview. Howlin, Marchant, Rutter, Berger, Hersov and Yule (1973) mention using a modified form in their intervention study with parents of autistic children. The data are utilised in helping to restructure the family's day in order to programme teaching activities most effectively, and also to ensure that parents have more time for themselves and for siblings (Howlin and Lask, 1985). However, no results have yet been published. McConachie (1982) studied nineteen young mentally handicapped children and their families, and found a variety of family patterns of cooperation, though 'mother as primary caretaker' was the most common. Fathers' involvement in concentrated interaction with their children seemed to be greater where the children were able to use words in communication, and fathers also seemed to have greater involvement in basic care activities with the handicapped child where there was a younger sibling.

In providing quantitative information, structured diaries and interviews about activities do not give a picture of the emotional quality of the interaction, nor of the parents' perceptions of the child's activities with and without them. Both of these qualitative aspects of interaction require additional methods of study. In itself quantitative description (e.g. of a high level of concentrated interaction with a parent) does not elucidate whether that interaction is helpful or too intense for the child. But the data give pointers to the range of differences which can then be linked to other information about the family in generating hypotheses about processes. Focussing on one or more ordinary days loses information about the impact of special events (clinic visits, starting nursery) upon a child. These periodic events may have an especially important effect upon everyday living in families of handicapped children. However, it seems potentially useful to collect detailed information about the ordinary activities (i.e. not pathologically focussed) of young handicapped children at home. This would provide illuminative background for the more detailed study of family interaction, and would provide guidance in fitting intervention strategies to the individual family.

CONCLUSIONS

Chapter 2 has reviewed well-substantiated conclusions in the literature about practical difficulties in the daily life of families of handicapped children, and the present chapter has evaluated the major methods used in obtaining that evidence. That evaluation is preceded by, and depends upon, discussion of the elements which might go to make up a conceptual framework of sufficient scope and flexibility to reflect the diversity in the subject matter. A fully-grounded understanding of the situation of families of handicapped children is necessary in order to begin to predict and to evaluate the outcome of intervention designed to promote the children's development.

Chapter Four

FAMILY REACTIONS TO THE HANDICAPPED CHILD

INTRODUCTION

Parental attitudes have assumed major importance in the study of child development. The primary influence on research used to be psychoanalytic theory, within which the major structures of the human personality are considered to be formed in infancy through the actions and attitudes of the mother. Thus the study of child development focussed on maternal child-rearing in a one-way model of causation. As studies of parents of mentally handicapped children multiplied in the 1950's, the causation model took a different form, i.e. parents' reactions were seen as neurotic, dysfunctional responses to the child's abnormality, and their child-rearing attitudes usually interpreted as caused by the child's characteristics. Generalizations about parents were thus made in terms of the IQ or diagnostic grouping of the child. As was described in Chapter 1, these one-way models of influence have largely been replaced by theories focussing on the interactive basis for development and on the ecological framework within which development occurs. Thus, mutual influence of parent and child is stressed, and individual differences become fundamental to research strategy.

The attitudes of parents of mentally handicapped children can be thought of on several different levels of meaning, any of which has apparent relevance in the consideration of intervention. Parents' attitudes are part of the ecological analysis of systems within which the child interacts and develops, and they in turn are shaped both by interactions with the child and by the wider systems of family and society values, by specific experiences, and by the services available.

The term 'attitude' is used loosely in the literature, to cover parent behaviour, perceptions, reactions, values, feelings, etc., and this chapter will be no exception. However, some definition of conceptual levels will be given here, to elucidate what is and is not addressed in the present review. At the most narrowly focussed level, parents' perceptions of the meaning of their own and their child's behaviour might be considered. The parent gradually builds up a picture of how he or she expects the child to behave, and through these expectations can anticipate and adjust to the child's behaviour. The parent also has plans for guiding the child's behaviour. Some research with parents of young handicapped children has adopted this level of enquiry, looking at decision points in parent-child interaction and asking the parent to explain the option chosen (Mogford, 1979a; Mitchell, 1980). Thus, as referred to in Chapter 3, at this level parents' attitudes are important sources of information, distinct from but closely aligned to parents' behaviour (Parke, 1978; Olson et al., 1982).

At the next level of generality, there are more stable parental attitudes, within a particular age-band for the child. At this level, such close correspondence with behaviour in particular situations would not be expected. However, overall groupings of attitudes (or of parents on the basis of attitudes) do show relationships with children's development. For example, mothers' accommodating (rather than authoritarian) attitudes have been shown to be significantly related to their positive and responsive interaction with two year old children, and these maternal variables in turn to children's general competence and sociability with strangers (Clarke-Stewart et al., 1979). Baumrind (1971) found fathers' authoritarianism negatively related to preschool girls' cognitive performance, and Radin (1973) found fathers' warmth positively related to cognitive performance in preschool boys. These and other findings hold up primarily for middle-class samples, however (Becker and Krug, 1965; Moss and Jones, 1977). Research at this level with parents of handicapped children has focussed on the possibility of generalized attitudes to the child's being handicapped. Individual differences have received little attention, largely because of this clinical focus, and links with parent behaviour have rarely been investigated. At this level of consideration of parental attitudes it is extremely important for valid interpretation that basic conceptual frameworks and assumptions are made clear, and this preparation often seems lacking. Much of the published work on attitudes of parents of mentally handicapped children is dated, therefore the implications for research of an ecological analysis (as outlined in the previous chapters) have not been considered by most authors.

These are the levels at which analysis of parental attitudes will mainly be addressed in the present review, i.e. questions concerning parents' ideas about child-rearing and about having a young mentally handicapped child, wherein expressed attitudes would be expected to be reflected in some way in behaviour toward the child. These are the levels which seem of most relevance in considering parental involvement in teaching their young mentally handicapped children. There are, however, two broader levels which could be considered, also of relevance to intervention. Firstly, there are parental reactions such as feelings of stress and marital discord, which are expected to be more transient (though still shaped to some extent by parents' basic outlook on life), and which are a reaction to the practical difficulties faced by parents, outlined in Chapter 2. Stress is clearly related also to the adequacy of service provision. It will affect parents' responses to their children and to intervention in an overall way, for example, by a parent being too depressed to participate in home teaching. Amelioration of such reactions (e.g. "increased family comfort", Brazelton, 1976) will be an important goal of intervention. Information about these types of parental reactions will be reviewed briefly in Chapter 6.

Secondly, parents' attitudes are to some extent a reflection of the society they live in; their overall attitudes to mental handicap and to current service philosophy (i.e. normalisation) are also of relevance. As might be expected, mothers of mentally handicapped children are found to have more positive general attitudes about mental handicap than mothers of non-handicapped children (Watson and Midlarsky, 1979). However, findings within the handicap group seem contradictory: mothers have been found to be generally more positive about integration for mildly rather than severely handicapped children (Siperstein and Gottlieb, 1978) but the opposite has also been found in the case of older children (Ferrara, 1979). The latter study asked parents of mentally handicapped children to indicate their attitudes toward normalisation activities firstly in general, and then for their own child; responses were more positive for the general condition. Ferrara suggests that parents of older, more severely handicapped children may be the most positive about normalisation because they have a lesser degree of personal involvement in the debates about changing services and opportunities, since the level of handicap of their own child necessitates significant adaptations to 'normal' living, while at the same time they benefit from a generally more positive climate about mental handicap. It is noted that parents' attitudes and behaviours (e.g. overprotecting their children) may be in apparent conflict; acknowledging this degree of individuality and complexity would seem of great importance in initiating services with parents.

PARENTS' REACTIONS TO A HANDICAPPED CHILD

A great number of different reactions have been referred to in the literature as typical of, or frequently reported by, parents when told that their child is mentally handicapped. Wolfensberger's (1967) summary lists 45 initial or early reactions, all negative, including shock, denial, grief, guilt, rejection, rage, impulses to kill the child, etc. Some authors suggest one or a few reactions as predominant, while others recognise the diversity of parents' reactions. Where the diagnosis is made months after the child's birth, and parents have suspected for some time (or even have had to fight medical denial of a problem) the reactions may be intermingled with relief that the situation is at least somewhat clarified (Booth, 1978).

It is clear that some of these strong initial reactions are affected by the manner in which parents are told: those parents who were told 'well' report primarily feelings of sadness rather than of anger (Cunningham and Davis, 1985a). They tend to have been told when together with the child, in privacy, by someone who conveyed sympathy and concern but who was positive about the future, and who was ready to talk with them again. When reassured of continuing support, parents may then be allowed to enjoy some of the ordinary positive feelings of parenthood, for example, the desire to help the child develop. One study has compared how parents react when the telling of the diagnosis of Down's syndrome is handled along the above lines (a 'model procedure'), with the reactions of parents who experienced the usual procedures in other health authorities (a contemporary control group). The contrast between the satisfaction expressed by the former group with how matters had been handled, and the dissatisfaction expressed by most of the control group was striking. It was also noted that the parents who experienced the model procedure were later more positive and confident in relating to support services (Cunningham, Morgan and McGucken, 1984).

Several authors have presented an analysis of parents' reactions in terms of stages. For example, a state of shock at the initial disclosure, i.e. a feeling of not being able to register or understand the news and thus withdrawing, will be followed by a reaction stage, during which emotions of denial, sadness, anger, etc. may be felt in a rush. Then gradually parents will enter an adaptation stage when they, for example, begin to ask questions about what can be done, and finally a reorganisation stage when they seek help and begin to plan ahead (e.g. Drotar, Baskiewicz, Irvin, Kennell and Klaus, 1975; Cunningham and Davis, 1985a). The series of stages has been likened by psychoanalytically-oriented writers to a process of mourning, for the expected ideal child, and the stages may be experienced in a recurring sequence (Ross, 1964; Canino and Reeve, 1980). It is suggested that the resolution of the mourning process may never be completed by some parents.

The literature evidence for a 'stages' analysis of parents' reactions has been reviewed by Blacher (1984b). She has noted problems of small sample sizes, lack of information about severity of handicap or ecological variables, and unstructured interview methods in much of the evidence. Thus professional inference has had a very great role in the description of stages of reaction. She also questions the extent to which parents can or will actually report reactions which imply weakness or anger in themselves. She concludes that the question of whether parents do experience sequential stages in adjusting to their child's handicap remains to be answered, but that it may provide a useful basis for determining professional helping strategies.

Other conceptual analyses of parents' reactions make more reference to the parent as a member of a society which has particular views of handicap. Thus, for example, they may emphasise parents' initial concern with coming to understand the nature and meaning in their everyday life of the child's 'abnormality' (Roskies, 1972). A personal construct theory analysis of parents' reactions stresses their diversity and individuality, depending on parents' previous expectations of themselves and of the child. It also suggests that, whatever the future improvements in public services and in public prejudice, the discovery that their child is handicapped will inevitably remain a crisis for parents, as the predictability of their lives is suddenly diminished (Cunningham and Davis, 1985b; McConachie, 1985).

Two other analyses have concentrated on the idea of 'crisis'. Wolfensberger (1967) outlines three types of crisis, which may be experienced simultaneously or successively. The telling of the diagnosis will precipitate a 'novelty shock' crisis, as already described. Wolfensberger also emphasises that it is the 'demolition of expectancies' rather than the facts of handicap which have impact at this time. The second crisis is regarded as a 'value' crisis, for example, coping with the physical demands of a severely handicapped child. Farber's (1959, 1960) analysis is similar to the last two types above, termed 'tragic crisis' and 'role-organization crisis', and linked in his research findings to socio-economic status of the family.

Finally, Lavelle and Keogh (1980) have drawn on attribution theory in order to understand parents' reactions and to relate feelings to behaviour. They suggest, for example, that if a disability is seen as internal to the child and stable, then expectations of the child may be low; however, if the disability is seen as changeable then parental efforts to help the child progress may be greater. They have found that parents of mentally handicapped children may attribute their child's success to luck rather than effort (and their child's failure to lack of ability), thereby receiving less reward for their and the child's efforts. The analysis also extends to the effect which the attributions of others may have upon parents, and to how parents' reactions to services may be affected.

> "...parents' attributions about their handicapped child's condition and about their own ability to deal with it may determine, at

least in part, the energy and persistence with which parents seek and utilize available supportive services." (Lavelle and Keogh, 1980, p.20)

The point to be made from this summary is not that any one analysis is necessarily better than another, but that parents' reactions to their child being mentally handicapped must be viewed:

a) in terms of individual differences,
b) in terms which allow for change over time,
c) in relation to familial and societal values, and
d) in relation to parents' knowledge of the current local system of services.

Parents' initial reactions will not be discussed further here, as they have been summarised many times in the literature. The focus of the present chapter will be on family members' reactions and attitudes a little later on, at a time when the parents might be being involved in teaching programmes for their young mentally handicapped child. However, the distinction between 'early' and 'late' reactions is somewhat artificial, in that many of the terms used (e.g. guilt, rejection) are the same, and also several authors suggest that the initial reactions remain strong. For example, Thurston (1959) suggested that even as much as fifteen years after the diagnosis parents of cerebral palsied children still felt grief, guilt and helplessness, and 21 per cent said they were too distressed to discuss the condition with outsiders. In a more recent questionnaire study, Wikler et al. (1981) used the concept of 'chronic sorrow' to describe parents' reactions, and stressed that parents who feel recurring grief and upset over a long time period are not abnormal or 'dysfunctional'. There are, however, dissenting voices. In a well-known paper, "The myth of parental attitudes", Roith (1963) asserted that many authorities were overgeneralising from a few cases met in the course of their clinical work. This process applied particularly to the picture which used to be held of parents of autistic children, who were regarded as being rather cold and withdrawn, this being interpreted as having a causal relationship with their child's difficulties. Properly conducted research has failed to support this supposition. Both Roith and Wolfensberger

(1967) suggest that authors have tended to copy each other's opinions, without conducting necessary controlled studies, thus creating a false impression of well-founded consensus about the long-lasting disturbed nature of parents' reactions to their child's handicap.

A number of the most commonly cited later parental reactions or attitudes will be discussed below, in particular the ways in which they might be expected to have observable effects on parent-child interaction. The discussion will be followed in Chapter 5 by detailed criticism of the methods by which information about these attitudes has been gathered.

Guilt

Guilt seems to be the most frequently cited parental reaction, and even regarded by some as reflected in every other reaction (Canino and Reeve, 1980). Usually it is suggested that this reaction is unrealistic, i.e. the parents fix their feeling of responsibility for the child's abnormality on imagined links with smoking or some unusual incident in pregnancy. It is also suggested that feelings of guilt may be a reaction to impulses to kill the child, or simply not wanting a handicapped child. Parents may be thought to feel guilt at fulfilment of rejecting feelings if they allow the child to go into short-term care (Bentovim, 1972b). Roith (1963) and others (e.g. MacKeith, 1973; Heifetz, 1980) have expressed grave scepticism, noting the varied, contradictory and unsubstantiated reasoning proposed; for example, parental guilt has been postulated as identifiable in reactions of hostility to professionals, and in reactions to the child construed either as rejecting or as overcompensating. The danger in such reasoning lies in lack of appropriate action being taken, such as parents' anger with poor services being dismissed or parents' real need for respite care being ignored while professionals concentrate on 'guilt feelings' etc. (Wilkin, 1979). Apart from case-study material, and ad hoc questionnaires to parents, the only attempt at measuring guilt in any psychometrically efficient way seems to be the study by Boles (1959), who compiled a lengthy comprehensive questionnaire to look at personality factors in mothers of cerebral palsied children. Interestingly, the Parental Guilt subscale was the only one not to have good split-half reliability.

The mothers of three to nine year old handicapped children were not found to have more guilty feelings than a control group, though they were found more protective.

Overinvolvement and overprotection

Given that feelings of guilt seem more a matter of professional speculation than of substance, it may be more profitable to examine some of the behaviours mentioned above which have been posited as reflecting such feelings. A number of authors have cited overinvolvement or overcompensation as a reaction of some parents. Thus parents are described as feeling that the child is specially entrusted to them, that only they properly understand the child, summed up as "too-good mothering" (Bentovim, 1972a). Or the pattern may be seen as affecting the whole family, with all routines centred around the handicapped child, the "too-cohesive family" (Schaffer, 1964). A seemingly inevitable corollary is overprotection of the child, and fostering overdependency.

Certainly for a family to be preoccupied constantly with one member is going to be a strain on all concerned and have several negative effects, including making it difficult to take risks and let the handicapped person move toward independence and autonomy. Likewise, intervention programmes which seek to increase the quantity or quality of interaction of family members with the handicapped child must surely be aware of the possibility of intensifying pressure and ignoring other possible interests and preoccupations of family members. However, a major problem with interpreting evidence about overinvolvement and overprotection lies in the use of the prefix 'over'. Firstly, the standard to which it refers is not made explicit. Schaffer (1964) cites fathers taking time off work to attend clinics as one part of the pattern of overinvolvement; yet use of the prevailing norm of lack of involvement of fathers in child-care may be quite inappropriate in terms of the needs created by the child's handicap. Parents' infrequent use of babysitters may be a mixture of reluctance to ask and a lack of proffered help; on the other hand, controlled studies tend to reveal that other parents of young children also go out together infrequently (Hewett, 1970). And some research has suggested that similar expressions of 'overprotectiveness' can be found in families with a handicapped child and in families with non-handicapped children (Jaehnig and Townsend, 1973).

The second part of the problem of interpretation arises from the negatively-toned labels often used by attitude scales. For example, some forms of the widely used Parent Attitude Research Instrument (Schaefer, Bell and Bayley, 1959) have the factor label 'overprotective', whereas Boles's scale (mentioned above) and the Maryland Parent Attitude Survey (Pumroy, 1966) use the label 'protective' (though it still may be reported by others as 'overprotective', e.g. Wolfensberger, 1967, p.345).

The findings do overall suggest that parents of mentally handicapped children are more protective (e.g. Boles, 1959; Klebanoff, 1959; Bell, 1964; Slouth, Kogan and Tyler, 1978). There is also evidence to link protectiveness with consequent child behaviours; for example, in studies of children with epilepsy, and with mild mental handicap, parental attitudes which encourage passivity are related to and seem to foster educational under-achievement (Hartlage and Green, 1972; Landman, 1979). Ferguson and Watt (1980) also found mothers of severely handicapped children more protective, reporting that they said they did some things for their children which they should do for themselves, that they did not like to ask neighbours to look after the children, that they worried about how other children would treat them, etc. However, the authors reject interpreting these reports as a generalised attitude of 'overprotection', as they did not extend to reports about the school situation. Thus when mothers had services they could rely on and professionals they could trust, they did not worry about the child and feel so protective.

Authoritarianism

Overprotection is an aspect of one of the two main dimensions found in studies of attitudes of parents to child-rearing, i.e. authoritarianism (the other being acceptance/rejection) (Martin, 1975). Studies tend to agree in finding mothers of mentally handicapped children more authoritarian or stricter than mothers of non-handicapped children, and children with other handicaps (except mothers of blind children) (e.g. Klebanoff, 1959; Cook, 1963; Pitfield and Oppenheim, 1964; Harper, 1984). Ricci (1970) did not; however, his study was poorly controlled and the reverse findings are probably explained by the control mothers being older and less well-educated, as these factors tend to be associated with more authoritarian attitudes (Dingman, Eyman and Windle, 1963). Cook (1963) found that mothers of severely handicapped children were more authoritarian than mothers of mildly handicapped children, but commented that this may simply be a reflection of the amount of care needed by the child.

How authoritarian attitudes relate to parental behaviour is not clear from the research. Some studies do find significant relationships, but with only limited shared variance (e.g. Baumrind, 1971). Brody (1969) found no attitude-behaviour correlations for the Parent Attitude Research Instrument, but found mothers who scored high on the Disciplinarian scale of the Maryland Parent Attitude Survey showed significantly more directive behaviours than did mothers who scored low. Unfortunately, when this latter scale was applied to parents of developmentally delayed preschoolers, no observational data on parent-child interaction was presented, and in any case parents of the delayed children were not found more disciplinarian than parents of non-delayed children (Slouth et al., 1978). The authors comment that the results might have been different with a more severely handicapped sample.

PARI scores have been found to relate to success in 'parent training': high scoring mothers of children with articulatory disorders were less successful in correcting their children's production of consonants after training than low-scoring mothers (Sommers, Furlong, Rhodes, Fichter, Bowser, Copetas and Saunders, 1964). As authoritarianism is held to be a major factor in all the PARI scales (Cohler, Weiss and Grunebaum, 1970), it may be suggested to be the differentiating factor in the mothers' success. No comparable within-group study seems to have been reported with mentally handicapped children.

Acceptance or rejection

Feelings of rejection, or simply ambivalence toward the child have often been described in the literature. Yet the term covers a multitude of interpretations, including parents' lack of confidence that they know how to love and care for an abnormal child; lack of interest in or enjoyment of the child; hostility towards or criticism of the child; unrealistic expectations of the child, etc. 'Acceptance' is even less well defined, and seems in many cases merely to be used by professionals to describe parents' acquiescence rather than any quality of their interaction with the child (Barsch, 1968; Roskies, 1972). Other authors attempt to distinguish between acceptance of the child, and refusal to 'accept' the disability, i.e. maintaining a hopeful and challenging stance about the possiblities for the child's future attainments (Russell, 1983).

Certainly there are several references in the literature to a shift in attitude to the child after a few months, when, for example, questions of the child's 'differentness' may be replaced by observation of the child's 'sameness', having ordinary problems such as catching colds, and beginning to interact in a way which is highly rewarding to parents (Roskies, 1972; Cunningham, 1983b). This reflection of the parents' growing confidence in themselves and in the child, taken in conjunction with the finding that parents do tend to make realistic assessments of their children's present abilities and difficulties (e.g. Boles, 1959; Wolfensberger and Kurtz, 1971; Wishart et al., 1980), seem to be the nub of what might remain as useful in the concept of 'acceptance'.

Generally attitude scale studies have not found parents of mentally handicapped children to be more rejecting than parents of non-handicapped children or only slightly so (Klebanoff, 1959; Dingman et al., 1963; Pitfield and Oppenheim, 1964; Cummings, Bailey and Rie, 1966; Cummings, 1976). Cook (1963) and Wetter (1972) suggest that mild handicaps are more likely to be associated with parental feelings of rejection. Only Ricci (1970) found mothers of mentally handicapped children significantly more rejecting than mothers of non-handicapped children. In contrast to both of these, Slouth et al. (1978) have found mothers of young children with developmental delay to be significantly <u>less</u> rejecting.

Using a rather different technique to measure acceptance-rejection (i.e. asking parents to rate their handicapped child on a list of 40 traits, then a non-handicapped sibling, an 'ideal child' and 'other' children on the same list) several studies have found that mentally handicapped children are rated more negatively by their parents than the non-handicapped and 'ideal' children. However, there are great individual differences, and the handicapped children may still be rated more positively than 'other' children (Peck and Stephens, 1960; Worchel and Worchel, 1961). Thus, 'more negatively' may not be the same as 'negatively', particularly when it is realised that classification of the trait labels as positive or negative was made by the researchers.

Whatever the methodological and interpretation problems of such studies (see below), the main criticism to be levelled is that

> "The acceptance-rejection-overprotection model has long been proven both theoretically and clinically meaningless, and it is about time that it be given a decent burial." (Roskies, 1972, p.299)

To conduct discussion about parents in these terms gives remarkably little insight into why and how parents and children might have difficulties in their relationships, and how they might be helped by others. For example, a static model of 'parental attitudes' fails to reflect the influence of service provision, and change over time (Wright, Granger and Sameroff, 1984). Several studies of young mentally handicapped children and their families have stressed finding a more positive picture in parents' reactions than they expected from the literature. They suggest that good early services, such as home visits from teachers and day-care facilities, have significantly affected parents' ability to cope, confidence in themselves and optimism about the future (Ferguson and Watt, 1980). When parents of younger and older children are compared cross-sectionally, the latter are found to be in need of expanded services, and report feeling less supported in their role and more isolated than the parents of young children (Suelzle and Keenan, 1981). One reason will be pressures created by the growing gap between the handicapped children's activities and those of their non-handicapped age-peers (Birenbaum, 1971). However, longitudinal studies are required in order to clarify what might be the long-term effects of improved services on parents' attitudes.

To summarise so far: the most commonly cited reactions of parents to their handicapped child tend not to stand up as general findings on closer scrutiny. The one possible exception to this conclusion is that parents are frequently reported as endorsing ideas or describing behaviour which could be summed up as 'protective'. These may be obvious reactions to the difficulties faced by their children in competitive society. On the other hand, some parents will need help to 'let go'.

> "The fact that Philip can find his way about outside he owes largely to my husband rather than to me. Left alone to decide I doubt whether I would have been brave enough to let him go out of my sight. My husband, however, was far-seeing and said, 'Unfortunately, we have to face the possibility that Philip will always lack the companionship of people of his own age. It is possible that if we can interest him in any pursuit at all it is going to be a lone pursuit.'" (Candy, 1976, p.11)

Even in the preschool years, the philosophy of preparation for independence is of relevance, perhaps evidenced by the large numbers of parents who currently seek an integrated preschool or school situation for their mentally handicapped children, so that the children are exposed to the demands of their age-peers (and in turn influence them and their parents). Thus, whether it involves helping parents gradually withdraw their support, or instead being careful not to pile yet more pressure on to parents' focussing on the child, the issue of protectiveness/overinvolvement seems relevant for professionals to consider in intervention.

Another reaction which seemed to emerge for consideration (though not demonstrated clearly by research focussed on 'rejection'), is the idea of parental 'acceptance' where that is taken to mean a combination of parents' self-confidence and seeing the child in more complex ways than primarily in terms of handicap. Personal construct theory suggests that helping parents to elaborate their system of construing the child in positive ways will be an important feature of early intervention (Davis, 1983; Davis and Cunningham, 1985; McConachie, 1985), as well as suggesting ideas on positive activities to do with the child. It may be that for fathers these are particularly important steps, if they lack confidence and knowledge about how to play with very young children, given that mentally handicapped children may take longer to develop spoken language, sustained attention, and so on (McConachie, 1982).

Thirdly, there is some suggestion in the literature that parents of mentally handicapped children are more authoritarian than parents of non-handicapped children, and that authoritarian attitudes may be linked to more directive behaviour toward the child. These characteristics may reflect necessary or obvious adaptation by parents to the child's difficulties (e.g. controlling the behaviour of hearing-impaired children, Malkin, Freeman and Hastings, 1976); on the other hand, they may be an overreaction and create pressure on the child to 'do things the right way'. It seems that degree of parental control may be another issue for consideration in intervention.

DIFFERENTIATING FACTORS

Fathers

Until this point in the chapter, the word 'parents' has been used loosely - most studies have included only mothers, and discussion papers allot at most a page or so to fathers as an aside. Before the author's own chapter (McConachie, 1982), there had been apparently only three published papers specifically about fathers of mentally handicapped children (Cummings, 1976; Price-Bonham and Addison, 1978; Gallagher et al., 1981, plus a brief critical reply to Price-Bonham and Addison - Wikler, 1979). There has since been one other published review of literature; however all but two of the articles referenced are pre-1976 (Lamb, 1983). On the other hand, there are many scattered references to fathers' attitudes and feelings, particularly in parents' own writings. For example, it has been suggested that to have a mentally handicapped child is harder for a father to accept than for a mother, because of its questioning his 'manhood', because he is cut off from the channels of information and services which the mother takes part in with the child, because the child will take much longer to develop (if ever) to the level at which father can involve him or her in traditional 'father-role' activities, and because the father's wish to take pride in his child's achievements in the outside world will be frustrated. However, several apparently contradictory beliefs can be found, such as that fathers should be told the diagnosis first since they are the 'strong ones' and will take it better. As with any such generalizations, it is likely that the range of individual differences will encompass any apparent contradictions.

Several researchers have used the theoretical perspective of Parsons and Bales (1955) (see Chapter 3) to suggest that the processes of adaptation to the handicapped child will be different for fathers and for mothers. Some evidence has been found to suggest that fathers have a greater tendency to be concerned about issues consistent with the instrumental role (e.g. the cost of providing for a young handicapped child) than mothers, and mothers a greater tendency to be concerned about issues consistent with the expressive role (e.g. the emotional strain of caring for the child) (Gumz and Gubrium, 1972). There is also some evidence suggesting that a father's primary mode of influence on the child may be indirect, for example, by relieving the strain on the mother, or by his attitudes influencing the whole family's acceptance or rejection of the child (Peck and Stephens, 1960; Cain and Levine, 1963). It is difficult to evaluate such studies in the light of change in expectations about the practice of parental roles, and of changes in theorising about parents' attitudes. There are also similarly conceived studies which do not find mother-father differences (e.g. Staton, 1972). Lamb (1976b) has noted that many studies on child-rearing have found paternal warmth a crucial variable, and suggested that the instrumental role of the father had been overstressed and the importance of the expressive component of the relationship with the child overlooked.

Other attitude scale studies comparing mothers and fathers have suggested much similarity and some differences. Sapon (1982) used the PARI and found mothers and fathers of young Down's syndrome children differed only on fathers being more likely to foster dependence in the child. (The structure of fathers' child-rearing attitudes on the PARI has been shown very similar to mothers' (Schludermann and Schludermann, 1970).) Another larger study showed mothers overall to score higher than fathers on understanding, acceptance and trust of the children, whose handicaps included diabetes, asthma, cystic fibrosis and hearing impairment (Tavormina, Boll, Dunn, Luscomb and Taylor, 1981). However, as this study encompassed children aged from five to 19 years, and did not include mentally handicapped children, its results may not be of relevance here.

A questionnaire study of mothers and fathers of young mentally handicapped children (who had all received a home-teaching service) found that parents agreed on how they described their children, but disagreed more in describing their own attitudes and feelings, particularly the parents of the more severely or multiply handicapped children. Fathers tended to be more negative than mothers, for example, in feeling satisfied with the child's progress, in feeling that services were appropriate, in feeling that friends offered the right kind of help, or in feeling delighted with the child's small achievements (Wishart et al., 1980). Fathers found the child difficult to understand and to play with. Cummings (1976) found that fathers of mentally handicapped children were markedly lower than fathers of non-handicapped or chronically ill children on items scaled as 'enjoyment of the child'. Both sets of authors concluded that fathers need particular help in intervention, and putting the results of the last four studies mentioned together, it may be that the kind of help needed is in understanding the child better, in observation of small changes and in how to facilitate children's development from an early stage.

General findings about discipline seem to indicate less dissension over handicapped children than over non-handicapped children, though in some cases this may be because it is left to one parent (Hewett, 1970). Carr (1975) found fathers of Down's syndrome children were said to be less strict than their wives more often than fathers of non-handicapped children were, and Gregory's (1976) conclusions about parents of hearing-impaired children were similar. Again, fathers being less strict may reflect lack of confidence. A series of small group discussions for fathers of infants with Down's syndrome found major concerns to be lack of understanding of the implications of the child's handicap, as well as difficulty in discussing the problem with friends and in supporting their wives who carried the major burden (Erickson, 1976).

The question of parents' differential reactions to the <u>stigma</u> of their child's handicap, and to the <u>sex</u> of the child have also been explored. Fathers have been found to cope less well with children whose handicap is obvious from their appearance (Cain and Levine, 1963; Tallman, 1965). Mothers' adaptability is generally related to variables other than appearance, such as children's level of competence. Evidence suggests that parents' perceptions of stigma are higher in the case of a boy (Levinson and Starling, 1981). It could be suggested simply that boys are seen as likely to have more troublesome behaviour (Farber, 1960); however, the difference in perceptions of boys and of girls holds for even the most severely handicapped children. Therefore, it seems that "a greater degree of subnormal behaviour may be tolerated for females than males" (Levinson and Starling, 1981, p.385). Because fathers (in their instrumental role) are expected to care more about sons' achievements, it has been suggested that fathers are less likely to accept the existence and extent of mental handicap in their sons (Levine, 1966), and to be generally more accepting of a mentally handicapped daughter (Grossman, 1972). However, several authors (for example, Greene, 1971; Wolfensberger and Kurtz, 1971; Staton, 1972; Cummings, 1976; Slouth et al., 1978) have not found such differences between mothers and fathers, and between sons and daughters, and suggested other variables such as social class and religious background were of more relevance than sex in explaining parents' attitudes to their child's handicap.

<u>Independent characteristics affecting attitudes</u>
In the research literature on parents' attitudes and adjustment to their handicapped child, a number of factors have been explored in subgroup comparisons. Where differences are found, however, it is rarely possible to interpret the mechanisms involved in any more than a speculative way, as many studies lack a clear conceptual background. An exception perhaps is the sociological research programme led by Farber in the mid 1950's to which reference has already been made, which proceeded from a complex theoretical perspective on family integration. One of the factors identified as having a significant effect on parental attitude was <u>social class</u>: Farber and others (e.g. Holt, 1958; Canino and Reeve, 1980) seem to agree that the higher the social class of the family, in some ways the more difficult is the process of adjustment, for example, through having had higher expectations for themselves and their children. However, Cain and Levine (1963) found higher social class fathers to be more adaptable in relating to their handicapped child, and Wolfensberger and Kurtz (1971) found higher social class parents more realistic in assessing their child's current level of functioning. It is difficult with many studies of

families of handicapped children (including Farber's) to judge the effect on the results of sampling deficiencies, i.e. the general bias toward white, skilled occupation, volunteer groups (and also the effect of unvalidated measures of 'adjustment'). Social class is a notoriously 'blunt instrument' as a measure, but through its associations with housing standards and levels of education, etc., may remain an issue for consideration in the evaluation of intervention (Osborn and Morris, 1979).

The racial or cultural background of parents seems to have been little investigated. However, it will obviously have an effect on parental attitude: for example, the Muslim belief that handicap is the 'will of God' may be expected to have a different effect from the Hindu belief in reincarnation. Vasquez (1974) using the PARI concluded that Mexican-American and black parents were more accepting of their (mild to moderate) mentally retarded child than white parents. Enwemeka and Adeghe (1983) related many Nigerian fathers' lack of interest in and financial support of their handicapped child to illiteracy and poor understanding of the real causes of the handicap. However, Okunade (1981) found Western Nigerian traditional communities to have more positive attitudes to handicapped children than Western-educated groups. There are obviously complex class as well as cultural factors at work in different settings, in need of research, in order to aid appropriate intervention. The one conclusion which is clear from cross-cultural community studies of attitudes toward disability is that generalizations do not hold true even from one neighbouring area to another (Mittler and Serpell, 1985).

The religious beliefs of parents have been an obvious source of hypotheses, positing that certain values and institutions may help parents to adjust to their child's handicap more easily than others. However, the research studies carried out have been poorly controlled for confounding variables such as size of family and social class, and have come to contradictory conclusions which will not be described here (Wolfensberger, 1967; Canino and Reeve, 1980).

A number of variables specific to the child have been investigated, in addition to the variable of child sex mentioned above. The type and degree of handicap has also been mentioned, with some specific differences in parent attitudes being found, usually against a background of overall difference from a non-handicapped control (e.g. Cook, 1963; Pitfield and Oppenheim, 1964; Cummings et al., 1966; Cummings, 1976). However, the categorizing is very broad, and a more interesting line of investigation is to enquire what characteristics of children are perceived by parents as significant. For example, in a study of young children with a variety of different severe problems in development, those children who were viewed as relatively more active and less irritable by their mothers received more positive caretaking and their mothers felt less confused (Affleck, Allen, McGrade and McQueeney, 1982). Studies which describe children's characteristics in more detail than simply diagnostic label or IQ score are to be welcomed (e.g. Mogford, 1979a; Wishart et al., 1980).

Sometimes, a diagnostic label can be seen as helpful, e.g. where the child's handicap is not highly visible and uninformed others might attribute deviant behaviour to poor parenting (Telford and Sawrey, 1977). Also other children may act more favourably to a child whose (mild to moderate) mental handicap is labelled than to one whose handicap is not (Budoff and Siperstein, 1978). However, generally parents are found to have great reluctance in accepting any label for their own child, even if they regard it as appropriate for other children (e.g. 'mental retardation') and they prefer euphemistic labels (Wolfensberger and Kurtz, 1974).

There has been very little investigation of differences in parental attitude according to whether the handicapped child has siblings or not. Authors seem to agree in suggesting that adjustment might be more difficult where the mentally handicapped child was the <u>first born</u>, and easier where there are other children to fulfil some of the parents' expectations (Wolfensberger, 1967; Telford and Sawrey, 1977), but this conclusion is not backed by thorough evidence.

Siblings

The attitudes of siblings themselves have received more attention (though still restricted by the general focus on mothers). However, researchers have generally relied on mothers' reports of siblings' feelings, and have tended to assume from the outset that the presence of the handicapped child will have detrimental effects on other family members.

Farber (1959) found a high proportion of siblings showing adverse effects, and showed a positive relationship with the severity of the handicapped child's dependence on the mother. McMichael (1971) and Kew (1975) also reported a number of adverse effects such as attention-seeking behaviour, jealousy, hostility and aggression, embarrassment and a reluctance to bring friends home. However, Kew's conclusions were drawn solely from social workers' assessments, and the families were unlikely to be representative of the population as a whole. These and similar reports are set in context by controlled studies. For example, Hewett (1970) found that mothers reported that 33 per cent of siblings of cerebral palsied children showed jealousy; this is the same percentage found by Newson and Newson (1968) for siblings of non-handicapped four year olds. Lonsdale (1978) made a similar point about reports of emotional disturbance in siblings. However, a major controlled study of siblings of three to 18 year old physically disabled children did suggest greater risk of psychological impairment in younger male siblings, especially those close in age to the disabled child, and in older female siblings, than in siblings of non-handicapped children (Breslau, Weitzman and Messenger, 1981; Breslau, 1982). Ferrari (1984) found same-sex siblings of chronically ill children were most at risk for maladjustment. In contrast to the findings of adverse reactions, Schaefer (1982) found older siblings of three to eight year old handicapped children to be less likely to show anger, jealousy or to hurt the child's feelings, and more likely to help, comfort, assume responsibility, and to be pleased with the younger child's progress than siblings of non-handicapped children. He comments that these differences applied more to families in which the child had a mental rather than a physical handicap where more rivalry might be evidenced. He found that age-spacing of the siblings made no difference, and Gath (1973) also found no differences whether the sibling was older or younger than the handicapped child. Thus, it seems that in addition to the use of control groups, future research with siblings should take account of such variables as the type and degree of handicap, age-spacing and birth order, and sex of the sibling, in order to more usefully predict adverse effects (Simeonsson and McHale, 1981).

When siblings themselves are interviewed, the reported incidence and severity of problems is low, and positive effects are frequently mentioned (e.g. Caldwell and Guze, 1960; Graliker et al., 1962; Grossman, 1972; McConachie and Domb, 1983). Siblings report having benefited through family cohesiveness being greater, and through gaining in maturity and understanding of others. Some authors have noted that siblings of handicapped children are rather likely to enter the caring professions, and have interpreted this as an 'adverse' effect, that is, taking on too great feelings of responsibility or "survivors' guilt" (Cleveland and Miller, 1977; Seligman, 1983). More carefully designed and controlled studies would be needed in order to evaluate this suggestion. Good sibling relationships are promoted by a positive marital relationship (Graliker et al., 1962; Schaefer, 1982) and also by positive parental attitudes toward the handicapped child (Caldwell and Guze, 1960; Minde, Hackett, Killou and Silver, 1972; Trevino, 1979). Thus the role of the family environment in promoting positive adjustment in siblings of mentally handicapped children should not be overlooked. Future research should aim at identifying "ecological factors as well as individual characteristics that contribute to adaptation" (Vadasy et al., 1984, p.165).

Grandparents

Grandparents are often the first to be told about a baby's birth, and they usually show keen interest in a child's development and achievements. Given that they have lived through times when mental handicap was not well understood, stigma for the family greater, and services limited, their reactions to the child's being handicapped are likely to be of as great distress and bewilderment as the parents' (Gabel and Kotsch, 1981). There are several anecdotal reports in the literature of grandparents consistently denying that the child is handicapped, putting a strain on relations with the child's parents (Bentovim, 1972a; Cunningham, 1982; Worthington, 1982; Glendinning, 1983). However, professionals rarely see grandparents directly, to convey information and to discuss implications of the handicap, and the grandparents may be reluctant to raise their worries with the child's parents, for fear of interfering.

One study of grandparents of autistic children looked at how grandparents and parents viewed each other and the child. Several significant differences between the generations were found, and in each case grandparents took a more positive view of the child or of their relationship with their own son or daughter. This might be interpreted as some evidence of greater 'denial' of the problems of the child by grandparents, or of lesser familiarity (Harris et al., 1985).

CONCLUSION

This review of reactions of other family members to a mentally handicapped child has produced a number of issues which seem worthy of further consideration, despite the variety of approaches and generally poor standard of research in terms of conceptual framework and design (and lack of clinical relevance). Three issues were summarised above: protectiveness versus promoting independence; the primacy of the 'handicap' in parents' eyes; parental authoritarianism or control. The examination of a number of independent variables has suggested other issues which might repay further study, such as potentially more problematic reactions of fathers to a handicapped child. However, it will be important for assumptions in research strategy to be made clear, and for multiple independent variables to be noted or controlled for, in order that interpretation of results be made on a sure footing. A third necessity in future attitude research is for well-constructed methods of measurement. The following chapter describes methods which have been used to measure attitudes of parents of mentally handicapped children, and analyses strengths and weaknesses in relation to the conceptual framework developed in Chapters 1 and 3.

Chapter Five

METHODS FOR MEASURING PARENTS' ATTITUDES

The overall conclusion of the previous chapter was that there are a number of issues to do with parental attitudes which might be of relevance in the planning of intervention. How might these attitudes be measured? The methods used in the studies reviewed above will be discussed here, before going on to more recent solutions to the question.

The methods can be categorized in various ways, along dimensions of formality, conceptual background and psychometric adequacy. A large proportion of the published literature has relied on informal methods which are affected by obvious biases. Many are comments on clinical cases (e.g. Kanner, 1953; Bentovim, 1972a), or other sources of experience, for example, noting experts' reasoning about parents' feelings of guilt (Roith, 1963). Into this grouping we might also put parents' own testimony, either on their own, or loosely grouped and contrasted with others' (e.g. Hannam, 1980).

More formal than these, but not rooted in a particular theoretical framework, are questionnaires to parents, based on 'common sense' or the findings of others, for which no evidence of validity or reliability is presented (e.g. Roith, 1963; Wishart et al., 1980). A problem attendant on such methods may be low response rate. Wikler et al. (1981) received only a third of questionnaires sent out, and then suggested that parents were reluctant to stir up hurtful feelings, i.e. using negative 'evidence' to support their conclusions about parents experiencing chronic sorrow. When questionnaires are returned, it is still difficult to interpret the validity of answers, as other feelings not asked about may be as important. This may particularly be the case when an explicit theoretical framework has been adopted (e.g. the psychoanalytic concept of mourning, or Parsons and Bales' theory of family structure) within which items are phrased and interpreted (e.g. Gumz and Gubrium, 1972). With less structured interview approaches, problems in classifying or interpreting responses may increase. For example, Cain and Levine (1963) interviewed parents about their handling of their handicapped child, and then rated responses in terms of 'adaptability' (i.e. flexibility, empathy and motivation). The possibilities for class-bias and misunderstanding in the ratings are obvious.

The advantages of parent attitude scales are the apparent care with which they have been constructed, and evidence as to their reliability. Those which have been designed for general use and have appeared most often in published studies of parents of mentally handicapped children will be discussed below.

The Shoben Parent Attitude Survey (Shoben, 1949) was the major forerunner of the PARI, based on psychoanalytic theory of maternal causation of neuroticism, and designed to assess parents' attitudes in relation to children's behaviour or personality problems. Parents indicate on a four-point scale their agreement with general statements of parental policy. The final version has 85 items scaled by agreement between sorters into Dominant, Possessive, Ignoring and Miscellaneous subscales. The items were selected for their ability to distinguish between parents of nine year old problem and non-problem behaviour children; however, several studies found that it was not useful in the prediction of adjustment in children (Schaefer et al., 1959; Becker and Krug, 1965). A modification of this scale was included in the battery of self-inventory instruments used by Cummings in comparing mothers and fathers of mentally retarded, chronically ill, neurotic and non-handicapped children, and it was found not to distinguish between groups (Cummings et al., 1966; Cummings, 1976).

The Parent Attitude Research Instrument (Schaefer et al., 1959) adopted a similar format (four-point rating, items expressed in the third-person) and was immediately a popular instrument. It consists of 115 items in 23 scales. The first factor analyses yielded five factors: Suppression and interpersonal distance, Hostile rejection of the homemaking role, Excessive demand for striving, Overpossessiveness, Harsh punitive control. Later analyses yielded two major factors, Authoritarian control, and Hostility-rejection, which were duplicated in a version devised for fathers. Criticism of the scale has been extensive. For example, predicted relationships with child behaviour are usually found only for upper middle class samples. Also, measures of authoritarian attitudes are strongly influenced by an acquiescent response set (e.g. many parents are found to agree with fundamentally opposing items) and by the respondent's educational level, so that the observed relationship between low educational level and authoritarian attitudes may in part be an artifact (Becker and Krug, 1965). The PARI has been used extensively with parents of handicapped children, so much so that Bell wrote a review of such studies in only 1964. Bell concluded that, rather than parental attitudes shaping child behaviour (which was the usual interpretation), in the case of handicapped children observed differences were a reaction to the care required by the child, and thus the normative basis for evaluating parents' attitudes as 'healthy' or 'unhealthy' should be invalid.

The Maryland Parent Attitude Survey (Pumroy, 1966) was designed to overcome some of the response set problems of the PARI such as social desirability. Items (expressed in the third person) were sorted as representing Disciplinarian, Indulgent, Protective or Rejecting attitudes. Ninety pairs of items are presented, with 45 items representing each of the four types, and the parent has to choose which most represents his or her own attitude. Low correlation has been shown with the social desirability scale of the Minnesota Multiphasic Personality Inventory. Brody (1969) found some correlations with observed parent behaviours, and no such correlations for the PARI. The sample consisted of mothers who were mostly high-school graduates, married to men in non-professional occupations (i.e. possibly not the usual upper middle class sample for whom attitude-behaviour correlations are found). A study of young developmentally delayed children using the MPAS found few differences from other parents of preschool children, no significant differences between mothers and fathers, and no more extreme scorers in the clinic sample than in the non-handicapped sample (Slouth et al., 1978). The authors suggest more differences might be found for parents of older, more handicapped children.

The Hereford Parent Attitude Survey (Hereford, 1963) was designed in order to monitor change following intervention with parents, and has 75 items in five scales, Confidence in the parental role, Causation of the child's behaviour, Acceptance of the child's behaviour and feelings, Mutual Understanding, and Mutual Trust. The majority of items were drawn from the PARI. This scale has been used with others in several studies by Tavormina (e.g. 1975; Tavormina et al., 1981) who has found that parents of mentally handicapped children score in between parents of non-handicapped and parents of poorly-adjusted children, and that mothers as a group score differently from fathers on some scales. It did not detect changes following counselling or training groups for mothers, but this may be either because changes did not occur, or that they took longer to occur than the period of assessment, or that they were not adequately measured by this instrument (Tavormina, 1975). The exception was in the Causation scale, where mothers trained in a behavioural framework came to see themselves as more able to determine the child's behaviour.

The Boles Inventory for Parents of Handicapped Children (Boles, 1959) was designed specifically for use with parents of children with cerebral palsy, but is similar to the above scales, in that many items were drawn from the Shoben Parent Attitude Survey. In a study of well-matched groups of mothers of handicapped and non-handicapped children, Boles found few predicted differences. Staton (1972) compared mothers and fathers of mentally handicapped children with part of this scale, and found no differences in guilt, 'unrealistic attitudes', and 'overprotective' attitudes.

General criticisms of these scales can be summarised as follows:

1) Most instruments are primarily measures of authoritarian child rearing attitudes.
2) The differences which are found between parents of handicapped children and parents of non-handicapped children are few, and are generally in the area of 'authoritarianism' which may simply reflect the reality of demands made by the child rather than generalized attitudes.
3) To describe these reactions negatively (overprotection, unrealistic, etc.) is to reflect professionals' psychodynamically-influenced

assumptions that parents are "neurotic victims of the child's untreatable impairment" (Heifetz, 1980, p.361). This view of parents has been long since thoroughly challenged (Wolfensberger, 1967) and the reality of parents' situations and positive adaptability recognised.

4) The attitude data derived is not clinically useful, though to be fair most scales were not designed to be so.

5) The scales appear to assume a generality of attitudes to child-rearing as a whole, across the age-span.

6) The comparative studies look for specific reactions to a handicapped child, ignoring the fact that many families have other children who also influence parents' general attitudes.

7) Thus, critical reviews conclude that attitude scales require to be phrased more specifically: to distinguish between attitudes and behaviour; to ask what parents feel rather than what they think; to be phrased in the first person; to be focussed on a particular child; to take account of different ages and situations; etc. (Becker and Krug, 1965; Cohler et al., 1970).

A number of scales used in published studies of parents of handicapped children have some of the features specified above. For example, the Parent Report of Child Behavior uses a four-point rating of items about a particular child, with underlying factors labelled both in positive and in negative terms. Internal consistency reliabilities are satisfactory, but no validity studies are reported. The use of the instrument with mothers of multihandicapped children suggested that factors of Positive Relationship, Obedience and Independence found in studies of mothers of non-handicapped children are not well separated, and that mothers of handicapped children perceive a positive relationship with the child as depending on a combination of compliant behaviours (Harper, 1984). This might be perceived as the mothers being more controlling (although the study did not include a comparison group), or might reflect reaction to differing degrees of child competence. Interpretation is also a problem with another scale which focusses ratings on a particular child, i.e. the Worchel Child Rating Scale (Worchel and Worchel, 1961). The structure of the scale is to compare ratings of the handicapped child with those made by the parent for other children or an 'ideal' child (see description above in the section on Rejection). No evidence of validity or reliability is given. The problems with this scale lie firstly in the degree of interpretation made by researchers in assessing parental 'rejection' from the original adjective ratings of the child, and secondly, the confusion in the ratings between the degree to which an adjective applies and the extent to which the child shows different behaviour in different settings.

In order to give parents more leeway in expressing their feelings about specific people and situations, some researchers have used sentence completion tests (Thurston, 1959; Appell, Williams and Fishell, 1964; Cummings, 1976). However, there are then great problems in interpretation and categorization of responses, and evidence of reliability is not provided. A third type is the Child-Rearing Practices Inventory (Pitfield and Oppenheim, 1964) designed specifically to distinguish parents of handicapped children from parents of non-handicapped children. It examines a broad base of attitudes, which factor-analyse into the usual two dimensions (strictness, acceptance/rejection). Its main difference from other attitude scales is that it is phrased in the first person, using a five-point scale of agreement. Subscales include lack of confidence, uncertainty in handling, and difficulties in setting limits, all of which are reactions which may have predictable observable behavioural correlates, and seem of obvious relevance for intervention. However, there is no analysis presented for how these attitudes might differ with children of different ages.

The approach adopted by some authors (e.g. Peck and Stephens, 1960; Cummings, 1976; Burden, 1978, 1981) is to utilise a battery of scales in order to assess attitudes. The problem is that without careful assessment of concurrent validity, by cross-checking of items between scales, a summation of data from poorly constructed instruments is itself just as poor, especially when small samples are used. Burden has chosen instruments which reflect the most commonly cited reactions of parents, but without reference to any theory of individual emotional or family functioning. (The problems with using citation as justification have been outlined above.) The battery is given only to mothers. However, the instruments chosen include the three types mentioned above as having some features which enhance their usefulness, along with a Self-Rating Scale (Judson and Burden, 1980) and the widely-used Malaise Inventory (Rutter, Tizard and Whitmore, 1970). At present, published results are limited to the Malaise Inventory (see next chapter) and the Worchel scale (Burden, 1985). The battery has been developed for use with mothers receiving comprehensive early services, who are compared with a group in another part of the country less well served. Conclusions presented so far emphasise the tenuousness of generalized interpretation of attitudes, and of the meaning of observed changes, when knowledge of individual circumstances is brought to bear.

ATTITUDES IN CONTEXT

The conceptual framework for the study of families of handicapped children which was outlined in Chapters 1 and 3 can be used to analyse the limitations of previous attitude research and to identify more fruitful approaches for the future. Many of the points have already been made in passing.

Research on attitudes of parents of handicapped children has generally been based on expectation of deviance, i.e. focussing on difficult, hurtful feelings to the exclusion of positive feelings about the child, and further than this, making judgements about parents' attitudes and feelings in terms of assumed psychopathology. Many research designs have used a clinical focus, comparing parents of handicapped children and non-handicapped children, and interpreting observed differences in terms of general statements about the effects of the child's handicap, ignoring both the extent of overlap between groups, and other sources of group differences. Research has generally used a static model, thus not following individuals over time in order to appreciate processes of attitude formation. Even those studies which have considered the question of change over time have frequently used cross-sectional analyses (e.g. Suelzle and Keenan, 1981) or asked parents to look back and/or to look forward from one point in time (e.g. Burden, 1980; Wishart et al., 1980).

Research into attitudes has made unacknowledged assumptions about cultural norms. For example, cross-cultural studies are lacking, and even within affluent English-speaking cultures researchers' strategies seem to represent questions about middle-class values rather than working-class values. The findings of clear relationships primarily in middle-class samples between attitudes and behaviour are open to a number of interpretations, and are not well understood. However, to speculate a little, there is perhaps a parallel in many recent findings of differences in clarity of links between parental attitudes and behaviour and child development depending on sex of parent and sex of child. For example, Clarke-Stewart (1980) found correlations over time of children's cognitive development with mothers' positive rating of the child and ability to engage the child in play much more strongly for girls than for boys. Pawlby and Hall (1980) have found significant relationships between maternal behaviour when children are aged 20 weeks, and child language development at 27 months, but only for girls. Davis (1979) found relationships between how mothers say they see their children and how they interact with them, again only for girls. He suggested that mothers perhaps have a more stereotyped set of constructs and thus less finely-tuned behaviour towards boys. Likewise, perhaps researchers on child development have stereotyped class-based ideas on the content of child-development research.

Few researchers have focussed on <u>fathers</u> of mentally handicapped children when considering parents' attitudes. Where fathers have been included, researchers have generally used the same strategy in describing their attitudes as is adopted for the study of mothers (e.g. Cummings, 1976; Slouth et al., 1980). However, some have taken note of the possibility that fathers' attitudes may have a different function and development in the family from mothers', e.g. having an indirect influence on the child through the mother. This is one stage more sophisticated than a unidimensional analysis, but lacks an overall conceptual framework of the <u>family as a system</u>, with its own individual values and structures, within which mothers' and fathers' attitudes can be better understood.

Looking at individual families as systems is incompatible with the almost exclusive concern in attitude research with group description. <u>Individual differences</u> within groups of parents of handicapped children have rarely been considered, and there seems to be no analysis of attitudes in terms of mother-father couples. The main source of concern here is the lack of clinical relevance of group analyses, even when independent variables such as religion and sex of child are considered. Additionally, since parents' attitudes such as feelings of hopelessness, and protectiveness toward the child, are clearly affected by the nature of services experienced, it becomes essential that research provides information in such a way as to improve the delivery of services appropriate to individual families.

There are a small number of studies of attitudes in the literature which have adopted research strategies with parents which overcome some of the conceptual inadequacies outlined above, and the methodological criticisms outlined previously. These will now be considered.

ALTERNATIVE METHODS

One approach has been to focus more specifically on a particular situation. Given current trends in intervention for parents to be involved in teaching their handicapped child, some researchers have looked at parents' perceptions of their role, including their role as teachers, and their teaching philosophy, and the relationship between these and their behaviour. Most usually, the conceptual level adopted is fairly broad, i.e. the examination of parents' beliefs and feelings about parent-child interaction, and values about child behaviour. The alternative is a more specific focus on parental explanations of specific classes or episodes of behaviour. For example, Russell and Russell (1980) adopt both strategies, and link them to behaviour with questions such as:

> "Do parents who believe that a child's cognitive development is relatively unaffected by environmental factors spend less time with, and interact in a qualitatively different way with their children (e.g. read fewer stories, play fewer cognitive games) than those who believe a child's home environment is very influential?" (p.4)

They use a non-schedule but standardised approach to interviewing, and relate derived information to detailed knowledge of family background and division of labour in the home. Unfortunately, their samples do not include handicapped children.

Other researchers have developed rating

instruments such as the Maternal Perceptions Questionnaire (Olson et al., 1982) and the Concepts of Development Questionnaire (Sameroff and Feil, 1984). The former has been used with mothers of non-handicapped children, and good correlations found at 24 months between the first factor of the scale - perceived language competence of the child - and measures of child and mother behaviour. Longitudinal studies are needed to tease out the relative influence of perceptions and actual behaviour on later development (Olson, Bates and Bayles, 1984).

> "Parent-child relationships are highly complex, interactional systems. Parent cognitions represent one potentially important source of variance in these complex systems, and their properties need to be carefully evaluated." (Olson et al., 1982, p.409)

Sameroff (1982) has presented an analysis of how parents' own theories of how development occurs may relate to ability to cope with child-rearing problems. The Concepts of Development Questionnaire is a short 20-item rating scale, incorporating both simple, categorical views (e.g. "an easy baby will grow up to be a good child") and more complex perspectives on development (e.g. "children have to be treated differently as they grow older") with which parents indicate agreement or disagreement. The wording of the scale can be criticised on the grounds of referring neither to the particular child nor to the parents' beliefs in the first person. Sameroff suggests that parents whose conception of development is more sophisticated should be able to work more effectively with the problems presented by the birth of a handicapped child, through consideration of alternatives and mobilisation of resources. For parents with a more simplistic point of view, apparently helpful intervention (e.g. increasing social support), has been found to increase rather than decrease stress, through confronting parents with questions not otherwise considered (e.g. other people's concerns about the child's future development(Wright et al., 1984). Thus, it is suggested parental beliefs need to be considered in interaction with other variables in the planning of intervention.

A structured technique for measuring broad attitudes to teaching has been applied to parents of handicapped children by Strom, Rees, Slaughter and

Wurster (1981). The Parent As A Teacher Inventory (PAAT) (Strom, 1982) includes a wide variety of statements (in the first person) about what parents want or expect of their child in play and communication and how they respond to specific aspects of their interaction with the child. Fifty items are grouped into five areas: Creativity (desire to encourage or suppress development of child's creativity), Frustration (parents' child-rearing frustration and reasons for it), Control (extent to which parental control of child behaviour is deemed necessary), Play (understanding of play and its influence on child development) and Teaching-learning (perception of own ability as facilitator). Studies on young non-handicapped children have previously shown PAAT to be reliable and valid. Strom et al. (1981, 1983) gave the PAAT to 101 parents at the beginning of a three-year home-based language programme for severely mentally handicapped children, aged from 20 months to twelve years. The internal reliability of parents' answers was high, and the mean total scores were within the range reported for various Australian and North American ethnic groups of parents of non-handicapped children. However, a small number of items were scored differently by parents of handicapped children, e.g. "It is all right for my child to spend a lot of time playing alone" and "I provide chances for my child to make up his or her own mind about a lot of things", both being scored lower than by parents of non-handicapped children (Strom, Daniels, Wurster, Rees and Goldman, 1984). When the parents of handicapped children who scored at the upper or lower extremes were studied further, it was found that these two groupings were discriminated in terms of success in the intervention programme (e.g. attendance, maintaining records, etc.). The researchers suggest that discriminating items may be used as a basis for counselling with low-scoring parents prior to entry into a parent-involvement programme (Strom et al., 1981).

The research on the PAAT described above does not assume deviance in the attitudes of parents of handicapped children, reports parents' attitudes about a specific child, phrased in the first person, and was related to making services more individually appropriate. However, the research as reported did not analyse any changes in parents' attitudes, thus it is not clear whether PAAT would be sensitive to change. Also no details are given about the parents, and no analysis is provided in terms of mothers and fathers, as groups or as couples, nor of family structures or routines. The domains covered by the scale appear not to be limited to a simplistic rating of authoritarianism. Indeed, the authors comment that "parents of intellectually handicapped children are often perplexed about the amount of control they should exercise over their children" (Strom et al., 1981, p.290), and that many parents were actively concerned with promoting the child's independence. Unfortunately, the structure of a standardized scale does not allow parents to indicate the relative importance to them as individuals of different aspects of the discussion, in the way that an interview would.

Other studies which have adopted a similar level of enquiry include Schaefer (1982), who used a 'Parent as Educator' interview in his battery of instruments, but presents no detailed data. McConkey, McEvoy and Gallagher (1982) used a 15 item inventory to elicit mothers' feelings about three situations in which they interact with their young mentally handicapped child. Factor analysis of the items yielded what they call the 'enthusiasm factor' ('I have lots of fun with child', 'I try to create new experiences for child', etc.). The study found evidence of mothers' increased enthusiasm about their interactions with their child following a six-week course to learn about play. The inventory was also given to 29 mothers who did not volunteer to attend the course, and they scored significantly higher (mean ratings of situations) on the 'enthusiasm factor' than those who enrolled. A discriminant analysis between the two groups accounted for 58 per cent of the variance and included, as well as the 'enthusiasm' scores, other attitude items such as feeling their child was happy to be left doing nothing, and reports of interaction such as fathers rarely joining in the children's play (McConkey and McEvoy, 1984). Thus, the results suggested a rather paradoxical picture for professionals: the course refusers felt confident and comfortable about their role as parents, but indicated low levels of playful interaction with the child at home. Those parents who attended the course seemed more aware of play needs, and also more self-critical. Independent variables, such as degree of the child's handicap and socio-economic status, were not related. The apparent paradox seems intriguing to follow up in more methodologically adequate research (e.g. drawing on direct observations, information directly gathered on the whole family, etc.), but again underlines the likely importance of considering the individuality of parents' attitudes in designing interventions.

It is also possible to look more specifically at parents' beliefs about and explanations of teaching. McGillicuddy-DeLisi (1982) interviewed the mothers and fathers of non-handicapped four year olds about hypothetical child-care situations, and found that their beliefs about the processes underlying child progress - such as direct instruction, self-regulation, identification, negative feedback, accumulation etc. - were related in a predictable and direct way to their observed teaching strategies. Parents' beliefs were shown to be both a source and an outcome of experience. For example, parents of only children and of three children differed reliably in the types of beliefs they professed; parents of only children tended more to believe in the efficacy of direct instruction, whilst parents of three children cited self-regulation, impulsivity and negative feedback as controlling processes. Some differences based on socio-economic status were found and also differences between mothers and fathers. The author suggests that "mothers' beliefs about development are differentiated to take into account different aspects of a child's performance, while fathers' beliefs are more generalised" across all aspects of development (p.295).

Again, the above research approach does not seem to have been extended to parents of handicapped children. Although parents' beliefs were compared with observed behaviour, information was not collected on family functioning in order to aid interpretation of mother-father differences. Also data was not presented in such a form that couples could be compared, in order to enquire what might be the effect upon a child of parents who thought similarly or differently about processes of child development. Parents' explicit philosophies seem rarely to be considered in interventions, except perhaps as explanations of difficulties after the event. For example, Baker (1977) looked at problems perceived by parents of mentally handicapped children in continuing teaching at home after a structured training course. The main perceived obstacle was limited time; however, many parents also cited points relating to lack of interest in and low perceived value of teaching, and also rejection of the 'behaviour modification approach' in interaction with their own child.

Repertory grid technique

A number of researchers have adopted the theoretical approach of personal construct theory, which can illuminate the process by which parents come to have beliefs about their children's development which are reflected in and in turn affected by their actions (Kelly, 1955; O'Reilly, 1977). Kelly argued that each of us strives to make sense of ourselves and of the situations we encounter, and that we "invent and reinvent an implicit theoretical framework which, be it well or badly designed, is our personal construct system" (Fransella and Bannister, 1977, pp.4-5). Parents attempt to build up a picture of their child (just as the child does at a simpler level of them) which will allow them to predict and find meaningful the child's actions. They also build up a picture of themselves as parents, which is constantly open to reconstruction. Kelly paid close attention to operationalizing the concepts in his theory (e.g. definitions of constructs, how to measure a construct system, etc.) which is a distinct advantage over attitude theory, which suffers from uncertain definitions and little attempt to describe how different attitudes interact and change.

Kelly developed repertory grid technique as a way of measuring construct systems. Constructs are bipolar discriminations (otherwise called values, feelings, attitudes, perceptions etc.) which relate to each other in various organised ways. Repertory grids involve elicitation of an individual's constructs and application of those to a range of elements (e.g. a list of people important in the person's life). The structure of the construct system can then be represented mathematically. For research with parents of handicapped children, grids have the potential to allow parents to speak for themselves (i.e. individualized content), but in a structured way which facilitates the search for general processes through comparison with others, and which also allows for measurement of change over time. Particular grids can focus on particular subsystems of an individual's construing, e.g. parenting.

There have been only a few studies of parents of handicapped children using grids. With one exception, these have used people as the elements, including the handicapped child, and perhaps the parents, or a non-handicapped sibling, or the 'imagined normal child' which the parents expected before the handicapped baby was born. One longitudinal study suggested that two separate groupings of mothers emerged over the interval of the child's first year of life, those who saw the handicapped child and the imagined normal child as very different and who continued to do so, and those who saw them less and less discrepantly. This second group seem increasingly to focus their construing of the child in ordinary terms (Vicary, 1983, 1985a). This change in focus was discussed above as a feature of what might be meant by 'acceptance'. Davis and Cunningham (1985) describe a study in which mothers completed a child characterisation sketch (i.e. asked to describe the personality of their child as fully as possible). Mothers of mentally handicapped children described their child in terms which differed remarkably little from those utilised by mothers of non-handicapped children. This finding suggests that research methods which are founded on an assumption of differing or negative perceptions (e.g. Worchel and Worchel, 1961) may distort how parents actually see their young mentally handicapped children.

McConachie (1986) used everyday interactions involving parent and child as elements in grids with mothers and fathers of 20 young mentally handicapped children. She noted marked differences in construing between fathers and mothers. Mothers who were involved in considerable daily concentrated interaction with their child emphasised the importance to them of the issue of teaching in their joint activities with the child, and the construct of teaching was closely associated with feeling they were doing a good job as a parent. In contrast, fathers who were highly participant with the child focussed on issues of how much they have to help the child to do things, and how much they perceive the child's handicap as affecting their joint activities. It seemed that mothers may take their everyday activities with the child relatively for granted, and thus focus their philosophy in terms of teaching and positive care of the child. For fathers, being highly participant is not something which can be taken for granted, and is construed by them in immediately relevant terms. It was the fathers who were least involved with their children who considered the issue of teaching as important, as if it might be a solution to their confusion about how to handle the child. This implies, rather paradoxically, that in beginning a teaching intervention, a professional worker might be 'talking the same language' with less-involved fathers and with mothers, and be ignoring the terms in which an already-involved father construes his activity with his child.

Other research on families using repertory grids has charted the process whereby a non-referred sibling comes to be viewed more realistically by parents in comparison with a behaviour-disordered child, through successful family therapy (Kotler and Chetwynd, 1980). Most studies have, however, used single-occasion grids. Dobson (1980) found mothers and fathers viewed their school-age mentally handicapped child more negatively than a non-handicapped sibling and said they had difficulty in applying the constructs to the handicapped child. She suggested that additional physical handicaps affected construing in similar ways to additional behavioural problems of the children. A study of parents of children with epilepsy suggested associations between parental expectations, and low self-esteem and academic functioning of the children; the authors assume a causal relationship in the direction written, but this is not substantiated (Long and Moore, 1979).

The research is thus limited and fragmentary, but where it is clearly linked to hypotheses derived from other variables it may illumine processes of change, and similarities and differences within parent groupings, and also within couples. For example, Humphrey (1977) found differences between mothers and fathers in a group of prospective adopters as to their expectations about parenthood. The studies reviewed have not related their results on parents' perceptions to broad-based theory about family functioning. However, other research on (non-handicapped) children with behaviour problems has done so, and also stresses the importance of parents' perceptions, showing that these are more related to marital discord and to parental negative behaviour toward the child than to the actuality of child behaviour (Christensen, Phillips, Glasgow and Johnson, 1983).

Kelly did not elaborate greatly the ways in which construing would be expected to be related to behaviour. Because of individual differences in the content of construing, relationships would perhaps be expected more clearly with structural variables than with the ideas contained in the grid (e.g. the number of different construct components, suggesting flexibility of response to situations, might be related to behaviour). Davis (1979) proposed very specific links between construing and behaviour of mothers of young non-handicapped children, and found hypotheses to be supported at chance frequency only. However, in a later study he did find clear links between parents' ideas about the effectiveness of praise, and their use or otherwise of praise in interaction (Davis, 1985). McConachie (1986) found significant relationships between the kinds of constructs which parents associated with teaching (e.g. controlling the activity versus freer approaches) and their observed style of interaction with the child on a teaching task. At a broader level of prediction, Pokela (1980) was able to discriminate between successful and unsuccessful foster parents on the basis of grid structural variables (and the content of the differences was not explanatory). Kaye (1979) noted that construing predicted behaviour of class teachers only when constructs describing children's specific behaviour (rather than e.g. 'shows good work') were used. Thus, it seems that the level of predictability of behaviour from construing is crucially dependent on the way in which the grid is derived. Some broadly conceived predictions seem capable of being supported by group differences on other variables; but specific individual predictions about behaviour in a particular situation are more difficult to capture.

Some repertory grid research has tackled the question of how people's ideas relate to a course of training, a relevant question for parents of mentally handicapped children who might be being helped to teach their children. It has been shown that trainee nurses' initial construing can predict drop-out from the course more accurately than knowledge of their personal circumstances (Heyman, Shaw and Harding, 1983). Stammerers' initial ability to construe themselves flexibly as a 'non-stammerer' is predictive of their degree of successful change following a course of speech therapy (Fransella, 1972). Ryle and Breen (1974) showed that repertory grids can identify problem areas for individuals (at the start of social-work training) and can indicate to what extent resolution of these problems has been achieved by the end of the course. It has also been suggested that the nature of the change in construing is cyclical; it goes through a process of initial tightening (i.e. focussing in on a few dimensions) then gradual loosening again, as new experiences and ideas become integrated into the system (Runkel and Damrin,

1961). Thus, a simple before and after measurement of change may miss key processes.

Potentially the use of repertory grids in research with parents would meet the requirement of focussing on individual differences, and since the content is personal it is not judged in advance as functional or dysfunctional. Using individuals' own constructs may overcome some problems of cultural or class specificity; relationships between parents' construing and behaviour (McGillicuddy-DeLisi, 1982), and teachers' construing and children's performance (Nash, 1973) have been shown stronger than the links with socio-economic status. The different ways in which individuals' grids can be compared allows for the emergence of attitudinal groupings within parents, which may prove to be of relevance in their response to intervention. The technique thus seems to have considerable potential clinical relevance in research with parents of mentally handicapped children.

CONCLUSIONS

In this chapter, the methodological limitations of research into parents' reactions to their handicapped child have been analysed, and linked to a discussion of the implications of applying a more satisfactory conceptual framework to the area of enquiry. Some alternative methods have been outlined which actually or potentially address a number of these implications.

The review and analysis should also have lent support to the contention that parents' attitudes and beliefs are a valid and important area of enquiry in the search for improved services to families of handicapped children.

> "...parental behaviour is, to some degree, controlled by knowledge of infant behavior, expectations about behavior differences, and early diagnostic labels. One component of a modification program should involve the alteration of parental attitudes, expectations, and knowledge about their infants." (Parke, 1978, p.82)

Certainly it is clear that parents need information: several authors comment on the link between lack of information and parents' confusion, hopelessness, etc. (e.g. Wolfensberger, 1967; Cunningham, 1979;

Long and Moore, 1979). Information about their child's handicap, and about all available services would seem essential in promoting clear "expectations and knowledge" (c.f. the above quotation).

But on what basis are parents' "attitudes" to be judged in need of alteration? The achievement of mutual understanding between professionals and parents requires two-way interchange and listening. On the one hand there may be parental attitudes which it can be suggested are less helpful than might be for their handicapped child. Many interventions are based on key assumptions - that the behaviour of a mentally handicapped child can be modified, and that parents' interactions can affect their child's development. Some parents may not share these assumptions, and thus they and their children are less likely to benefit from the intervention offered (Lavelle and Keogh, 1980; McConkey and McEvoy, 1984). On the other hand, parents <u>do</u> have particular philosophies and assumptions of their own, and where methods can be devised for making these clear, professionals may be able to adapt to and learn from them, not simply assume that they must be altered. Research into parents' attitudes seems to be at a stage where description, and development of methods (i.e. hypothesis derivation) is required before judgements (i.e. from hypothesis testing) can be made.

Chapter Six

STRESS

The material examined in this chapter is hard to place in relation to the preceding reviews. It does not fit clearly in Chapter 2 as it is about feelings, though these are largely in response to daily pressures of living; however, stress is more situationally related than the parental attitudes reviewed above in Chapter 4. It is important to include a review of the area for conceptual completeness, and because of the obvious felt relevance for parents of stress and its causation.

'Stress' requires definition: generally, it seems to be used as a description of an individual's response to events or changes (Beckman, 1983). It is thus measured in terms of psychiatric disturbance, or ill health, etc. However, it is also used in the sense of an individual's perception of the events or circumstances themselves, i.e. the individual's 'response to stress'. This brings in the necessity to measure parents' needs in relation to daily pressures and the frequency and nature of significant events they experience, and also to hypothesise the nature of coping mediators in individual family systems and ecologies (Crnic, Friedrich and Greenberg, 1983).

Psychiatric disturbance

Some studies have surveyed parents of handicapped children using a standardised psychiatric interview. For example, Wing (1975), looking at 100 families of severely mentally handicapped London children up to the age of 14 years, found that 57 per cent of mothers and 20 per cent of fathers had had mild or severe psychiatric symptoms at some time since the child was born. The ratio is greater than the two to one ratio of women to men with psychiatric problems in the general population (DHSS, 1972), suggesting mothers are more at risk, which is what would be suggested by the evidence presented in Chapter 2. The great majority of the mothers attributed their symptoms to the worry of having a handicapped child; only a few fathers did so.

Gath (1978) suggested that the incidence of psychiatric problems found in parents of young Down's syndrome children was not greater than in some other populations of parents facing difficulties (e.g. poor housing, twins), but other studies of parents have stressed that both mothers and fathers seem to show significant psychological disturbance in comparison with parents of non-handicapped children (e.g. Cummings et al., 1966; Erickson, 1969; Cummings, 1976). A particular pattern was suggested by Fox (1974). He found an excess of high 'hysteria' or 'extraversion' for fathers, using the _Middlesex Hospital Questionnaire_, a psychiatric self-rating index (Crown and Crisp, 1970) (though n.b. his sample seems to be small and self-selected). Fox regarded hysteria as an acquired trait:

> "A facility for brashness, over-dramatization, and a refusal to be intimidated by authority or status, have become necessary for obtaining the best from our services" (p.64).

Most studies of psychiatric disturbance lack information about key subject variables: for example, one dimension that has been suggested as related to stress is increasing age of the handicapped child (Farber, 1959; Gallagher, Beckman and Cross, 1983). But parents have been shown to experience difficulties from an early age, as Erickson's MMPI study (1969) included only parents of children aged three years or less.

Emotional and physical problems

A measuring instrument which has been widely used, particularly in British studies of parents of handicapped children, is the _Malaise Inventory_, adapted from the Cornell Medical Index, and developed by Rutter, Tizard and Whitmore (1970). It measures emotional and physical symptoms (e.g. 'Do you feel tired most of the time?') with a 'yes'/'no' answer; it lacks statistical sophistication, but seems to have considerable face validity. Generally it has been found that mothers of handicapped children score significantly higher than comparison groups of mothers of non-handicapped children (Bradshaw and Lawton, 1975; Tew and Laurence, 1975; Butler et al., 1978; Burden, 1980; Wishart et al., 1981; Carr and Hewett, 1982; Chetwynd, 1985), particularly when the child's mental and/or physical handicap is severe.

However, mothers of young children who have received some form of early services are more usually shown to have low scores (Burden, 1980, Ferguson and Watt, 1980, and Wishart et al., 1981, British samples; Waisbren, 1980, Danish and American samples). Waisbren stresses the similarity of the stresses experienced by parents of developmentally disabled and non-handicapped infants, e.g. difficulty in sleeping, or in letting go of worries, reduced physical health, etc. Bradshaw and Lawton's finding of no difference in stress with children's age may perhaps be explained by their sampling: successful applicants to the Family Fund generally have children over the age of two years, and are severely disabled, and so parents all experience high levels of stress. Rather than looking at child age per se, it may be of greater relevance to study key points in the family life cycle (e.g. child starting school) for evidence on changes in stress (Byrne and Cunningham, 1985).

The above studies do not clearly show whether the child's age is related to the degree of maternal reactions of stress; however, it seems that the availability of some form of early intervention to meet parents' needs can do a great deal to alleviate such feelings.

Few studies have looked at fathers' feelings of stress. Generally no difference is found from fathers of non-handicapped children (e.g. Kazak and Marvin, 1984) although, as for mothers, severe and multiple handicap in children may cause greater stress (Wishart et al., 1980).

Resources and stress

Fairly recently, a scale has been developed which combines both definitions of stress, i.e. it looks both at parents' feelings and at their reported resources (or lack of resources). The <u>Questionnaire on Resources and Stress</u> (Holroyd, 1974) was developed to measure family response to a handicapped family member. It has 285 true/false items in 15 scales, i.e. parent problems (poor health, low mood, excess time demands, lack of social support, etc.), family problems (lack of family integration, financial problems, etc.) and problems of the child (physical incapacitation, lack of activities, difficult personality characteristics, etc.). (Shorter versions have since been developed, for example, by Friedrich, Greenberg and Crnic, 1983.) The questionnaire is deliberately multidimensional, and most items reflect upon interaction between the child's behaviour and the parents' reaction (e.g. "If X were more pleasant to be with it would be easier to care for him"). There have been limited but successful attempts to measure the scale's reliability and validity. Greater problems are reported by mothers of mentally handicapped and behaviour-disordered children than by fathers (Holroyd, 1974), and the scale also distinguishes clearly between mothers of handicapped and of non-handicapped children, and between groupings of mothers of children with different types of problems (Holroyd and McArthur, 1976; Friedrich and Friedrich, 1981). For example, mothers of Down's syndrome children reflect greater family integration than mothers of either autistic children or children attending a psychiatric clinic (Holroyd and McArthur, 1976). Stress has been shown related to child characteristics in some studies. For example, Beckman (1983) found a positive correlation between stress and the number of extra care-giving requirements of the child (e.g. special feeding, handling and medical problems) for a sample of handicapped children aged three years or less. In contrast, Friedrich (1979) found a negative relationship between reported stress and severity of handicap, in a sample of children of widely differing ages and handicaps. Bristol (1982) (and Bradshaw and Lawton, 1975, above) suggest that stress is more strongly related to individual family resources, than to the severity of the child's handicap, and Friedrich (1979) found marital integration the strongest predictor.

These apparently conflicting results suggest most clearly that parental stress cannot be described as a unitary phenomenon. It may be related to the child's age, to diagnosis or to severity of handicap, and may be greater for mothers than fathers; but the results must be related to models of family functioning and to knowledge of the services being received in order for replicable conclusions to be drawn.

Marital integration

Marital integration or discord has been seen by different authors either as a reaction to the handicapped child, or as a mediating variable affecting the experience of stress by family members, depending on their theoretical point of view.

Having a handicapped child does seem to put a strain on the parents' relationship. Mothers of handicapped children have been found to report lower marital satisfaction than mothers of non-handicapped children (Friedrich and Friedrich, 1981). That study utilised the Locke-Wallace (1959) Marital Adjustment Inventory, a widely-used 15-item self-rating scale. Gath (1978) however used a well-researched interview approach to assessing the quality of a marriage, from replies to questions about decision-making, and measures of expressed criticism, etc. (Quinton, Rutter and Rowlands, 1976). She rated nearly a third of marriages as 'poor' two years after the birth of a Down's syndrome child (and none of the control group marriages). She commented that

> "... the advent of the mongol baby was not as likely to mar a good marriage as to turn a moderate or somewhat shaky marriage into a poor one." (p.66)

Farber (1959) made a similar observation, even though his studies covered a wider age-range of children. Both self-ratings and interviewer ratings are open to various sources of bias (such as expectation of difficulty) but the finding seems robust despite that. Waisbren (1980) suggested a complex interaction of factors:

> "... when parents relate well to their developmentally disabled child, they internalize some of the strain, experience physical symptoms, and perhaps displace their negative feelings onto a spouse." (p.350)

Generally, good sibling relationships are expected to be facilitated by a good marital relationship.

Conflicting statements have been made about whether handicapped children's parents are more likely to divorce. Those who conclude so have often presented no evidence (e.g. Love, 1970). Other evidence is unsatisfactory. In a longitudinal study of spina bifida children, Tew, Laurence, Payne and

Rawnsley (1977) concluded that the divorce rate for parents with a surviving child was nine times that for the local population. However, they compared figures for their cohort, followed for ten years or so, with a census rate per year and so seem to have overestimated by about the ratio they found (Stevenson, Graham and Dorner, 1978). Of 58 couples, six had divorced in the time. One American study looked at divorce rates in several groups of parents of young mentally handicapped or genetically impaired children, attending a genetic counselling service. In general, the authors found a lower divorce rate than in the general population, but suggested that young parents having a first born male child, and mothers in their early thirties having a first child were groups at greater risk for divorce (Roesel and Lawlis, 1983). Chetwynd (1985) interviewed 91 New Zealand mothers of mentally handicapped children around nine years of age. She found that twice as many of the sample were bringing up their children on their own as would be expected in comparable general population samples. However, generally reviews of the evidence conclude that divorce rate is not necessarily raised in parents of handicapped children (e.g. Longo and Bond, 1984). A controlled longitudinal study of Down's syndrome children concluded:

> "The findings of our study are a testament to the ability of ordinary families to meet the challenge of bringing up a child with Down's syndrome and of coping with all the practical and emotional problems that this undeniably entails. ... The overwhelming impression gained from our study is of children who, in the great majority, enjoyed their own lives and were a source of much pleasure and pride to their families." (Carr and Hewett, 1982, p.13)

Certainly, where one parent is left to cope on her (or his) own, the strains are great (Tew et al., 1977; Beckman, 1983), but whether the child's being handicapped precipitates parental separation is not proven.

It seems an important consideration for services not to further increase the strain on the parents' relationship. For example, Townsend and Flanagan (1976), in evaluating a programme to encourage home care rather than institutionalization of children, commented that counselling with the mother alone tended to result in increased marital conflict as well as a decision to keep the child at home, and that this conflict could defeat the real purpose of having the child grow up in a facilitating environment.

Coping and social support

The overwhelming impression from the research into parental stress is of variability, undoubtedly partly a reflection of the quality of the work, but also apparently evidence of wide individual differences and thus lack of easy prediction (Bradshaw and Lawton, 1975). One family in which the parents are no longer young or very fit, living in poor housing, with a severely mentally and physically handicapped child, may seem to cope with any circumstance and welcome opportunities to do more for their child, for example, by working on a teaching programme. Another family, in better objective living and financial circumstances, with a less severely handicapped child, with considerable support from statutory and voluntary services, may nevertheless experience severe levels of strain. Thus, levels of stress experienced seem to be as much to do with parents' perceptions, roles and coping strategies as with unalterable features such as the parents' or the child's age. At least in this case, services can then attempt to relieve stress in families through individually flexible intervention (Beckman, 1983).

Understanding how parents cope in different ways requires consideration of various mediators. For example, there seems to be good evidence for the nature of possible predisposing factors in depression in women, including lack of paid employment and of a confiding relationship (Brown and Harris, 1978). Services may need thus to concern themselves with the nature of the social support available to mothers of handicapped children, and, for example, not unwittingly pressure them to refrain from seeking employment. The effect of such predisposing factors is mediated by individual psychological mechanisms, such as the experience of 'learned helplessness' which promotes depression (Seligman, 1975) and the role of attributions (Abramson, Seligman and Teasdale, 1979). Thus services need to be structured in ways which let parents experience being competent and solving problems, in control of what happens to them, exercising choice, expressing anger, etc. in order to combat helplessness and depression. Direct attempts may be made to help parents through interventions which emphasise making coping self-statements (e.g. 'I know I can get through this tantrum - she will stop screaming in a few minutes if I stay calm') and overcoming negative thoughts (e.g. Kushlick, Smith and Gold, 1984; Schilling, Gilchrist and Schinke, 1984; see Chapter 10). Parents of children with cystic fibrosis have been studied using the Coping Health Inventory for Parents (McCubbin, McCubbin, Patterson, Cauble, Wilson and Warwick, 1983). This instrument looks at parents' ratings of the usefulness of various coping strategies under three headings: maintaining family integration, cooperation and optimism; maintaining self-esteem, psychological stability and social support; understanding the child's medical needs through other parents and professionals. Such an emphasis on parents' strengths and self-esteem seem a long way removed from the types of assessment of parental reactions detailed in Chapter 4.

The study of families perceived as 'coping well' with the child, in order to learn what sustains them (Gallagher et al., 1980; Longo and Bond, 1984) necessitates a wide ecological framework for the research. For example, several studies have been made of families' networks of social support - not simply asking parents whether extended family members and neighbours are helpful (c.f. Chapter 2), but assessing which people play a helpful role, in which ways and how often. An example would be use of the Social Support Questionnaire (Sarason, Levine, Basham and Sarason, 1983). The parent lists for 27 items the individuals who provide support in the situation described, and how satisfactory this is (e.g. 'console you when very upset', 'will help in a crisis, even if it puts them out'). From such information, analysis can be made of the size of the parents' network of support, how closely knit it is (i.e. how many of the individuals know each other well), and what gaps there may be in relation to particular functions. Kazak and Marvin (1984) found that small, closely-knit networks of support are associated with raised stress for mothers and fathers of handicapped children, perhaps because of lack of flexibility. Waisbren (1980) also found that highly supportive family networks, while increasing parents' positive feelings about the child, could be associated with greater stress. Chetwynd's (1985) analysis showed that greater stress in mothers was associated with feelings of isolation and with the number of breaks or holidays they had experienced. Such findings imply interventions which would extend networks of social support for families (e.g. through weekend fostering schemes for children), and which would help parents to negotiate more helpful, responsive relationships with grandparents and other family members. However, the introduction and timing of such intervention needs to be tailored to individual parents and families (see Chapter 5 re. Sameroff). The simple idea that support has the same positive impact on all parents needs to be examined more carefully. What from the professional's view may seem like a simple strategy for helping parents with their child may have quite different meanings from the parent's viewpoint.

The view of parents as coping and resourceful in the face of stress is not yet well developed either in the literature or in some approaches to intervention. Such respect for parents' individuality would feed into parent-professional relationships based on partnership and equality. This philosophy for intervention is discussed further in Chapter 10.

Chapter Seven

INTERACTION AND DEVELOPMENT

INTRODUCTION

Parent-child interaction plays a vital role in child development. Historically, this view derived from observation of children reared in institutions, who received physical care but lacked consistent social interaction, and whose development was consequently retarded (Spitz, 1945). Current theory regarding the interactive basis of development characterises the parent's role as influencing the child's developing ability to direct his or her own actions on the basis of a world which is socially constructed (Mogford, 1973). Thus, interaction does not simply promote the development of skills; it allows the child to develop intentions and an understanding of self (Shotter, 1974). This occurs through the 'intersubjective' development of communication. That is, actions of the baby are not simply reflected back automatically by the parent in terms of their physical consequences. Instead, the parent interprets the meaning of the actions, so that only some actions are judged to have relevance and coherence, as intentions or as potential communications. It is:

> "...only because mothers impute meaning to 'behaviours' elicited from infants that these eventually do come to constitute meaningful actions so far as the child himself is concerned." (Newson, 1978, p.37)

Studies of both handicapped and non-handicapped children show that mothers intervene in the child's activity to avoid failure and frustration, and to help make environmental events accessible. Bruner (1976) has described as 'scaffolding' the process by which parents highlight the significance of certain acts of the child, and make obvious the associations the child needs to solve a particular problem. Infants are active participants in interaction. However, a handicapped child is one whose disability or disabilities interfere with the normal pattern or rate of development; for example, Down's syndrome infants are frequently hypoactive. If mentally handicapped children are less active and equal partners in interaction, then they may need to have their experience structured or 'scaffolded' for them more vividly and for longer. However, handicapped children are all different individuals, with differing profiles of development, temperamental characteristics, etc. Therefore, when an intervention programme begins to consider the role of parents not simply as interaction partners, but as change agents, great potential flexibility will need to be built in both to observation and assessment methods, and to suggested strategies for facilitative interaction (Vietze and Anderson, 1981).

All interaction between individuals is embedded in an ecological system. It is influenced indirectly by the actions and attitudes of others inside and outside the family. Feinman and Lewis (1984) have classified such influences on dyadic interaction under four headings:

1. the physical presence of other people, to form triads and larger groupings;
2. the extent to which a dyad is isolated from or integrated within social networks;
3. the social experiences and relationships which each dyad partner has outside the dyad;
4. the ways in whch others modify dyad partners' perceptions of each other, thus influencing dyadic interaction.

When researchers observe interaction they usually take a small segment of time, spent in play ("a phenomenon grossly over-represented in psychological studies of pre-school children" - Mills et al., 1985, p.12), distorted by the very process of being observed, and then they theorise about the properties of the interaction in isolation from those wider networks of influence. An important case in point is the study of father-child interaction. Where a father is asked to interact with his child while being observed, a distinctly unusual situation may have been created. Many fathers rarely play with toys with their young children on their own (Russell, 1979a). When researchers try to infer the nature of the father-child relationship from the observed interaction, they are on very shaky ground. Hinde (1979) has made clear in his analysis of relationships that interaction is only one element in their definition. The links between observed interaction, daily involvement and the quality of relationship between father and child, and mother and child, may be of an entirely different nature.

These conceptual issues have not at all been solved, sometimes not even addressed, by the available research on parent-child interaction. For example, researchers face the dilemma of whether to measure the frequency of occurrence of events (and at what level of specificity to measure) in order to reduce the extent to which the observer requires to make inferences, or on the other hand to rate qualities of the interaction (e.g. sensitivity, responsiveness) which procedure in fact turns out to produce higher reliabilities between observers (Cooper et al., 1974; Lytton, 1980). Theoretically, the quantity and quality of various aspects of interaction, its timing and synchronicity, are all important to the discussion. However, methods of observation and analysis lag behind. The study of parents of mentally handicapped children is particularly lacking. For example, much of the latter research is concerned with describing only the behaviour of the parents, and characterizing it as controlling, or warm, etc. It is often then not sufficiently realised in interpretation that qualities such as warmth apply to the interaction and not to individual parents, who might behave rather differently with another child, or in another situation, or given different support services to relieve their anxiety.

The present chapter first summarises some aspects of the study of mother-child interaction as they might be relevant to the study of young mentally handicapped children. Then in Chapter 8 a comparison will be made of mothers and fathers in interaction with their non-handicapped children, in the context of a discussion of the basis of such research. Finally, the literature pertaining to parents in interaction with their mentally handicapped children will be reviewed in Chapter 9, along with discussion of the conceptual problems in interpreting any differences from the observed interaction of parents and non-handicapped children.

STUDYING MOTHER-CHILD INTERACTION

A number of longitudinal studies in recent years have attempted to answer questions about the role of environmental influences in child development, and about the balance between factors inherent in the child's physical status and factors in the environment, focussing particularly on the role of parental care-taking practices. Underlying this activity has been the goal of identifying what might be the most positive influences on later child development, and their promotion in families whose children are considered 'at risk' for later problems (Bradley and Caldwell, 1978).

Studies have varied in sample composition, sample size, frequency of data-collection, and length of time interval studied. For example, Bee, Barnard, Eyres, Gray, Hammond, Spietz, Snyder and Clark (1982) followed 193 healthy, able, North American infants and their mothers to four years of age, with nine data collection points; Epstein and Evans (1979) followed 53 North American infants and their mothers from working-class backgrounds to seven years of age, but with only two data collection points; McLaughlin, Morrissey, Empson and Sever (1981) followed 60 disadvantaged English children and their mothers to two and a half years of age, with four data collection points. Findings are markedly consistent: the child's later intellectual or language skill is predicted by provision of appropriate play materials, affectionate, nonrestrictive and non-punitive caregiving, responsiveness to the child, and language teaching, modelling or stimulating (Clarke-Stewart, 1973; Bradley and Caldwell, 1976; Clarke-Stewart et al., 1979; Epstein and Evans, 1979; Ramey, Farran and Campbell, 1979; White, Kaban and Attanucci, 1979; Jay and Farran, 1981; McLaughlin et al., 1981; Bee et al., 1982; Olson et al., 1984). The general magnitude of predictive relationships obtained has been surprisingly similar in studies with children with differing levels of performance (Bradley and Caldwell, 1976; Ramey et al., 1979; Bee et al., 1982), i.e. multiple correlations in the range of .50 to .65 between early environmental measures and later IQ. These predictions outweigh considerably those generated by, on the one hand, information about perinatal status alone (excluding severe handicapping conditions) (e.g. Bee et al., 1982), and on the other hand, broad demographic indicators such as socio-economic status (e.g. Clarke-Stewart et al., 1979). The quality of mother-child interaction is the most (or among the most) potent predictor at intermediate ages of later child cognitive, language and social functioning. But in addition Bee et al. (1982) and McLaughlin et al. (1981) have shown that a broader assessment of stress and support in the family can add significantly to the magnitude of predictions in relatively disadvantaged samples.

This brief summary of findings about the importance of interaction to child development will now be discussed in more detail, in order to consider which variables might be associated with individual differences between parents and their children in the styles of interaction they develop. These will be presented under the headings of child variables, situation variables and parent variables.

Child variables

A variety of child characteristics have been shown to be related to differences in parent-child interaction. (Some will be considered later, e.g. sex of child along with sex of parent, and mental handicap as a chapter on its own.) For example, first born children are found to be treated differently from later born children. They are more dependent in their activity, and their mothers more interfering at four years (Hilton, 1967), and in their second year, mothers spend twice as much time interacting with them as do mothers of later born children (White et al., 1979), with better organisation of the environment and provision of play materials (Bradley and Caldwell, 1984). There may also be effects of the sex of the child here - Jacobs and Moss (1976) found that the decrease in time spent with later born children was minimal where the second child was male and the first born female. However, it seems likely that such interaction differences do not arise primarily from common characteristics of the children so much as from their parents' behaviour. A similar conclusion could be drawn about interaction with twins. Lytton, Conway and Sauve (1977) found the twin situation more influential than social class differences in shaping parent-child interaction, for example, in demonstrating fewer verbal and affectionate interchanges between children and parents.

A second example is the comparison between

pre-term and full-term babies. Differences in early interaction are found (e.g. Field, 1977a; Bakeman and Brown, 1980; Crnic, Ragozin, Greenberg, Robinson and Basham, 1983), but seem not to be predictive of later social or cognitive development, though birth status in itself does predict later cognitive levels (Bakeman and Brown, 1980). As Dunn (1975) argues, it would not make biological sense if difficulties in the first few days and weeks (e.g. problems in feeding) had long-term consequences. However, Crnic, Ragozin, Greenberg, Robinson and Basham (1983) showed that apparently less successful patterns can persist from four to twelve months. They found that mothers of pre-term infants gave more social signals which were not reciprocated by the infant. A pattern developed and persisted in which when the mother was active the child was not, this pattern being accompanied by less overall mutual positive affect. Thus, a 'vicious circle' may arise out of the two basic factors of the child's initial difficulties and early problems in parental handling (Papousek and Papousek, 1983).

Children's changing social and motor capabilities as they develop affect interaction with parents. For example, mothers remain the predominant initiators of interaction but this declines over time (Green, Gustafson and West, 1980, 6-12 months; Clarke-Stewart and Hevey, 1981, 12-30 months). Some measures peak at one age and then decline, e.g. visual attention and interactive play peak at 18 months. Children gradually show an awareness of self, and begin to direct the behaviour of adults between 18 and 24 months (Kagan, 1982). Other child variables which affect parenting style over time include temperament, and how the parent in turn perceives the child's temperament (Thomas and Chess, 1977; Affleck, Allen, McGrade and McQueeney, 1984).

Such studies reflect on the one hand the variability in mother-child interaction, and on the other hand the consistency in some measures over time (Escalona, 1973). In terms of variability, for example, Clarke-Stewart and Hevey (1981) observing mothers and children interacting naturally at home on several occasions noted a range from one per cent to 97 per cent of periods in which the mother spoke to the child. In terms of consistency, over half the correlation coefficients over time were significant. However, there has been considerable discussion in the literature about how to conceptualize and thus to measure consistency.

Vietze and Anderson (1981) stress the form, timing and sensitivity of interaction in their definition of parent-child interaction style, not simply the frequency of particular behaviours of one or other participant. One solution is to record the interactive function of the dyad's behaviour, leaving aside its content and meaning (Escalona, 1973; Bakeman and Brown, 1977, 1980). Another solution has been to rely on overall ratings of the quality of interaction, e.g. in terms of responsiveness, rather than to concentrate on frequency counts. Ratings seem to reflect higher consistency measures than frequency counts (Clarke-Stewart and Hevey, 1981; Crnic, Ragozin, Greenberg, Robinson and Basham, 1983) and to provide higher predictions of later child cognitive competence (Jay and Farran, 1981).

Infants have been shown to react very quickly to experimentally-induced changes in style of interaction. For example, they smile and look more when the mother concentrates on imitating them (Field, 1977b); they become distressed when the timing and responsivity of mother's behaviour is altered (Tronick, Als, Adamson, Wise and Brazelton, 1978; Trevarthen, 1981). However they also react simply to rate changes, displaying more positive interactions to too-fast than to too-slow temporal style, and most positive interactions to the natural style (Arco and McCluskey, 1981). Thus frequency, as well as timing and sensitivity, of interaction seems important to the infant. It has previously been shown that children are not helped by parents who overstimulate, ignoring the child's pace and need for time in which to respond (Ainsworth and Bell, 1969). Parents who take a highly active role may in effect interfere with the child, and delay the development of new skills, e.g. language (Nelson, 1973). On the other hand, patterns in which mothers give less visual attention to infants and less stimulation have also been implicated in later delayed development (e.g. Thoman, Becker and Freese, 1978). In this last study, the three infants who were later found delayed in development did not differ on early observations from the rest of the sample on measures such as wakefulness or crying. However, the authors conclude that:

> "One cannot attribute the distinctive qualities of the three individual pairs primarily to differences in the mothers. Behaviour patterns of a dyad, within a systems approach, must be

> viewed as an expression of ongoing adjustments that each member of the dyad is making to the other." (p.112)

The authors then provide evidence of mutual effects through detailed analysis of individuals, showing how infants might give 'mixed messages' to mothers, who express their uncertainty in reduced responding.

Thus, whether frequency counts or qualitative measures are used, parent-child interaction style has been shown to reflect considerable consistency over time from the first months. It also varies greatly between dyads; however, the evidence so far presented does not suggest that the variability is related in any simple way to broad categories of child variables.

Situation variables

There is a certain amount of evidence available to suggest what one would expect anyway, that parents and children interact differently in different situations. The issue is of interest here because in studying social interaction with young children, and relating the observations to cognitive development, researchers have used a variety of settings, tasks and instructions.

At one extreme are rigorously controlled laboratory conditions and artificial tasks; at the other extreme are procedures involving observations in the home with the minimum of interventions (i.e. other than the presence of the observer or recording apparatus). Each setting may be appropriate for answering certain types of questions. However, experimental method may also be used in the home setting, and naturalistic-observational method may involve interventions - the differences lie on a continuum (Thoman et al., 1978). Studies of mother-child interaction, including those reviewed above, have often used more than one setting, in order to test experimentally derived hypotheses in terms of naturally observed interactions (e.g. Baumrind, 1967; Lytton, 1980; Clarke-Stewart and Hevey, 1981).

Nevertheless, other researchers have posed the basic question of whether observed mother-child interaction differs according to physical setting in predictable ways. An early study of unstructured play suggested that mothers were more hostile and restricting and interacted with and helped children less at home than in a laboratory situation

(Moustakas, Sigel and Schalock, 1956). Similarly, Belsky (1980) found that mothers attended to, responded to and stimulated children less frequently at home, which is hardly surprising. Infant functioning was not much affected by the setting. However, accompanying differences implied by the setting are, firstly, the mothers' expectations about the situation (e.g. competing pressures at home) and, secondly, the instructions given.

Expectations have been shown important in studies which compared interaction when parents knew they were being observed with times when they did not know. For example, positive reactions to the child increase when parents are knowingly observed (Patterson and Reid, 1969), and also parents structure activities more (Zegiob, Arnold and Forehand, 1975). These findings apply also to mothers of 12 month old infants who offered and demonstrated toys more in unstructured play, engaged in more interaction games and vocalized more when aware of being filmed (Field and Ignatoff, 1981). It would be important to consider whether certain groupings of parents would be affected by these manipulations more than others (e.g. fathers versus mothers,parents of handicapped children versus parents of non-handicapped children) (Cox, 1975).

In terms of instructions given by the researcher, these usually differ between home and laboratory setting. For example, parents may be told to go about their usual routine at home, and in the laboratory to act as if they had some free time with the child. Belsky (1980) used these instructions, in order to replicate others' work, thus confounding setting and instruction in his comparison. However, it could be argued that the two settings can never really be compared, in that to create a situation in the laboratory which is comparable to home is impossible, and to create a situation at home which is comparable to the laboratory is to lose much of the ecological validity of the observed situation. It can be concluded that cross-setting generalization about interaction may not be warranted; on the other hand, it may be that the setting affects interaction and yet leaves rank differences between dyads relatively unaffected (Lytton, 1980).

The task given to the parent-child dyads has also been systematically varied; in very many studies a structured task is compared with an unstructured or free play situation and considerable differences found, particularly in the parents' behaviour (Hatfield, Ferguson and Alpert, 1967). For example, parents give more instructions and suggestions and ask more questions in a structured task than in a waiting room situation (Bee, Van Egeren, Streissguth, Nyman and Leckie, 1969; Bates, 1971) and use more controlling behaviours in difficult tasks than in easy ones (Osofsky and O'Connell, 1972). Again these findings imply caution about generalization from specific tasks to other situations of parent-child interaction. A teaching-task situation may offer information about parents' teaching strategies; it does not offer information about how parents and children interact at home, and this may be particularly true for fathers if the teaching-task situation is an unfamiliar one for them, as will be discussed further later.

Parent variables

Generally research into the relationship between parent variables and parent-child interaction has focussed on broad demographic categories (socio-economic status, education level, race) rather than individual differences such as level of depression or the parent's own experiences as a child. Despite recent theoretical emphasis on parent-child interaction and family interaction as systems of mutual influence, there are still few guidelines as to what variables to examine. Vietze and Anderson (1981) suggest parents' temperament, attitudes about children and experience of parenting. There are some indications in the literature which support the suggestion that "adult individual differences can moderate the effects of children" (Bates and Pettit, 1981, p.338; Crittenden and Bonvillian, 1984). Also, as was described in the Introductory chapter, maternal depression seems to affect interaction with young children not in terms of overall warmth or negativity but in terms of the quality of 'meshing' of the interaction (Puckering and Mills, 1982). The mothers in that study were described as having escaped by early marriage from an unhappy home life, having quickly had children, and then finding themselves "short of inner and outer resources and in a disastrous marriage" (p.3). Findings in a study of mothers who were previously in care as children showed similar patterns (Dowdney, Skuse, Rutter, Quinton and Mrazek, 1985). Also, mothers from disrupted families of origin (i.e. parents divorced or died before they were 16 years) have been found less contingent in their responses to their infant's vocalizations, and to talk, smile, present objects, look and touch the infants less, while no differences were detected in the infants' behaviour from the children of a matched control group of mothers from non-disrupted families of origin (Pawlby and Hall, 1980). When the infants were five months, 'disrupted' mothers were less likely (35%) to say they saw the child as a person than 'non-disrupted' mothers (75%) (Hall, Pawlby and Wolkind, 1979).

Thus, quite apart from the attitudinal variables and ideas about child-rearing which were discussed in Chapters 4 and 5, there are a number of other indications of parent variables which might be of key importance in understanding parent-child interaction differences, i.e. variables which reflect parents' experiences and roles in past and present family systems.

However, the primary focus in research on parental differences in interaction style with children has been on social class. Generally consistent social class differences have been found, particularly in structured situations, such as middle-class mothers giving fewer direct commands and more indirect commands (Bee et al., 1969; Zegiob and Forehand, 1975), less physical help (Bee et al., 1969; Phinney and Feshbach, 1980), more positive feedback (Bee et al., 1969; Brophy, 1970; Phinney and Feshbach, 1980). In play situations, middle-class mothers participate more actively (Zunich, 1961; Ramey et al., 1979), and spend more time in distal interaction (e.g. watching, talking) with infants (Field and Pawlby, 1980) than working-class mothers. These patterns do not imply homogeneity within class groups. For example, McLaughlin et al. (1981) found considerable variation within a disadvantaged group of mothers and children, and Phinney and Feshbach (1980) described two separate patterns within their working-class sample of mothers in semi-structured interaction with their three year olds, a 'negative-intrusive' style (negative statements, imperatives, pointing, moving pieces and physical guidance) and a 'positive non-directive' style (positive and neutral statements and questions).

There are those, however, who argue that social class is not related to differences in mother-child interaction. In contesting previous results they point, for example, to the different meanings the research process may have for middle-class versus working-class families, with the latter mistrusting researchers who tend to categorize their life-styles and interaction patterns as deficient. The unfamiliarity of a structured interaction situation may likewise affect the groups differently (Brophy, 1970). Using a laboratory setting, but asking participants to do what they usually did at home, Harmon and Kogan (1980) found very few social class related differences in interaction between white mothers and their three to five year old children. They used detailed coding of interaction, and the lower-class parents were familiar with one of the researchers. The authors conclude that massive social changes (including the effects of television) since the 1960's may have decreased variability between class groups in parent-child interaction patterns. On the other hand, a similarly structured contemporary study did find some differences, such as the middle-class mothers and children spending more than twice as much of the observed time in mutual play as lower-class dyads (Farran and Haskins, 1980). However, when the actual interaction was examined further, few group differences were found in the participants' frequency of initiations and responsiveness; it was the length of mutual play episodes which differed. Lower-class mothers were not found generally more controlling than middle-class mothers; they made more suggestions to their children, but the latter were more often engaged in no clear activity, a state which elicited suggestions at a higher rate from both groups of mothers.

Thus, social class differences in mother-child interaction may possibly be magnified artificially by situation, expectation and coding method, and at any rate are of much less significance than the wide within-class variability in interaction styles.

Several social-class difference studies also confounded the variable of race or cultural background. When race is looked at in isolation, it is not found predictive of interaction style (e.g. Zegiob and Forehand, 1975). Apparent cultural differences (within one country) may be primarily a product of maternal level of education (Laosa, 1980, comparing Anglo-American and Chicano mothers), reflecting the extent to which minority group parents have been socialised in the norms of the dominant society. However, some studies have found evidence of fine-grain differences in cultural patterns and expectation of interaction. For example, Steward and Steward (1973) observed Anglo-, Mexican- and Chinese-American mothers and their young sons. The Mexican-American mothers tended to repeat their instructions in the same format, and to use verbal interaction little, particularly praise, in contrast to the other two groups. Dixon et al. (1984) identified a similar pattern in Kenyan mothers, who were agriculturalists living in a small, tight-knit society (c.f. the Mexican-American mothers' origins). In comparison with white American mothers, they used little praise in teaching, as their culture emphasises teaching children not to rely on external reinforcers, but rather to value complying with tasks required by their family or group. Teaching strategies were directed toward the child completing tasks the correct way; American children and their mothers were more playful and exploratory. Even within white Western cultures, study of mother-infant interaction has suggested slight differences in distal interaction, such that British mothers seemed more instructional and used more toy-related play, as opposed to North American mothers who seemed more socially oriented (Field and Pawlby, 1980). Thus, cultural context may inhibit generalizability of findings about mother-child interaction style. Observed interaction requires to be interpreted within the broader context of the cultural goals of the society, as widely contrasting maternal and child behavioural styles may be appropriate in achieving contrasting cultural goals. This calls into question the usefulness of applying any single definition of 'optimal' maternal interaction style.

Parent variables such as social class, cultural background, IQ and level of education are not, of course, unrelated. Thus findings of parent-child interaction differences related to level of education are very similar to those cited above for social class. For example, better-educated mothers have been reported to use more positive reinforcement, more questions and descriptions, and fewer commands and specific task instructions (Streissguth and Bee, 1972; Clarke-Stewart, 1977). Lytton (1976) found mothers' educational level the variable most discriminative of group differences in control behaviour, but it was not related to the degree of warmth exhibited.

It should perhaps be reiterated that demographic variables such as those reviewed above are much less predictive of children's later functioning than interaction variables. Bakeman and

Brown (1980) agree with Lytton (1976) in suggesting that the variable of maternal educational level makes "a substantial unique contribution to accounting for the variance" (p.446) in child cognitive development. On the other hand, Olson et al. (1984) found that the correlation of social class with children's competence at two years was dissipated when mother-child interaction variables were controlled for in a path analysis.

Thus, although relationships can be shown between parent-child interaction and variables such as social class and parental education level, the importance and meaning of such relationships may be much less than was previously assumed. One factor behind this reassessment is the recognition of the necessity of conceptualising dyadic relationships within an ecological framework. For example, as mentioned above the assessment of mothers' degree of social support (past and present) is important in understanding differences in interaction style and in predicting the child's later competence. There is also research evidence to show that less well-educated women not only have fewer sources of social support, but also that they are less able to mobilise those sources in a crisis (Eckenrode, 1983).

However, the major and glaring omission from most previous research strategy in parent-child interaction has been the role of fathers. The word 'parents' has been used above in general statements, or to refer to particular studies which included mothers and fathers, but the research reported, most notably the longitudinal studies, has usually focussed on mothers only. Findings relevant to a discussion of mother-father differences or similarity will be reviewed in the following chapter.

Chapter Eight

COMPARISON OF MOTHERS AND FATHERS

INTRODUCTION

The review of literature in this chapter will not attempt to be fully comprehensive given, for example, the wide-ranging and recent survey available in Lamb (1981a) of the father's role in child development. The areas of study to be considered are attachment, early interaction, dyadic versus triadic situations, naturalistic versus structured situations, interaction with boys versus girls, paternal sensitivity, indirect influences and highly involved fathers.

First, however, it is necessary to discuss the context in which such research has been carried out. That is, when studies of father-child interaction became more frequent in the 1970's, the strategies largely mirrored those which had been adopted for the study of mother-child interaction, for example, cross-sectional glimpses of children of different ages in 'natural' or semi-structured dyadic interaction with father. Often the fathers were the partners of mothers who had previously been studied, and who usually had traditional role division, i.e. father working outside the home, mother at home (e.g. Lamb, 1976b; Clarke-Stewart, 1978). For the convenience of researchers, in naturalistic observation studies fathers have usually been observed with the child shortly before the child's bedtime (e.g. Lytton, 1976; Belsky, 1979; Blurton-Jones, 1980) rather than sampling across the day, which might be the more usual procedure with mothers. Thus, a number of constraints can be posited which would seem to affect the data. For example, sustained dyadic interaction in play with toys may be a less familiar or comfortable situation for some fathers (see Chapter 3) than it can be assumed to be for mothers; the expectations of fathers in being observed behaving as 'a father' may influence their behaviour in unpredicted ways; the novelty of the father returning home from work, and also the child's possible tiredness, may influence observed interaction considerably; the couples included in the studies do not reflect the role structuring and relative involvement with the child of families in which e.g. both parents work; and finally, observation of dyadic interaction excludes study of the effect of the couple's relationship on the interaction with the child, and of the more ecologically valid situation of triadic interaction. These points, where there is evidence relating to them, will be further examined below.

The important theoretical point to be kept in mind while examining the available research is thus that parent-child interaction takes place within a family and community context. It is suggested therefore that study of a dyad should take into consideration how their interaction might be affected, for example, by the presence of others (e.g. Clarke-Stewart, 1978; Belsky, 1979) or the birth of a new sibling (Dunn and Kendrick, 1982). The necessity of acknowledging mutuality of effects has already been stressed; but effects may also be indirect rather than direct, for example, the child affecting the parents' relationship, or the father influencing the child through the mother. However, it must be said that relatively little work in this area has been done, given the complexity of the concepts and of developing appropriate models for data collection and analysis (Belsky, 1981; Lewis, Feiring and Weinraub, 1981; McGreal, 1981).

Attachment

A significant portion of early father-child research focussed on the question of the child's attachment to figures other than the mother. Verbal report of attachment to fathers and to other family members was, however, available as early as 1964 (Schaffer and Emerson), counteracting prevailing assumptions that fathers were very much less important attachment figures than mothers (Bowlby, 1969). For about a third of infants studied, at the age of six to 18 months, the primary attachment seemed to be to the father. Observational studies have confirmed attachment (i.e. children demonstrating behaviours such as approaching and asking to be held) to fathers as much as to mothers, particularly when in a relaxed situation (Lamb, 1977a). When distressed and with both parents present, infants do however tend to turn preferentially to mothers (primary care-takers) (Kotelchuk, 1976; Lamb, 1976c). During the second year of life, observed at home, boys begin to show significant preferences for their fathers on attachment measures (Lamb, 1977b). These findings, however robust, may still be culture-specific: in Sweden, where fathers are more involved in caretaking than North American fathers, a significant attachment preference for mothers is found in home observation (Lamb, Frodi, Hwang and Frodi, 1983).

Explanation of these findings is looked for in observation of the quality of early interaction between parents and children. For example, there are differences in how fathers respond to sons and to daughters, and there are differences in the style of interactive play offered by fathers and by mothers (see below). But, first, there has been considerable study of father-baby interaction, to assess its quality and fathers' 'competence'. Positive correlations have been found between the quality of early father-infant interaction and later father-infant attachment, as has also been found for mothers (Chibucos and Kail, 1981).

Early interaction

A series of studies by Parke and colleagues, of middle-class and working-class fathers, have shown that fathers when observed with their infants are generally very interested and active participants in early interaction, holding and looking at the infant, touching and talking, at least as often as mothers, whether or not mothers were present (Parke and Tinsley, 1981). Both mothers and fathers adjust their speech similarly when talking to their infant, and change their rate of speech similarly when play-sessions and feeding-sessions are compared (Parke and Sawin, 1980). Thus, fathers' interest and competence as early interaction partners have been demonstrated.

But as Lamb (1981b) observes,

> "Although the fathers were capable of behaving sensitively, they tended to yield responsibility for child tending chores to their wives when not asked to demonstrate their competence for the investigators." (p.462)

That is, when the actual amount of daily interaction is considered, fathers are found to have much less contact with their infants than mothers. This information has usually relied on parental reports. However, Rebelsky and Hanks (1971) made 24 hour tape recordings of children, at two weekly intervals up to three months of age, and found the average number of fathers' vocal interactions per day with the infant was 2.7. Such a finding cannot be explained simply in terms of lesser time being available. Mothers' vocal interactions increased over the three months, fathers' decreased. This strategy of unobtrusive, long-duration recording does not seem to have been repeated in recent years, but would be necessary in order to reveal information about the actual experiences which may have impact on the child's social development.

Mother-father differences in 'natural' interaction

So far, parents' potential similarity in interaction with their children has been stressed; however, against this background some differences in style have been studied extensively. In what is otherwise a 'theoretical vacuum' (McGreal, 1981), the issue which has seemed to be being considered again stemmed from the past assumption of fathers' essential redundancy in child-care. That is, it has been proposed that if mother-father differences are found, this would be taken as evidence of fathers' complementary contribution to the child's socialization (e.g. Lamb, 1981b). However, the extent to which the research strategies adopted may of themselves magnify the finding of differences has not been sufficiently acknowledged. The simplistic nature of the theorizing is reflected in a lack of research into individual differences, and families as systems.

Even in the first few weeks, some differences in interaction style between mothers and fathers have been reported. Yogman (1982) has reported that fathers tend to touch infants with rhythmic tapping patterns more than mothers do, and mothers to vocalize in soft, imitative repetitions more than fathers do, in face-to-face interaction. Both parents play repetitive 'games' but fathers more so than mothers, particularly limb-moving games. At around eight months of age, differences are also found. In studies conducted both in laboratory and at home, fathers play more bouncing and lifting games than mothers, and mothers present toys more and watch the child (Lamb, 1977a; Power and Parke, 1982). However, these differences are not found consistently. A comparable study in Sweden did not find differences in play styles, though it did find that mothers were more likely to hold, tend to, vocalise to, smile at and display affection towards infants than fathers (Lamb, Frodi, Hwang, Frodi and Steinberg, 1982a). Belsky (1979) criticised studies such as the above for using 'non-representative situations', and took his analysis from naturally occurring units of interaction (father alone with child versus mother alone as well as all three together) during two two-hour observations at home. He stresses that there is no such thing as psychologically equivalent times of day for mothers and fathers in families with traditional role division. He observed around the time of the father's return home from work, a natural ('ecologically valid') time for observing both dyadic and triadic interaction. He found that mothers and fathers of 15 month old children differed on only two out of fifteen behaviour categories, i.e. mother stimulated the child, and did basic caretaking activities, more than the father did. Fathers did engage in more 'vigorous-motion' play than mothers, but the difference was not reliable.

Studies of older children have repeatedly found differences between mothers and fathers in triadic interaction observed at home (n.b. siblings might also be present, e.g. Lytton (1980)). Parental roles seem to become more differentiated between 15 and 30 months (Clarke-Stewart, 1978). Generally mothers are found to interact more with the child, both in terms of amount and in proportion to the time they are available, than fathers. However, when social-physical play is considered, fathers either are found to engage in such play more than mothers (Lytton, 1980, two year olds) or an equal amount (Clarke-Stewart, 1978). The latter study instead revealed the different quality of maternal versus paternal play style: fathers were less likely to choose toys or teaching-type activities, interacted in briefer episodes, and gave more praise. Children in turn were more cooperative and interested in play with their fathers.

Lytton (1980) points out that amounts and types of play observed may be greatly affected by the time of the observation. His study observed children when fathers came home from work, and when

> "mother, after a long day's dealing with the child, is glad to let him take over and to retire from 'play duty', often to prepare supper." (p.271)

Clarke-Stewart (1978) observed triadic interaction at the weekend, which may explain the greater emphasis on similarities between mothers and fathers in her results. She also gives an example, rare in the literature, of within-couple analysis, again emphasising similarity. There was also, however, further evidence of complementary differences in maternal and paternal roles, in that the father's amount of social-physical play correlated highly with the mother's talking to the child and playing with toys. That is, mothers who show qualities of interaction identified as most likely to promote child development seem to have partners who engage most in social-physical play. Clarke-Stewart speculates whether this might be an 'optimal paternal role'.

Studies of children older than about two and a half years are rarely of 'naturalistic' interaction, perhaps because of children's growing responsivity to the camera/observer (Lytton, 1980). The exception are studies in the operant tradition, seeking baseline or comparison data for purposes of behaviour modification. For example, Wahl, Johnson, Johansson and Martin (1974) observed four to six year old children at home with their families, and found no difference between mothers and fathers in terms of their reponses to children's deviant (defined as annoying, or a cause for concern) and non-deviant behaviours. An interesting comparative analysis has been made of the style of interaction between parents and child, and siblings and child, suggesting that it is quite usual for sibling relationships to be based on coercion. That is, siblings were more likely to be negative than positive to each other, and to cease aversive behaviour only when the other complied (Baskett and Johnson, 1982; Wahl et al., 1974). (This is mentioned here as an additional example of the necessity of collecting background data for intervention, in order to choose reasonable and individually-appropriate goals.)

Siblings have been little studied, despite their salience in young children's lives and effects on parent-child interaction. Dunn and Kendrick (1980) have, for example, shown considerable changes in mother-child interaction after the birth of a second child. These include decreases in maternal attention and play, increases in confrontation, and an increase in the proportion of interactions initiated by the child. Mother-child interaction has also been studied in a triad with a familiar same-age peer of the child. Mother-child interaction was found to facilitate sustained attention to a play object, but boys were at their most creative with a peer (Cohen and Tomlinson-Keasey, 1980). Siblings have been shown to be better at understanding children's communications than non-siblings (Weist and Kruppe, 1977). Also siblings and peers adjust their language in talking to younger children in a way similar to parents, but not as subtly; they seem to rely more on repetitions and directives (Wilkinson, Hiebert and Rembold, 1981).

Parent-child interaction, assessed in a dyadic situation, has been shown to change considerably in triadic interaction. Both quality and quantity change. Clarke-Stewart (1978) found that mothers initiated less talk and play with the child, and were also less reinforcing and responsive, when the father was present than when they were alone with the child. Belsky (1979) made similar suggestions for the change in father-child interaction. In the triad, parents may variously be described as sharing the interaction with the child (Belsky, 1979; Lytton, 1980), or as mother being more responsible for interaction with the child (Golinkoff and Ames, 1979; Pedersen et al., 1980), or as a variety of patterns (Miyake, Wakai, Tajima, Seki, Gotoh and Usui, 1978). However, even when parents' interaction with the child is equal in amount, it may still be that fathers are less alert and responsive to child signals. That is, in traditional role families, it may generally be someone else who clears up the accidents (Berko-Gleason, 1975). The general pattern of a decrease in behaviours in the triadic situation does not always hold for young infants; some behaviours increase. Fathers and mothers were found to smile and explore the baby more when their spouse was present (Parke and O'Leary, 1976) and the authors suggest that parents may stimulate each other by commenting on the baby's appearance or actions.

Belsky, Gilstrap and Rovine (1984) included analysis of data within couples, and found a high level of father involvement with the baby associated with a high level of couple interaction (which might be interpreted as either cause or effect). Marital interaction was unrelated to the degree of mother involvement in taking care of the baby, which suggests that mothers' activity is more directly dictated by the baby's needs.

There are thus a number of complex issues to be considered in choosing a setting for naturalistic observation of parent-child interaction, and for judging the comparability and generalizability of the results. Russell (1979b) has supported the argument that it is not ecologically valid to study fathers interacting alone with young children for extended periods of time, with evidence from a large study of families in which 80 per cent of fathers reported that they did not regularly spend time alone with their children at home, and 60 per cent never had this experience at all. However, even if the triad is 'the most characteristic social unit' for fathers (Pedersen et al., 1980), methods for studying and interpreting the observed interaction are still at an early stage of development.

Structured interaction

Parent-child interaction with older pre-school children has usually been studied in structured dyadic situations. Generally the findings are of much similarity of mothers and fathers, and a few differences (e.g. Pakizegi, 1978; Golinkoff and Ames, 1979; Davis and Hathaway, 1982; Frankel and Rollins, 1983). For example, in a sorting task fathers gave more statements and non-verbal instructions, while mothers asked more questions and gave more irrelevant information (Barton and Ericksen, 1981). Osofsky and O'Connell (1972) also found that fathers were more likely to intervene with physical help, whereas mothers more often encouraged the children's efforts. Bright and Stockdale (1984) found that fathers controlled and directed children more than mothers. Golinkoff and Ames (1979) found more differences between parents in a free-play triadic situation than in the structured situation. It should perhaps be noted that all of the above studies were conducted with relatively well-off and well-educated parents.

Interaction with boys and with girls

Before going on to review what the observed mother-father differences might mean, there is one other factor to consider, the sex of the child. Boys and girls do behave significantly differently, and the nature-nurture controversy in explaining the origin of differences will not be gone into here. Certainly some parent-son and parent-daughter interaction differences are accounted for by differences in the children's behaviour (e.g. Snow, Jacklin and Maccoby, 1983, an entertaining study of fathers' and twelve month olds' behaviour in a hazard-filled waiting room). However, when mothers and fathers are compared, it is clear that they show contrasting patterns of differential interaction. Both mothers and fathers are influenced by the infant's sex in the weeks after birth (when little is known of the child's characteristics), but after this period the majority of the studies of mother-child interaction show no significant differential treatment of the sexes up till about 18 months. In contrast, there is considerable evidence of differential treatment by fathers, such as encouraging boys to explore and to play with objects, while encouraging girls to vocalize (Power, 1981, reviewing 39 studies of sample sizes of 20 or more). Toward the end of the second year of life, both mothers and fathers seem active in promoting stereotypically sex-appropriate behaviours in boys and girls (Fagot, 1974). The differences in interaction patterns of fathers may well relate causally to the attachment differences in children in the second year of life, mentioned above.

<u>The meaning of mother-father differences</u>

The studies reviewed above thus suggest that mothers and fathers in traditional role-divided families typically evolve rather different play styles, and that when both parents are present fathers may be more salient figures for the child than mothers. The father's role as playmate, and lesser amount of interaction (particularly in care-taking activities), does not, however, appear to prevent his being seen as an attachment figure as well (Lamb, 1976b). Thus, father's role in socialization of children may be posited to be one of novelty, social-physical play, and sex-role differentiation.

A number of questions may be asked about this summary, however.

(1) Firstly, it is expressed in terms of the one-way effect of the father on the child, and not in terms of what the child learns about the structure of the world through the process of interacting with two parents who differ. What might be the effect of lesser frequency and amount of

interaction with father? Is it simply that he provides variety and novelty?

(2) Secondly, to consider the family as a system, are all effects direct, or can indirect chains of effect of one family member or one relationship be detected as acting on others?

(3) Thirdly, to what extent are the observed results of research on interaction artifacts of the methods adopted? For example, it has already been argued that there are no psychologically equivalent times of day, nor equally familiar interactive settings, for mothers and for fathers in traditionally role-divided families. Thus, comparisons of ecologically dissimilar settings may inevitably produce results which favour difference. But further than this, there is the question of how parents may conceive of their roles differently in triadic interaction, whether being observed or not. For example, do mothers 'pull out of the limelight' in that situation? Does each member feel they are expected to act in particular ways, for the camera, or for each other?

(4) Finally, as a broader type of problem of method, to what extent are mother-father behaviour differences tied up with roles? For example, what differences in results might be found from study of primary-caretaker fathers, or families in which both parents have paid work?

These questions will be discussed in three further sections, i.e. evidence relating to differences in sensitivity of response of fathers and mothers; discussion of patterns of influence in the family system; and research on families with non-traditional role-division.

Sensitivity

As fathers are generally less familiar with their young children than mothers, spending less time in interaction with them, it might be expected that they would be less skilled in interaction. For example, they might be less contingently responsive, and less carefully adjust their language level to that of the child. Several researchers have suggested that this is not so. In Clarke-Stewart's (1978) study, ratings of mothers' and fathers' interaction did not differ for responsiveness or effectiveness. Belsky, Gilstrap and Rovine (1984) found fathers to be as sensitive to changes in infant behaviour as mothers are. Fathers have been found to decrease their mean length of utterance, reduce syntactic complexity, increase redundancy, etc., in their speech in a similar way to mothers, to children from a few months old through to two and a half year olds (Golinkoff and Ames, 1979; Parke and Sawin, 1980; Wilkinson et al., 1981).

However, these studies seem to be the exception rather than the rule. In most studies of responsivity in play, mothers of infants (up to twelve months) are shown better at reading infant cues than fathers (Dickie and Gerber, 1980; Power, 1981). For example, when infants showed signs of losing interest in a particular toy, mothers would shift their focus in response to the infants' becoming interested in a new toy. Fathers were found more likely to ignore the new object and to engage in physical play, or to try to introduce another toy thus clashing with the child's interest (Power, 1981). Fathers' greater tendency to have sex-stereotyped expectations in play with young children could also be seen as evidence of lesser sensitivity than mothers to the fine detail of child characteristics. Fathers of infants who had experienced respiratory distress syndrome were found not to differ from fathers of normal healthy infants in interaction (e.g. laughing, smiling, games, total activity), whereas the two groups of mothers did differ (Field, 1981). On rating their high-risk infants, it seemed that fathers were aware of differences in responsivity and attentiveness, but they did not appear as disturbed by it as the mothers did. Belsky (1981) has suggested that fathers and mothers may be affected by different kinds of characteristics of children. Fathers, in favouring physical play, may be most affected by children's energy level, whereas mothers, in favouring social games and toy play, may be more sensitive to individual differences in responsiveness. However, the direction of causality could be either way, for example, fathers choosing to initiate physical play because it is 'easier' in terms of fine-tuning. The implications of parents' differential sensitivity to the decreased attentiveness and responsiveness of children with handicaps will be explored below.

There have been several studies of fathers' language interactions with their children which have suggested differences too (though small numbers, and variation in age of the child and observational setting in these linguistic studies seem to have led to some contradictory results). Weist and Stebbins (1972) and Weist and Kruppe (1977) have reported a lesser ability in fathers as opposed to mothers in understanding the precise meaning of two to three year olds' utterances. The researchers also suggest that fathers are not much better at understanding the speech of children than unrelated adults or non-parents. Berko-Gleason (1975) suggested from a small study that fathers' language at home did resemble mothers' in some features, but that fathers used more rare words, and more direct imperatives. In a story-telling situation, fathers concentrated on telling a good story, whilst mothers spent more time interacting, and ensuring the child's understanding. Berko-Gleason suggested that "fathers can be seen as a bridge to the outside world" (p.293).

These suggested differences in mothers' and fathers' speech to and understanding of their children have been confirmed by some later studies. In a laboratory play session with a constructional toy, fathers provided and elicited more different items of information than mothers. They seemed to be testing, confirming and displaying children's knowledge, as opposed to mothers who supplied labels only when children did not already know them (Masur and Berko-Gleason, 1980). Rondal (1980) noted that fathers provided greater lexical variety than mothers and more often asked children for clarification. He suggested the last may be because of greater difficulty in understanding the child (see above). However, it may also represent testing the child, or greater curiosity about the child's activities, or setting higher standards of intelligibility for the child than mothers do. Rondal found that fathers more often used long utterances than mothers did; however, Malone and Guy (1982) found the opposite, and age of the children does not seem to be an explanation. (In more naturalistic studies - recording interaction for 25 to 30 minutes at home - mothers and fathers did not differ on mean length of utterance to the child (Hladik and Edwards, 1984) nor on other syntatic or semantic features studied (Kavanaugh and Jirkovsky, 1982).)

Rondal did not find that fathers were more directive than mothers. He stressed the degree to which fathers' language was adapted to the child's expressive level. Parents were observed in three settings and this affected parents differentially on only two out of nineteen language measures; in each case parents were more alike in the structured situation than in free play or at mealtime.

However, it has generally been in naturalistic studies at home that mothers and fathers have seemed most similar (see above). Rondal, and Malone and Guy (like Berko-Gleason), conclude that mothers' and fathers' speech to the child differ sufficiently to require adaptation by the child to the differences.(1)

The study of reciprocal interaction between children and their parents thus suggests that fathers' role is more than simply adding a novel stimulus. In traditional role families at least, they seem to stretch children's capacities and to accustom them to not being automatically understood by adults. The literature is presently not able to provide answers to the question of under what circumstances and at what ages, redundancy or variety in parental behaviour might be in the infant's best interest (Belsky, 1981). However, an interesting comparison arises from Clarke-Stewart's (1978) study. She found that differences in parents' behavioural style were positively associated with children's cognitive and social development, but that differences in attitude to the child were negatively associated with child outcome measures (Clarke-Stewart, 1980). That is, it is suggested that a variety of stimulation may have a positive influence on children but that inconsistency in approach to child-rearing, on the other hand, may have a negative influence (see also McConachie, 1985).

Indirect effects

So far all the analysis presented has been in terms of a direct link between father and child. However, many researchers have considered the possibility of fathers' influence being greater indirectly, through the effect of their relationship with the mother (e.g. Lynn, 1974; c.f. Chapter 4). Lately, Belsky (1981) has pointed out that several reciprocal links can be posited in a family system. He comments that we have information about parents' and children's mutual influence, and some information from family sociology about children's effects on the marital relationship and the effect of the marital relationship on parenting. But two paths of influence have been largely ignored in this triangle, i.e. the effect of being a parent on the marital relationship, and the effect of the marital relationship on child behaviour and development. The present review will comment only on directions of effects within the mother-father-triad.

Several studies have suggested that mother-child interaction has a direct effect on children's cognitive development, whereas fathers' influence is indirect. For example, Radin (1976) reported research on four year old children in which fathers' expectations of daughters were positively and significantly correlated with their cognitive functioning, though their observed behaviours were not. In contrast, mothers' stimulation of the children was related to daughters' cognitive functioning. Radin suggests that mothers' behaviour is affected by fathers' expectations. Similar interaction/child functioning correlations were found by Clarke-Stewart (1978) for younger children. By performing cross-lagged correlational analysis, she was able to suggest that the paternal behaviours most closely associated with children's intellectual competence (e.g. being able to engage the child in play, rating the child high on competence) were more likely to be a result than an antecedent of the child's functioning. She posited a chain of influence from mother to child to father to mother in her sample of traditional role-divided families.

The nature of the mutual influence between mother and father has been speculated on, and researched, by several authors. One line of questioning is focussed on how parental expectations of each other affect interaction. For example, Radin (1976) suggests that as father-child interaction has usually been observed with mother present (quite apart from observers, who may be of either sex), the nature of the interaction may be coloured by fathers feeling that they need to meet role demands such as that of being the 'disciplinarian'. Power (1981) notes that on interview fathers are more likely than mothers to report promotion of sex-differences in their child-rearing goals, which may in turn affect how both parents feel fathers should act towards their children (e.g. that they 'ought' to rough-house with a boy child). There are also suggestions as to how mothers may act in accordance with expectations. Lytton (1980) suggests that father's presence seems to spur mother on to be 'on her best behaviour', i.e. that she gives significantly greater positive response to child compliance when father is present than when he is absent. Observer effects on interaction have been studied carefully, but the expectancy effects of mothers and fathers on each other require comprehensive study also, given that parents are frequently being observed in triadic interaction.

Another form of mutual influence is the effect of parents' behaviour on each other. As has been mentioned above, the presence of two parents tends to decrease the amount of interaction each has with the child, although mutual discussion of a newborn infant may increase interaction. With older infants, it has been shown that the amount of focussed attention given to the child is balanced by the amount of attention parents give to each other. Less focussed actions such as holding, cuddling, and feeding solid food to the child were not affected by parents' conversation (Pedersen, 1981). Children's behaviour in turn was linked to the balance, with increased initiations especially to mother when parents were not conversing. In a similar study, of 15 month old children, Belsky (1979) found that when the content of conversation was about the child, fathers' interaction with children increased.

Thus, at many levels, the mother-father relationship can be shown to affect the interaction of each with the child. The levels include not only conversational behaviour and role expectations, but also mutual warmth or hostility, marital satisfaction, etc. Complex conceptualizations of the levels of influence are offered by Parke (1979) and Russell and Radin (1983), and include also the introduction into the network by each parent of influences (e.g. other children and adults, television) from outside the family triangle. Thus, research which limits analysis to the direct influence between father and child misses out important explanatory indirect links through ignoring that the father is also a partner to the mother.

Family structure and change

In the past few years there has been evidence of an interest in studying fathers and mothers who adopt nontraditional family roles and structures. Partly the interest seems to have been in the old question of fathers' competence as parents. Review of results suggests that "high father involvement in the context of a two-parent family does nothing to impair the child's adjustment or ability to function well" (Radin and Russell, 1983, p.31)!

More illuminating is the question of whether observed mother-father differences are largely fixed by gender role, or determined by differences in care-taking. An early study was that by Field (1978) of primary versus secondary care-taker fathers of four month old infants. She found that primary care-taker fathers were like primary care-taker mothers in some ways (e.g. more smiling, more imitative grimaces and vocalizations than secondary care-taker fathers), but like all fathers in other ways (e.g. more poking and game playing than mothers). She suggested that the effect of greater care-taking was to increase familiarity with the infant, and thus to know, for example, that infants enjoy being imitated. This study looked only at three-minute bouts of behaviour. A longitudinal study in Sweden has attempted to address the same issue with observations at home. Fathers who said before the birth of the child that they planned to take extended paternity leave have been compared with 'traditional' fathers. Generally no significant effects have been found for the amount of intended or actual involvement of fathers, on interaction patterns at three months and eight months, or on attachment at eight months and sixteen months. Such differences as there are are related to parental gender (Lamb et al., 1982a, b, 1983). A similar conclusion was reached by an American study of dual-earner families (Pedersen, Cain, Zaslow and Anderson, 1982).

One effect of changes in cultural expectations about fathers' roles has been an increase in providing fathers with opportunities to learn 'fathering skills'. For example, one study used a videotape shown to fathers shortly after the baby's birth, and designed to illustrate ways of interacting with babies, and to model fathers' basic care-taking of infants. In a controlled follow-up, fathers who had seen the videotape were more contingently responsive in their interaction with their infants, and changed and fed them more often (Parke, Hymel, Power and Tinsley, 1980).

An intervention study with four to twelve month infants, employing a series of lectures and discussions, found an interesting effect in the follow-up triadic observations. Trained fathers and untrained mothers were found to talk more with the child than trained mothers and untrained fathers (Dickie and Gerber, 1980). It was suggested that one effect of the training was to heighten awareness of father-child interaction, and thus for mothers to deliberately 'step back' from being the central figure in interaction with the child. This effect has certainly been suggested in other studies as a by-product of research method (e.g. filming mothers interacting alone with the child shortly before filming the triad, Clarke-Stewart (1978)). But it may also be a more general effect of changes in role-expectations within a couple. In the Swedish study, employed mothers seemed to avoid 'stealing the limelight' in terms of play interaction from fathers who were highly involved in child-care (Lamb et al., 1982b). However, a contradictory result was reported by Pedersen et al. (1982), found that fathers in dual-earner families played little with their five month old infants, when observed in the evenings at home. They suggested that working mothers tended to inhibit the fathers' interaction through needing to establish their own interaction with the child.

Once again such considerations make any simple comparison of 'naturally observed' interaction patterns of mothers and fathers fraught with difficulty, whether dyadic or triadic interaction situations are chosen. That is, most studies of father-child interaction have been conducted with a particular sub-grouping (white, middle-class, traditional-role, North American), and the effects on the data and conclusions imposed by their particular ecology are as yet largely uncharted. Parents have particular goals in socializing their children within a particular cultural context, and what constitutes 'competence' in one culture may be dissimilar from competence in other cultures (Ogbu, 1981). This consideration will affect the choosing of an appropriate research strategy as well as how value judgements are made about parents' effectiveness.

NOTE

1. Smith and Mullis (1984) have noted that where studies of parent-child dyads in verbal interactions have used two-way analysis of variance (factors of child sex and parent sex), this procedure will probably have had the effect of reducing apparent differences between mothers and fathers. That is, because the child is the same within a couple, three-way analysis should be conducted, using blocks of each child within sex.

Chapter Nine

INTERACTION WITH YOUNG MENTALLY HANDICAPPED CHILDREN

INTRODUCTION

In considering the interaction of young mentally handicapped children with their parents, a number of factors would tend to suggest that differences will be observed in comparison with parent-child interaction where the child is not handicapped. These factors, and observed differences, were briefly outlined in Chapter 1 and will be discussed more fully here. Factors which might affect interaction include the whole context of the daily care of the child, for example, reactions of friends and neighbours to the child's handicap, additional caretaking burdens, ambiguous expectations for the future, more frequent separations through hospitalization, pressure to do special teaching with the child, etc., etc. (Ramey, Beckman-Bell and Gowen, 1980).

There are also the possible direct effects of mental, sensory or physical handicaps. Both theoretical and experimental justification has been presented above for regarding interaction as fundamental to child development. Mothers' behaviour has been shown to be carefully timed in response to particular periodic infant behaviours, or to phases of maximum arousal (Schaffer, 1977a). This suggests that impairment in the infant (e.g. sensory impairment, pain, irritability, etc.) will affect the cues available to the mother or other adults around which to time or phase interaction, for example, making the cues ambiguous or less salient. Findings from a number of studies indicate consistently that mentally handicapped infants and young children are relatively inactive and less responsive than non-handicapped children (e.g. Buckhalt et al., 1978; Jones, 1980; Berger and

Cunningham, 1981a, 1985; Gunn, Berry and Andrews, 1981). However, it is also evident that many observed behaviours do eventually develop to a comparable level, even though delayed, in children without major sensory impairment, e.g. eye contact (Berger and Cunningham, 1981b) and referential looking (Sorce, Emde and Frank, 1981) in Down's syndrome children. These children also are found to go through the same stages in attachment formation, but at a slower pace and showing less distress at separation from their mothers (Blacher and Meyers, 1983). Thus, mentally handicapped children's behavioural characteristics may be expected to have a direct effect on parent-child interaction. However, the comparative differences from parents and non-handicapped children may lessen or disappear when the groups are matched on developmental level, rather than on chronological age.

To jump ahead, the research evidence does indicate, though not consistently, that there are differences in parent-child interaction even when mentally handicapped and non-handicapped children are matched on some developmental index. However, this finding has been and can be interpreted in several ways. Firstly, the emphasis has been on 'handicapped' interaction style, at the expense of exploring individual differences within groups. This is despite repeated findings of greater variance in the parent-handicapped child samples than in the comparison groups (e.g. Eheart, 1982). It is also an unsatisfactory averaging procedure, to use as a yardstick for comparison the interactions of parents and non-handicapped children, given the well-documented wide range of individual differences in style (e.g. Escalona, 1973; Mahoney, 1983). The experience of having a mentally handicapped child should not therefore lead to parents being expected to be homogeneous in anything so detailed and variable as styles of interaction with their child.

Secondly, there are problems in any matching procedure for children whose aetiology, particular disabilities and behavioural characteristics will be so diverse. Matching on mean length of utterance (e.g. Rondal, 1977) or cognitive level in play (e.g. Eheart, 1982) leaves out of consideration, for example, the fact that the children are of rather different chronological ages, a feature which parents may well be taking into consideration in judging the appropriate content and style of interaction. Also, as was described above, it may be inconsistency of the child's responding, rather than the child's level of competence, which eventually depresses mutual interaction with the parent (Thoman et al., 1978). Thus, simply matching children on one index does not necessarily 'equalise' the context of interaction, and does not imply a simple conclusion of parental responsibility for observed differences between handicapped and non-handicapped dyads.

Thirdly, however, many researchers have interpreted observed interaction differences in terms of parental effects and also have assumed that differences represent deficiencies on the part of the parents of handicapped children. For example, parents are described as presenting their children with an impoverished socializing experience, through being overly directive or intrusive (e.g. Buium, Rynders and Turnure, 1974). The reasons behind the development of such differences in style are usually not specified, but may be suggested to be anxiety or depression felt by the parents associated with the child's handicap, or even simply pressure felt by them to 'show off' the child when being observed. The general implication is that parents are seen as increasing the child's handicap by deficient interaction. This interpretation has, however, been challenged occasionally, by the suggestion that observed differences are a necessary and adaptive response to the child's learning style or learning difficulties (e.g. Crawley and Spiker, 1983).

> "Measures used with the normal infant may not be equally applicable with a handicapped infant. For example, the lack of some behavior in the parent of a handicapped infant may not be interpretable in the same way if the infant is lacking a sensory modality to which the parent is adapting." (Walker, 1982, p.230)

To begin to resolve the issue requires detailed exploration of the variety of interaction styles, rather than merely counting the comparative frequency of various parental behaviours. It will, however, remain extremely difficult to tease out cause and effect relationships between parental interaction style and child competence or difficulties.

Ultimately, the 'difference' hypothesis is not proven anyway. Many of the more detailed and more recent studies have stressed instead the similarity of parents' strategies of accommodating to the child's developing competencies, whether handicapped or non-handicapped (e.g. McConkey and Martin, 1984). This and other theoretical issues will be referred to during the review of literature below. They have been touched on here in an attempt to establish some of the issues to be kept in mind, and some of the reasons which make the research difficult to interpret.

MOTHERS

Early interaction

Recent studies of pre-term infants have highlighted a number of issues of interest to the study of young mentally handicapped children and their parents. As has been mentioned already, group differences between pre-term and full-term infants in terms of mother-child interaction tend to disappear with time. But the degree of stress reported by parents, taken in conjunction with early interaction patterns, can be found to predict later problems such as hyperactivity, attentional problems and language delay (Kysela and Marfo, 1983; Marfo, 1984). A feedback loop can be identified whereby infants whose mothers are under greater stress are less responsive and less clear in the cues they give. In turn the mothers have less positive feelings, and are less likely to respond to infant cues (Crnic, Greenberg, Ragozin, Robinson and Basham, 1983). It is not hard to see how a similar circular effect might apply in the case of a child identified at birth as mentally handicapped. The longer-lasting effects of caring for a pre-term infant seem to include what has been termed 'maternal burn-out'. That is, Barnard (1981) has described how, as pre-term children develop and become more like full-term infants in their behaviour around eight months of age, their mothers may become increasingly less sensitive to the baby's cues, smile less at the baby and give less praise than mothers of full-term infants. It is as if mothers have put in so much effort in the early months, for minimal reward, that now they cannot do so. Mothers may remain less positive in teaching interactions even when the child is 24 months old (Barnard, Bee and Hammond, 1984).

This type of interaction pattern can be manipulated to some extent. For example, the experimental condition of asking mothers simply to imitate the infant's behaviour (at three months of age) has been shown to result in maternal activity contingent on and matched to the infant's activity, prompting more infant gaze and smiling. This facilitation of infant cues and maternal responsiveness is interpreted as potentially of benefit to the developing interaction (Field, 1977b).

There have been few studies of the early signalling behaviours of mentally handicapped children. Berger and Cunningham (1981a) first demonstrated patterns of differences between non-handicapped and Down's syndrome infants in development of smiling, gaze and vocalising. They also showed that mothers of Down's syndrome infants initially vocalized less, but from about five months significantly more, than the mothers of the non-handicapped infants. They suggested that maternal overstimulation might be partly responsible for inhibiting the infants' signalling. This seemed to be confirmed by experimental manipulation of interaction, in which maternal imitation was associated with more smiling by the Down's syndrome infants, but not by the non-handicapped infants. These mothers were involved in an early intervention programme, which might mean that they felt they had to 'try harder' in stimulating the child (at least when being recorded). However, it may be that mothers of non-handicapped children reduce in total amount of stimulation at this time, but become more contingent, as their infants' behaviours are more predictable (Parke and Tinsley, 1981).

Berger (1980) makes another point of importance in considering possible intervention strategies with parents of handicapped infants. He notes that smiling and face-to-face gazing decline naturally toward the end of the non-handicapped infant's first six months of life in favour of exploration and manipulation of objects. Thus, it is important that any intervention take note of age-appropriate fluctuations in behaviour, and not attempt, for example, to increase the frequency of gaze simply because it is assumed to be at a depressed level in a Down's syndrome infant.

Mother language

The study of interaction with older infants becomes more complex, and more varied, as the children are capable of a wider range of activities. Many early comparative studies focussed on mother-child language, and these have been reviewed by Mitchell,

D.R. (1976, 1980). Briefly, when mothers of mentally handicapped children are compared with mothers of non-handicapped children of the same age, they are found to use more demands and requests (Marshall, Hegrenes and Goldstein, 1973; Buium et al., 1974; Breiner and Forehand, 1982; Cardoso-Martins and Mervis, 1985), more controlling behaviours such as prohibitions (Kogan, Wimberger and Bobbitt, 1969; Kogan and Tyler, 1973) and less labelling of objects to which the child is attending (Cardoso-Martins and Mervis, 1985). These studies were of children aged between two and seven years, and were conducted both at home, in 'natural' as well as structured interaction, and in the laboratory. None of them compared home versus laboratory interaction. Greater differences were found by Buium et al. (1974) between the two groups in teaching situations as opposed to play. In contrast, Davis (1985) found mothers of Down's syndrome children gave more commands in a play situation than mothers of non-handicapped children matched on age (and also those matched on ability level); in a structured teaching situation, the group differences disappeared. Handicapped children's mothers are also found to show more warmth (Kogan and Tyler, 1973) and more rewards (Breiner and Forehand, 1982). It was found that mothers tended to give more orders during 'therapy' than during play (Tyler, Kogan and Turner, 1974), and that over time, there was progressive reduction in warm and positive behaviours (Kogan, Tyler and Turner, 1974). Campbell (1973) showed that all mothers increased their activity in situations which they perceive as difficult for their child. Other differences found between handicapped and non-handicapped children's mothers include giving a higher frequency of physical cues relevant to a task (Smith, Filler, Bricker, Robinson and Vincent-Smith, 1973), dominating the interaction more (Wedell-Monnig and Lumley, 1980, deaf children) and using a higher number of utterances and a lower mean length of utterance (Buium et al., 1974).

One of the weaknesses of matching mentally handicapped and non-handicapped groups by age is that the children may be contributing rather different patterns of behaviour to the interaction. The last three findings can each be commented on in the light of research which considers the interaction between the mother's behaviour and the child's developing competence. Firstly, in a longitudinal study of the interactive play of Down's syndrome children, McConkey and Martin (1983) have shown that mothers tend to shift from physical prompts to gestural prompts in play at about 18 months, i.e. when the child begins to be able to successfully complete simple actions with toys such as putting a ring on a stack. Thus, mothers are adapting their helping strategies closely to the child's needs - which may be an explanation of the greater use of physical cues reported above. Secondly, the ratio of mothers' to children's initiations in interaction changes over time in favour of domination by the child (Clarke-Stewart and Hevey, 1981), which might explain why mothers of handicapped children appear to dominate more. Thirdly, a comparative study of younger Down's syndrome and non-handicapped children (i.e. around 13 months chronological age) confirmed Buium et al.'s finding that mothers spoke to their Down's syndrome infants more than mothers of non-handicapped children did (Buckhalt et al., 1978). But they found no difference in mean length of utterance. They disputed the previous research conclusion that mothers of Down's syndrome children were presenting a linguistically-impoverished environment, and suggested instead that each group of mothers was responding appropriately to the language level of the children. Thus Buium et al.'s two year old non-handicapped group were conversing at a level to which mothers had adjusted, whereas the Down's syndrome children were largely preverbal at that age.

Thus the research comparing maternal interaction with mentally handicapped and non-handicapped children of the same age has yielded results which are difficult to interpret, primarily because mothers' behaviours have been looked at without reference to their context, i.e. the children's preceding and consequent behaviours. Another important point to consider is the great variability of mothers of handicapped children. A growing body of research has now looked at reciprocal interaction and matched children on the basis of developmental level.

Mother-child interaction

An early study of mother-child interaction with infants of "atypical behaviour" (i.e. pica, failure to thrive, etc., not congenital problems) was exemplary in its awareness of the conceptual problems of such research, even though its observation method was primitive. Greenberg (1971) discussed general problems in child-rearing research such as the lack of study of what actually happens (rather than e.g. relying on ratings of parents' attitudes), the conceptual remoteness of parental data from child data, and problems in sampling (such as grouping mothers on reported social class rather than on detailed knowledge of background or personality characteristics). He also pointed out that 'identical circumstances' for observation (such as a structured task in a laboratory setting) may in fact suit some parents and not others. He gave no statistical information on his filmed observations, but reported that mothers of atypical infants more often had an apparently fixed facial expression, and organized the play with the child poorly. Some were inactive, some were very busy, and some alternated between vigorous activity and apparent apathy.

Later studies have provided a micro-analysis of sequences of interaction and have tended to confirm reported disturbances in the interaction of mentally handicapped children and their mothers. For example, several studies have demonstrated less successful synchrony of turn-taking (Jones, 1977, 1979, 1980; Berger and Cunningham, 1983). Mogford (1979b) has described in detail how some mothers are very successful in interaction with their children, and others less successful.

> "...unsuccessful mothers were 'at odds' with their children so that either each was engaged in different activities at the same time, or the child was systematically failing to comply with his mother's suggestions, and yet the flow of his own play was constantly interrupted." (p.78)

The clashes and reduced contingent responding mean that children derive less feedback for their initiations, such as informative expansion of their utterances (Jones, 1980), and that mothers derive less reward for their participation (Mogford, 1979a).

The behaviour of mothers of mentally handicapped children has been characterized as including more initiations (Mogford, 1979a; Davis and Oliver, 1980; Jones, 1980; Eheart, 1982), more commands and less feedback to the child (Cunningham, Rueler, Blackwell and Deck, 1981; Eheart, 1982) and more semantically unrelated conversation (Petersen and Sherrod, 1982) than mothers of non-handicapped children matched in terms of competence. The matching indices included cognitive level in play, utterances per minute, mean length of utterance and assessed developmental level. The interaction situations included laboratory free play and structured task. There are, however, conflicting findings. Several authors have not found mothers of handicapped children more directive (Terdal, Jackson and Garner, 1976; Rondal, 1977; Mogford, 1979a), the first study only finding them more directive when observed in a structured task. Davis and Oliver (1980) found the handicapped children's mothers less directive; however, this study was unusual in not distinguishing directive questions from other question forms, and the effect of leaving these out from the category of directive utterances is not known. This study was also unusual in having all working-class rather than middle-class subjects. The observation situation does not explain the conflicting findings about maternal directiveness, as all of these latter studies, except Rondal's, used laboratory free play situations too.

One possible factor is suggested by Cunningham et al.'s (1981) observation that the mothers of the handicapped children might have been more affected by the situation of being observed. Jones (1980) reported that the Down's syndrome children's mothers repeatedly referred to 'teaching' the child when they were in verbal interaction, whereas the mothers of the non-handicapped children saw 'chats' as enjoying the child's company. Osofsky and O'Connell's (1972) study of non-handicapped children reviewed above suggested that parents would use more controlling behaviours in difficult tasks than easy ones, and teaching might well be seen as challenging the child more than a 'chat'. There may be an interaction with age in the case of the handicapped children, as Gunn, Clark and Berry (1980) found that from three months to 17 months one child's mother gradually used more directions and tried to do more teaching. But McConkey and Martin (1984) found that mothers' demands decreased again when Down's syndrome children were around 21 months of age, as the children were then able to carry out simple correct actions with toys. As children's verbal abilities increase, mothers tend to change from demands (at the sound imitation stage) to increased commenting or questioning at the two-word level (Price, 1984), and mothers are generally more responsive proportionately to handicapped children's behaviour as child competence increases (Brooks-Gunn and Lewis, 1984).(1) The studies which observed no difference in directiveness did not involve children of a consistently different age from those studies which did. Mogford (1979a) took account of the possibly different meanings of the observation situation for the two groups, by trying to provoke similar pressure on the non-handicapped children's mothers through her instructions. Most studies do not make clear the exact context of the observation for the mothers, and do not ask what mothers' perceptions of the study are. Eheart (1982) did and found more mothers of handicapped than non-handicapped children said that they were trying to change their child's behaviour in the play situation. Such information might cast light on conflicting findings.

There is an additional explanation of the possible greater directiveness of mothers of young mentally handicapped children. Rather than it being determined by parents' perceptions of the importance of teaching, to some extent modified in response to children's changing levels of competence, it may also be a reaction to the different quality of behaviours which mentally handicapped children bring to interaction. A delayed child generally initiates less and may be less responsive verbally and non-verbally. A questioning style by mothers may produce few appropriate responses, but directions may be much more successful in eliciting behaviour, on the basis of which the dyad can then focus interaction (Leifer and Lewis, 1984).

> "One possible explanation for the lowered responsiveness observed in handicapped children is that they have failed to take turns in mother-infant interactions, and their behavior is not controlled by the verbal and non-verbal cues that affect the behavior of normal children. They do not respond because events that signal to normal children that a response is appropriate do not function in the same way for them. Mothers may use explicit cues because these cues are more efficient in eliciting a response than descriptive or non-directive statements." (Rogers-Warren, Warren and Baer, 1983, p.252-3)

On the topic of maternal feedback, researchers have noted that mothers of handicapped children tend to be less responsive to cooperative behaviour than mothers of non-handicapped children (Cunningham et al., 1981; Eheart, 1982), and indeed to give poorly differentiated consequences to appropriate or inappropriate behaviour (Terdal et al., 1976). But this observation cannot be divorced from consideration of the general nature of the children's behaviour. Generally the handicapped children are described as less responsive and initiating less, thus providing parents with less adequate information as to the level of language they can comprehend. Consequently, parents may fail to adjust their interaction sensitively enough (Cunningham et al., 1981).

Again there are dissenting voices. Jones (1980) found that the mothers of the Down's syndrome children used significantly more 'support techniques', i.e. on failing to elicit a desired response they would carefully reduce the level of their initiation, for example, by modelling or prompting a child response. Other studies have found mothers as responsive (Terdal et al., 1976; Vietze et al., 1978), or even more responsive (in terms of speed of response - Davis and Oliver, 1980) than mothers of non-handicapped children. These studies suggest that the children's lower level of activity had not affected mother's behaviour. Vietze et al. (1978) found that this held true primarily for mildly mentally handicapped children, but that the less predictable behaviour of two year old severely handicapped children had eventually affected the interactive style of the mothers. Cunningham et al. (1981), apparently using a similar definition, found the opposite, that mothers were less responsive to the more able group.

There are thus two issues here, whether mothers are as generally responsive, and whether the content of that response is sensitive to the child's level. There is, in summary, mixed evidence as to whether mothers are affected in terms of responsiveness, despite the depressed level or ambiguous nature of the child's cues. However, the evidence seems clear that reciprocal turn-taking in interaction is less successful. In terms of the latter question, there is much evidence that mothers are sensitive in attuning their behaviour to the child's level, in a similar way to mothers of non-handicapped children (Rondal, 1977; McConkey and Martin, 1984). Mogford (1979b) has noted that, to an observer, mothers who are successful in interaction may appear to be over-interpreting their children's intentions and capabilities, but that further study (e.g. of videotapes) will usually confirm their interpretations. Willingness to make such interpretations is based on greater intimate knowledge of the child, and is also part of the way in which infants come to attach meanings to events, and to discover their own powers.

A longitudinal study of Down's syndrome children and their mothers also emphasised the extent to which mothers were attuned to their children's play levels, and adapted their actions according to the toys provided (McConkey and Martin, 1983). The authors comment, however, that the mothers had quite reasonable but fixed expectations about how to play with different kinds of toys (dolls, a ring-stack). This meant, in effect, that they limited the kinds of help that they could have given their children, if they had used the toys in more flexible ways (e.g. giving more models of self-pretend play, before applying the actions to the doll). This is an example of where using non-handicapped children and their mothers as a standard is inappropriate, when in effect handicapped children's mothers might be helped to be even more supportive to their children's levels of activity.

Those studies which found mothers of handicapped children to be more directive and to dominate the interaction more than mothers of non-handicapped children have frequently interpreted this to mean that the mothers are intrusive and thus insensitive to the children's cues. However, directiveness and sensitivity can be shown to be quite separate dimensions, integrated by different mothers into their style in different ways (Crawley and Spiker, 1983). Firstly, for non-handicapped children, an 'authoritative' style that combines clear and firm expectations with warm and sensitive responsiveness has been found facilitative to child development (Baumrind, 1971). Secondly, the appropriateness of maternal directiveness is related to the interaction style of the child; a child who is passive may initially require more direction by the mother. Crawley and Spiker (1983) found that mothers' sensitivity rating was not related to the child's developmental quotient, and suggested that:

> "Mothers who merely respond sensitively to child initiations without providing the child with a minimal level of direction or without elaborating on the child's play may not provide an optimally stimulating environment for a young child with Down syndrome." (p.1321)

Thus directiveness needs to be examined in a more differentiated way than it has been in previous research, and perhaps its separateness from sensitivity confirmed in studies which use more demonstrable measurements than ratings.

FATHER-CHILD INTERACTION

Fathers of handicapped children have been even more invisible in parent-child interaction studies than they were in studies of parents' attitudes and feelings. This may well be a reflection of the workings of services for handicapped children, since detailed research has usually gone hand in hand with intervention. Since services operate largely during weekdays, and mothers are under pressure to be full-time caretakers, fathers are excluded by default.

Of the studies identified in the literature, only two involve a comparison with non-handicapped children's families, and only one has contrasted triadic with dyadic interaction. Mitchell, W.M. (1980) found that fathers of Down's syndrome children were very similar to fathers of non-handicapped children in home observations of interaction, except that they were more likely to be found teaching their children (even though the observations were made just prior to the children's bedtime). A more structured study of play interaction at home with four to seven year old children stressed similarity of mothers and fathers, but noted several differences between handicapped and non-handicapped groupings (Stoneman, Brody and Abbott, 1983). In dyadic interaction, parents of Down's syndrome children more often adopted teacher and manager roles with their children. The Down's syndrome children were less contingently responsive to their parents than were the non-handicapped children; however, the Down's syndrome children were more responsive to fathers' teaching than to mothers' in the triadic situation. This was interpreted as fathers' greater novelty in teaching - the content of their joint activity was not reported, nor was the quality of fathers' interaction style measured. The parents of Down's syndrome children were found to be "extremely contingently responsive", as if they were under more of a pressure to respond since each initiation by the child was felt to be important. However, this may also represent a developmentally appropriate decline in responsiveness by parents of fluent non-handicapped children. In the triadic situation, fathers of Down's syndrome children and non-handicapped children alike were found to retreat into the observer role or solitary activity, while mothers continued their manager role in much the same way as they had in dyadic interaction.

The other available studies of fathers of mentally handicapped children have contrasted mothers and fathers in play or structured teaching sessions. The general conclusion is of very few significant differences between mothers' and fathers' behaviour in interacting with the child. For example, a case study of a four year old language-impaired boy (compared with his non-handicapped cousin) found no evidence of lesser competence of the father in adjusting his speech appropriately to the boy's level (Cramblit and Siegel, 1977). There have also been three studies of Down's syndrome children and their parents. Cheseldine (1977) recorded play sessions at home, and found that mothers and fathers differed only on use of expansions of the child's utterances. Mitchell, D.R. (1976, 1980) observed dyads in a laboratory teaching task and found very few categories on which mothers and fathers differed. These exceptions included greater use of high levels of physical help to the child by fathers (c.f. Golinkoff and Ames, 1979), and Mitchell, J. (1976) found fathers' mean length of utterance to the child significantly shorter than mothers' (c.f. Malone and Guy, 1982). Mitchell, D.R. also found that couples resembled each other closely on most categories of behaviour (c.f. Clarke-Stewart, 1978). Battersby (1982) observed a teaching situation at home; she found no significant differences between mothers and fathers, and couple similarity on mean length of utterance. The children in these studies were of mean age four and a half, five and a half and two and a half years respectively and sample numbers were eleven, eight and seven. Thus no difference in parental sensitivity to the child's level of activity is suggested by these studies, unlike the studies of non-handicapped children reviewed above.

A larger study of 21 young mentally handicapped children and their families also tended to find a lack of difference between mothers and fathers as groups and as couples, within a wide variety of styles of interaction (McConachie and Mitchell, 1985). However, there were some fine-grained differences which tended to support the idea that fathers' responses were less finely-tuned to children's changing activity (c.f. Power, 1981). For example, fathers remained stable in style of interaction between two separate filmed sessions whereas mothers varied on some variables, and also fathers differed in style depending on external characteristics of the child, whereas mothers did not. Fathers elicited more negative behaviour than mothers did, particularly when they used commands in giving directions, and the children made more errors when fathers used simply verbal directions without gestures (and these patterns did not apply to mothers). Fathers who tended to dominate the interaction elicited less compliance from children, and in turn complied less themselves with the child's initiations. When mothers took control of interaction they seemed to be more successful.

These studies of mothers and fathers in interaction with mentally handicapped children are very limited, in terms of short observation sessions, structured tasks, and lack of observation in the more ecologically valid situation of the triad or family group. Research on non-handicapped children suggested that observed parental similarity might be greater in a structured task setting (Golinkoff and Ames, 1979; Rondal, 1980). Cheseldine (1977) underlines the point that parental interaction varies with different situations, finding that both parents used language in different ways when playing with bricks as opposed to playing with dolls (c.f. McConkey and Martin, 1983, 1984).

CONCLUSION

Research into the interaction of parents and their young mentally handicapped children has suffered from several limitations. Most obviously, it has not been linked in to any conceptual framework of family functioning (see Chapter 3). The very few studies which have included fathers have been limited almost exclusively to artificial situations for interaction, with no background information available as to the family's usual patterns of interaction including father's level of involvement. Analysis of indirect as well as direct effects on interaction has been impossible. The paucity of studies and the generally small samples do not allow for any analysis in terms of child sex or age, or of services being received by the families. The question of possible cultural differences has not been touched on.

In terms of method, many studies have looked at parents' behaviour separately from the children's behaviour. Where an interactive framework has been adopted, it has generally been restricted to immediate contingencies, ignoring various natural contingencies which might be operating and would require analysis of longer sequences (Vietze et al., 1978; Jones, 1980). The many conflicting findings of single-occasion studies have to some extent been clarified by longitudinal studies; however, none of the latter included fathers. A major problem in interpretation has been the almost universal presentation of results in terms of group differences. Thus emphasis has been placed on 'handicapped' style rather than on the wide range of individual differences. Similarly mothers and fathers have been compared, but little information is available on couples.

Parents' interaction with their young mentally handicapped children is a potent source of developmental stimulus. Research as yet has provided few guidelines as to how parents may be helped to maximise its benefits. Firstly, it is impossible to make recommendations for individual parents from correlational studies of the effect of aspects of parental interaction style on cognitive and social development in children. The correlations derived are significant, but account for a relatively low proportion of the variance in the results (Hess, 1980) and individual results are of low replicability (Clarke-Stewart et al., 1979). Secondly, for reasons discussed above, it is difficult to interpret observed differences between parents of handicapped and parents of non-handicapped children, that is, whether they represent hindrance or help to the children. The following chapters will examine the questions of how knowledge about interaction has been applied to intervention programmes, and of which parental variables have been studied in gauging the individual appropriateness and success of intervention.

NOTE

1. Interestingly, it has been shown that non-handicapped five year old children show a similar ability to adapt the level of their speech depending on the developmental level of a

handicapped child. They are more directive, and provide less information, the more handicapped the child. These adjustments are interpreted as increasing the likelihood that messages will be understood and responded to (Guralnick and Paul-Brown, 1980).

Chapter Ten

INVOLVING PARENTS IN TEACHING

INTRODUCTION

The kinds of service interventions which have been developed over the past 15 years have attempted to respond to various aspects of the situation in which parents of mentally handicapped children find themselves. Those aspects which have been outlined above include:

- the demands of daily living, including not only practical and economic demands but also the children's increased need for supervision and stimulation;
- emotional reactions to the child's being handicapped, and attitudes to the child's upbringing;
- potential problems in establishing rewarding interaction with the child, given reduced or unclear initiations by the child associated with less successful meshing of interaction.

From an early stage there was some recognition that intervention required to involve parents actively, not only to improve effective services to the children but also to support the family system. Several explicit programme philosophies have reflected this dual goal (e.g. Lillie, 1974; Denhoff and Hyman, 1976; Bricker and Casuso, 1977; Beveridge, Flanagan, McConachie and Sebba, 1982; Brynelsen, 1983; Cunningham, 1983b). For example:

> "When we initiated our family involvement program, our goal was to teach parents specific intervention skills to assist them in becoming more effective change-agents with their child. Although this is still our ultimate goal, we

> have learned that other family needs must often be met before parents are able to learn to apply education intervention strategies. We have found that one needs to approach parental participation and education from a comprehensive base. Isolated skill training with parents often is not effective." (Bricker and Casuso, 1977, p.2)

The areas included in programmes may encompass:

- social and emotional support to family members;
- exchange of information between parents and professionals;
- parent participation as members of the team, in assessment, decision-making, etc.;
- development of positive parent-child relationships;
- liaison between families and networks of community services.

(Beveridge et al., 1982)

Programmes thus go beyond awareness of parents' feelings to offering practical support and advice, as Wolfensberger (1967) recommended in reviewing earlier counselling interventions for parents. Yet educational aims for the children need not dominate at the expense of the emotional support which parents may require at times. Such support may come best from other parents, either informally as part of an educational programme, or in an organised parent-to-parent programme (Pugh, 1981). Parents may be involved at several different levels of decision-making; in the Infant Development Programmes in British Columbia parents are even included in the management and monitoring teams (Brynelsen, 1983). Parents often need help to find their way through the maze of different statutory and voluntary service possibilities which may be available but an ultimate aim of programmes will be to develop parents' confidence in dealing with other professionals on their own (e.g. Bromwich, 1981). Any one service intervention is simply a part of the network of ecological systems which impinge upon the family of a mentally handicapped child.

This broad-based approach to planning services might be thought of as the best of current practice. The emphasis on parental involvement in educational services for their children did not only evolve through trial and error (as in the above quotation). It was influenced by a number of historical trends of which a few will be mentioned briefly. Firstly, institutional care for mentally handicapped people had been seen as the treatment of choice till the 1960's at least, in theory offering specialist training, care and employment from the time of the first asylums established in the nineteenth century. However, policy ideas changed considerably in Britain during the 1960's, partly in response to increased awareness of the true nature of institutional care, and perhaps partly in response to increased knowledge about the real needs of families (e.g. Tizard and Grad, 1961; Carnegie UK Trust, 1964). In 1971, the White Paper 'Better Services for the Mentally Handicapped' put forward as government policy the principle of 'community care', in which obviously families had to play a major role. At the same time, the Education Act of 1970 brought all mentally handicapped children into the responsibility of the Education Authorities. Secondly, the perceived role of parents in general education had been changing. The Plowden Report (1966) 'Children and their Primary Schools' argued that increased parental understanding of education was necessary in order to attempt to correct the imbalance in achievement of children from different social class backgrounds. This policy of greater parental involvement in schools carried the implicit assumption that parents needed to change. It was, however, accompanied gradually by a recognition of the rights of parents to contribute to changes in schools. Also, in response to the lack of preschool provision, parents set up a very successful network of playgroups. The results of early intervention programmes, for example, in the USA the Head Start programme to counteract educational disadvantage, underlined the importance of parents' being involved, so that initial beneficial effects did not quickly wash out (Consortium on Developmental Continuity, 1977; Lazar and Darlington, 1979).

Thirdly, early intervention had as one part of its basic rationale the idea that the first five years were essential in terms of the child's learning. Developmental theorists such as Bowlby (1951) had suggested that relatively small events could have major positive or negative consequences for the child. Later educational thinking softened this emphasis, and also re-evaluated the idea of there being 'critical' early periods for learning, in favour of the idea that there may rather be 'optimal' periods and conditions for child development (Clarke and Clarke, 1976). This left room for effective later remedial intervention. However, the importance of environmental influences on early intellectual development was established. Finally, during the 1950's and 1960's, there were major advances in the education and training of mentally handicapped people. For example, it was shown that careful structuring of learning could bring about considerable results, not necessarily related to measured IQ levels (Gold, 1973). The development of behaviour modification as a technology arising from learning theory was set in motion by the publication of Skinner's 'Science and Human Behavior' in 1953. Thus, a successful approach to teaching mentally handicapped people was being developed which lent itself to wide application in the training of teachers and paraprofessionals, and also parents.

Thus, the focus on parental involvement in the education of their young mentally handicapped children seems in retrospect inevitable. It has undergone many changes in philosophy, from training parents to carry out professionals' programmes, through to 'parents as partners'. The development of current philosophy will be discussed later in the present chapter, following a summary of the kinds of involvement programmes which have been described in published literature. One of the major questions which has as yet to be answered satisfactorily is how individual differences between parents relate to the degree of success of different kinds of intervention programmes. Therefore a thorough review will be made in the following chapter of such parent variables as have been considered in the evaluation of programmes.(1)

The area of 'parental involvement' presents great problems of word-usage. This is partly because a few words have been used in many different ways, partly because vocabulary reflects changes in philosophy over time, and partly because of the different perspectives of parents and of professionals. As an obvious example of the last, parents might well be surprised at professionals' plans for their 'involvement', given their constant responsibility for their children; 'involvement' here will refer to a systematic introduction to strategies of teaching their children. It is hoped that the various meanings of words such as 'programme', 'services', 'intervention', 'learning' and 'teaching', will be clear in context. Finally, the term 'parent training' will be used extensively in this and the next chapter, even where it is basically inappropriate to the philosophy of the intervention under discussion. It will be used to mean the active transmission of knowledge and skills to parents by professionals, and is appropriate for the majority of interventions reviewed, particularly those of the 1970's, which had a clear base in behaviour modification principles.

PARENT-CENTRED EARLY INTERVENTION

The multitude of programmes for parents of young mentally handicapped children which have been described in published literature can be summarised in various ways. The approach taken here will be to describe differences firstly in organisational structure and secondly in the teaching content, as these reflect programmes' aims. Obviously there is a range of possible service structures and mixes of different types at different times (Karnes, 1977). However, three basic structures can be discussed.

Structure: Parent Workshops

Workshops for parents have been a very popular form of intervention (popular in terms of numbers of reports in the literature). They have generally taken the form of a six to twelve week course, often held in the evenings, to which parents come without their children. The evening will often be structured in two halves, with some form of presentation, for example, about how to observe a child's current abilities, and then an opportunity for small group discussion, with parents focussing on how they can work with their own child. The structure allows for parents to give each other mutual support, to talk with a variety of professionals, and to plan and receive help in carrying out a teaching programme for their child (e.g. Mash and Terdal, 1973; Bidder, Bryant and Gray, 1975; Cunningham and Jeffree, 1975; Tavormina, 1975; Attwood, 1978; Firth, 1982). Parents themselves may later be recruited as instructors to work alongside professionals (e.g. Ball, Coyne, Jarvis and Pease, 1984). Evaluation has generally been restricted to reports of attendance levels, parents' expressions of satisfaction, and number of teaching programmes carried out successfully with children. More searching evaluations tend to reveal less positive results, however. For example, it may be found that parents do not actually carry out programmed teaching as intended (McConkey et al., 1982; Gardner, 1983; Salzburg and Villani, 1983; Baker, Prieto-Bayard and McCurry, 1984; Hornby and Singh, 1984), and parents of older children have difficulty in successfully implementing programmes with only this degree of support (Firth, 1982). However, in the short term, studies which have measured parents' teaching skills following a short course have tended to show that parents can successfully acquire skills (Mash and Terdal, 1973; Tavormina, 1975; Sandler, Coren and Thurman, 1983 - see Chapter 11, section on measurement of parents' skills). Few reports of workshops have presented results in terms of children's progress, perhaps because the interventions are usually short-term. The results are mixed, either finding no difference from control children (e.g. Kiernan, 1978) or changes as expected (e.g. progress on skill checklist - Heifetz, 1977a; increased frequency of child play - McConkey et al., 1982; increase in complexity and types of utterances - McConkey and O'Connor, 1982).

A number of measures have been introduced in order to overcome certain limitations of the workshop structure described above. For example, some workshops are accompanied by occasional home visits in order to help parents apply their learning, and to discover what practical impediments may exist in the home (e.g. Saunders, Jordan and Kiernan, 1975; Heifetz, 1977a; Emerson, Hood, Pitt, Palmer and Sinclair, 1981; Gardner, 1983). Others have accompanied the group course with manuals of instruction (e.g. Larsen and Bricker, 1968; Baldwin, Fredericks and Brodsky, 1973; Baker, Brightman, Heifetz and Murphy, 1976; Perkins, Taylor and Capie, 1980) for parents to refer to, and to help workshop attenders explain the course to non-attenders in the family. Another modification has been to invite parents to a three week intensive workshop, wherein parents progress from one set of skills to another at their own pace of achieving competency (O'Dell, Blackwell, Larsen and Hogan, 1977). Other courses have been based around videotaped instructional units (e.g. Coleman, Ganong and Brown, 1981; McConkey et al., 1982; McConkey and O'Connor, 1982). One further development has been to base the workshop, not in a university setting or a clinic, but in the child's school (e.g. Cunningham and Jeffree, 1975; Saunders et al., 1975; Hattersley, 1979; Boucher, 1981; Gardner, 1983). The advantages can include making links with the child's school curriculum so that parents and teacher can work together in the future; however, in practice, such joint programming can be very difficult to implement (Saunders et al., 1975). Another benefit is meeting on familiar ground, so that potentially all parents can be involved, not simply the confident volunteers. One result may be lower attendance figures, however. Another difficulty may lie in teachers' lack of training in working with parents and with groups, so that they, for example, find it difficult to encourage parents to answer each other's queries rather than 'being the expert' (Cunningham and Jeffree, 1975; Karnes and Teska, 1980). However, it does seem that when workshops are based in a school, they may more easily become part of the long-term support services offered to parents by the school (Hattersley, 1979; Boucher, 1981).

Only very occasionally do workshop reports mention that a member of the family other than the parents has been involved. However, there have been a few reports of workshops specifically for siblings. Weinrott (1974) described a summer training camp for teenage siblings, where they followed a behaviour modification course, and then applied their new knowledge at home with their mentally handicapped sister or brother. The aim was that the time they spent together should be as productive and positive as possible, therefore the siblings learned strategies for minimizing disruptive incidents and ways to help their brother or sister to become more independent. Hart and Walters (1981) also described a workshop for siblings which included information on behaviour management and teaching skills.

Structure: Centre-based programmes

It would be impossible either to list centre-based programmes, or to summarise the diversity of their features. The purpose of including this heading is primarily to consider the advantages to parents of having a central resource which allows them, for example, individual consultations, and some form of shared care of the child.

One early-established British example was the Nottingham University Toy Library, run by psychologists, to which parents and children came for regular consultations aimed at promoting the child's development and parent-child interaction. Some regular nursery playgroups were attached, for example, a weekly group for blind children (Newson, Newson, Head and Mogford, 1979). Another example is the Anson House Preschool Project, which incorporated an integrated nursery classroom on four mornings per week, and which also involved parents on an individual basis in teaching their children (Hogg, 1979). Thirdly, there is the Honeylands family support unit which incorporates a staffed playgroup and short-term respite care, and from which a home-visiting service operates (Green and Evans, 1982, 1984). Others are reviewed by Parker and Mitchell (1980).

As Newson et al. (1979) stress, the needs families "present on joining (the toy library) are diverse and apparently fairly independent of the child's type of handicap" (p.51). Thus, in order to help families in a thorough and flexible way, it may be essential to have extended opportunities for individual discussion and observation of the child. Also, there are some parents who will not ever feel at ease in a group discussion. Given a structure for parent teaching work which involved both individual and group sessions, parents at Anson House rated group discussion as enjoyable but not particularly helpful (Beveridge et al., 1982). However, extended opportunity for informal contact with other parents was important and sustaining. Again, a centre-based intervention may offer this opportunity more easily than a workshop structure.

The other important feature of centre-based interventions is that often they share the child's care with the family for some part of the day (which workshops and home-based interventions do not). It has frequently been noted that what parents want most from a preschool setting is to be able to rely on a teacher's competence (e.g. Buckley, 1981; Turnbull and Turnbull, 1982). Winton and Turnbull (1981) asked parents to rank-order features of an ideal preschool for their handicapped child, and found they placed parent involvement as of low importance. A very few day-care settings also offer respite total care (e.g. Callias and Carr, 1975; Green and Evans, 1984). As was noted in Chapter 2, the facilities which parents seem to agree would be of most value are a flexible system of respite care, including babysitting and minding after school. They tend to be more divided on whether short-term total breaks are desirable (e.g. Lonsdale, 1978), but they are an essential support for many families (Green and Evans, 1984).

Formal evaluation of centre-based programmes

for young mentally handicapped children, given the broad-based nature of their intervention, is a difficult matter and has therefore been undertaken primarily for specific projects within total schemes. Also as a centre will generally serve a total population, control groups are difficult to establish. Where evaluation of centre-based programmes for high risk children has been carried out, it seems generally that a small-scale intervention may have little demonstrable effect (Woollacott, Graham and Stevenson, 1978, one year, one day a week), but a long-term, large-scale intervention will show clear beneficial results in terms of child progress (Ramey and Campbell, 1984, five years, five days a week). The latter study established a randomised control group by offering health services and nutritional supplements, thereby reducing to five per cent those families who refused to accept the randomisation. Whether a limited intervention might have more beneficial effects for mentally handicapped children than for high risk children cannot be judged from the available literature.

Structure: Home-based programmes

One problem mentioned above for workshops, i.e. possibly serving only confident volunteers, has formed a major part of the rationale for establishing home-based programmes. They pose no transport or babysitting problems for parents, and take place on parents' 'own territory' thus perhaps permitting greater confidence in discussion with the professional home-visitor. The home-visitor can potentially adapt visiting times and interaction style to individuals, thus minimising some of the factors which may lead to parents dropping out from workshop interventions (Baker, Clark and Yasuda, 1981; Cunningham, 1983b). Home-based programmes are particularly appropriate for rural communities (Shearer and Shearer, 1976; Brynelsen, 1983), and can be backed up by radio and correspondence course (Mitchell, 1977; Ashby, McGaw, Perry and Grant, 1978). The model has proved to have wide applicability including in Third World countries, e.g. Jamaica (Thorburn, 1981), and the World Health Organisation structure of community rehabilitation programmes, e.g. in Botswana (Sebina and Kgosidintsi, 1981).

The differences in content of various home-visiting programmes will be discussed below.

The purpose of this section is to discuss potential problems with the model and to consider overall evaluation of its effectiveness. Generally, a home-based programme involves a home-teacher visiting an individual family at regular intervals, assessing the child periodically, and deciding with the parent on developmentally appropriate activities for the parent to carry out with the child. In the Portage system (originally developed in Portage, Wisconsin) (Bluma, Shearer, Fishman and Hilliard, 1976), the home-teacher has a resource of activity cards linked to a developmental checklist, and from the cards draws up an instruction and recording sheet for the parent to follow and fill in during the week before the next visit. The parent will have three or four activities to carry out per week (though other home-teaching programmes tend to target fewer). As the aim is for each activity target to be achieved by the child within the week, the home teacher needs to be able to rewrite targets into small steps as well as using checklist items (about 50 per cent new targets, Shearer and Shearer, 1976). Home-teaching programmes usually operate a close back-up system, with supervision meetings for all home visitors every week or so. The initial training is short and health visitors, social workers, psychologists, other parents, etc. have all become successful home teachers (e.g. Rayner, 1978).

A number of British authorities have copied the Portage model - Bendall (1985) identified 116 in 1982/3 - and it has been tried out in at least 75 nations world-wide (Shearer and Loftin, 1984). Where data are reported, the original findings of increased acquisition of checklist skills over baseline are replicated (e.g. Smith, Kushlick and Glossop, 1977; Revill and Blunden, 1979; Barna, Bidder, Gray, Clements and Gardner, 1980; Glossop and Castillo, 1982). However, this is not a very strong indicator of effective intervention, as non-programmed skills form the majority of those acquired. Repeated testing may provide opportunities for learning, or parents may be extracting general principles and applying them to all the children's activities (Revill and Blunden, 1979). There are several other possible explanations, and one cautious summary of the evidence has concluded that a Portage-style programme "perhaps accelerates the child's rate of development in some cases" (Clements, Evans, Jones, Osborne and Upton, 1981). Other programmes have used geographically distant, or historical, control groups, and find comparative gains on standardized developmental tests (e.g. Ludlow and Allen, 1979; Sandow, Clarke, Cox and Stewart, 1981; Cunningham, 1984). Thus, a general effect of such intervention, at least over a period of two to three years, seems to have been demonstrated. What the nature of the content of that intervention requires to be has not been clearly shown (see below).

In contrast to the Portage model, some other home visiting programmes visit less frequently (e.g. every two weeks or every two months, Sandow and Clarke, 1978; six-weekly, Cunningham, 1983a) and do not require that parents keep detailed records. Both of these features may be reactions to criticisms which have been made of home-based programmes. For example, it is argued that frequent, prolonged visiting may set up a dependency of the parent on the home-teacher which is ultimately undermining to the parent's confidence (Gray and Wandersman, 1980; Berry and Wood, 1981). In prescribing new and time-consuming activities, the home-teacher may overburden an already hard-pressed parent, increasing feelings of inadequacy. Formal sessions may be hard even for highly motivated parents to integrate in to the daily routine (Harris, Wolchik and Weitz, 1981). In addition, even though parent and home-teacher collaborate in choosing the week's activity(ies) (Revill and Blunden, 1979), a home-based model may give little opportunity for the learning of general educational principles, and independent construction of teaching programmes by parents (Berry and Wood, 1981).

Another undermining feeling may be guilt at 'not doing enough' (Sloper, Cunningham and Arnljotsdottir, 1983; Cunningham, 1984). The underlying value-system of the intervention is that mentally handicapped children can progress faster, and that any indication of faster progress is good and important. This sets up an implicit expectation upon the parents who have daily care of their child, a felt pressure to do 'good activities', which may mean that they inevitably feel they have partially failed their child. On the other hand, it is certainly reported by many parents that they gain great satisfaction and relief through being able to do 'something to help the baby' (Cunningham, 1983b). Recording of activities provokes the same ambivalence, with many parents reporting having found it an unwelcome effort (e.g. Holmes, Hemsley, Rickett and Likierman, 1982), yet liking to be able to see the changes in the child's behaviour (e.g. Sloper et al., 1983; Cunningham, 1984; Beveridge, 1985).

One further problem in the structure of home-based programmes is that they tend to focus intervention and pressure on one family member only (i.e. the mother), the possible problems of which are largely unexplored. It may be desirable to the family to involve siblings in limited ways. For example, Schreibman, O'Neill and Koegel (1983) describe a home-based intervention with eight to 13 years old children, helping them to work with their autistic siblings on academic skills. Another problem mentioned by parents is the ending of the programme when the child starts school; few schools will offer parents a continuing opportunity to participate in a coordinated programme (Land, 1985). Finally, as the home-based programmes mentioned so far all are based in a developmental/behaviour modification model of child learning, they focus on the child's skill acquisition rather than on parent-child interaction, and thus may ignore or even magnify potential problems (as outlined in Chapter 9). The next section discusses the question of the content of parent involvement programmes.

Content

Many early intervention schemes with parents, both workshop (e.g. Tennant and Hattersley, 1977) and home-based (e.g. Watson and Bassinger, 1974) were explicitly based on behaviour modification principles. Reviews of parent training had shown that parents could learn and apply techniques successfully; but these studies were mostly of parents of children with behaviour problems. Cunningham (1975) outlined the difficulties in transferring the approach to parents of mentally handicapped children:

> "Although behaviour modification provides a constructive, easily mastered approach to the training of child behaviour, the permanence and totality of the learning disability limits its applicability and sufficiency for parents of mentally handicapped children. They must be concerned with long-term objectives and sustained treatment. They do not have the solace that after the treatment the child will be normal,..." (pp. 177-8)

He pointed out that the essential issues for parents of mentally handicapped children were how to generalize and maintain learning, and most especially how to decide what to teach.

The general solution adopted was to base teaching on what was known about normal developmental progressions (e.g. Shearer and Shearer, 1976; Jeffree, McConkey and Hewson, 1977), including the development of language (e.g. McConkey, Jeffree and Hewson, 1979; Clements et al., 1981, 1982) and of play (e.g. Newson et al., 1979; McConkey et al., 1982). Thus, parents would require a certain amount of continued support from developmental experts, but might still become relatively independent programme designers, having acquired skill in task analysis and in behavioural teaching techniques. However, there are a number of drawbacks to this model. For example, because developmental checklists do not allow for analysis of the constituent skills in any one behaviour, they may not provide a guide for how to teach that behaviour. A more thorough theoretical analysis of the development of particular behaviours may be required, e.g. the lattices developed by Bricker and Bricker (1976) from Piagetian theory. Secondly, the order of skills development may be different for mentally handicapped children from that of non-handicapped children. For example, for many handicapped children physical or sensory disability will alter the course of development; it may even be appropriate to introduce the teaching of reading when language skills are still not well developed (Buckley, 1985). Thirdly, checklists may not cover some areas of development (e.g. social and emotional development) which parents consider important. Finally, the individuality of mentally handicapped children and their families is such that it is hard to see how any general prescription of goals can be effective (Kiernan, 1981; Cunningham, 1983b).

One general assumption underlying the content of programmes as outlined above appears to be that parents must necessarily learn to do something special and different in order to promote their handicapped child's development. However, when parents' existing teaching interactions with their children are examined, it is found that many are already successfully using teaching strategies (e.g. Cheseldine and McConkey, 1979; Beveridge et al., 1982) and that pressurising the child to attain certain short-term goals may disrupt interaction (Mogford, 1979a; Wright et al., 1984; Vicary,

1985b).

Recently, a number of interventions with parents have more explicitly considered how to match intervention goals of child progress with what is known about helpful parent-child interactions (e.g. Mogford, 1976; Kogan, 1980; Bromwich, 1981; Affleck, McGrade, McQueeney and Allen, 1982; MacDonald, 1982; Walker, 1982; Cunningham, 1983b; McCollum, 1984). Thus, they aim to train parents' observation skills and to enhance their responsiveness to children's activity. Parents learn to extend children's responses and to help them overcome barriers to exploration, the ultimate aim being that children will be able to direct their own learning and play (Mogford, 1976). Lombardino and Mangan (1983) describe their language-focussed intervention thus:

> "... emphasize the importance of training parent-child dyads in the context of naturally occurring activities (i.e. caregiving, play) which provide for opportunities to use communication/language as a vehicle for social interchanges motivated by multiple purposes (e.g. to request information, to provide information, to express feelings)." (p.360)

Parents' enjoyment of their children is an important guiding principle, and also the facilitation of parents' confidence in themselves as able to help their children progress (Bromwich, 1981). Of fundamental importance is the recognition of the unique characteristics of each family and each parent-child interaction (Kysela and Marfo, 1983). The intervention techniques adopted therefore include headings such as listening, observing, discussing, commenting positively, modelling, encouraging, etc. (Kogan, 1980; Belsky, Goode and Most, 1981; Bromwich, 1981; Hornby and Jensen-Proctor, 1984). Success of intervention is judged in terms of observed interactional sequences and also in terms of the emotional tone of interaction (see Chapter 11, section on measurement of interactional skills), and thus is usually presented in terms of individual rather than group change (e.g. Bromwich, 1981). However, Kogan (1980) presented results of a controlled study with children who had mild or moderate learning difficulties, which suggested that parents and children had significantly changed, as a result of intervention, their frequency of certain behaviours (e.g. smiling, ignoring, negative voice, lead taking) towards the norm for the children's age group.

Given the difficulty of specifying exactly the nature of such flexible intervention approaches, it may be that parents are in some ways more dependent on the intervener's experience and expertise than with techniques which are clearly trainable. Cunningham (1983b) describes attempting to "inform parents of management and training techniques as part of the immediate stimulation activities", and to "explain the significance of developmental processes", as well as encouraging parents to create a balance between the child's needs and their own in the daily routine. How parents' acquisition of this model of parenting could be assessed is not at all clear.

The rationale for interaction-based intervention is derived from the results of basic observational research and longitudinal studies linking interaction with child intellectual progress (see Chapter 7). Thus, for example, Ramey et al. (1980) outline these apparently justified, very general implications for educational programmes:

- recognizing the infant's active role in interaction, and thus e.g. the effect of specific infant characteristics on parents;
- the need to build on the infant's present repertoire of behaviours, and thus the importance of extended systematic observation;
- the use of naturally-occurring reinforcers in interaction, and intrinsic to certain activities;
- the use of daily routines as educational settings.

However, more specific implications seem less justified, since the original research was not designed with the intention of guiding or evaluating intervention (Clarke-Stewart, 1977). As was discussed in Chapter 9, though correlational analysis has given rise to conclusions about optimal patterns of mother-child interaction for promoting child cognitive and social competence, these cannot be used for making recommendations for individual parents. Also the generalizability of the research is constrained by the conceptions of the researchers and by the nature of the sample. Gray and Wandersman (1980) have stressed the limitations of the definition of 'competence' adopted by such research. If the competitive definitions of competence applied by a 'striving' culture are inappropriate for certain social groupings, then they may be even more inappropriate for people with severe learning difficulties and their families.

A second point to make in relation to this question of using research conclusions is that a very particular definition of parenting has been used. Most obviously, interactional research and interventions have concentrated on mothers to the virtual exclusion of fathers. But more than that, there are dimensions of parenting left untouched by research, for example, what Newson (1979) has called 'unreasonable care'. 'Parenting' is thus more than 'care-taking'; it is more direct and intimate, "including anger and discipline as well as love and support" (Hess, 1980, p.149). It is this partiality which children may need for emotional development, and which may be at odds with the interventionist's view of the 'parent as teacher'. Newson (1979) also stressed the long-term view which parents take of the child's upbringing. This perspective may have several consequences, such as tolerance of the child's idiosyncracies, and a feeling of ultimate responsibility for the child. That is, parents are inevitably at risk for feeling that the child's behaviour and progress (or lack of it) reflects on them. Professionals, on the other hand, can console themselves with the extent of their efforts; the nature of their responsibility is much less intense. In terms of tolerance of the child, the parent (but rarely the professional) may be concerned about the effect on the child's self-esteem of continual special efforts toward change, with the possible implicit message to the child that he or she is at present unacceptable (Turnbull and Turnbull, 1982). As one very pessimistic commentator has put it:

> "Far from teaching them to be better mothers and better able to help their children to develop competences which will be valuable to themselves and to society, (home visitors) may have led the mothers to adopt perceptions, expectations and behaviours which are psychologically damaging to themselves, which inhibit the growth of their children and which are dysfunctional in society." (Raven, 1980, quoted in Reader, 1984, p.249)

The third point to make concerns the fallacy of taking specific implications from research on interaction with non-handicapped children and applying them to interaction with handicapped children. This step is made clearly, for example, by Bromwich (1981) in reporting on her work with high-risk infants. She notes that parent-infant interaction will sometimes be distorted, and describes the development of intervention strategies on a 'positive interaction model'. Yet the initial research on which the model is based had not attempted to identify processes by which unsatisfactory interactions may develop nor how they may be ameliorated. This seems clearly an area in which attractive ideas are being put in to service models before the requisite basic research has been carried out; this was shown, for example, by the paucity of relevant, broad-based research into interaction between parents and handicapped children found for review in Chapter 9.

This is not, however, to say that parent-child interactions should not be considered in intervention with handicapped children. On the contrary, it seems essential that intervention studies at least monitor their effect upon interaction within the family. However, at this stage of knowledge it seems premature to decide what are 'good' interactions and what are 'bad' interactions, in ignorance of long-term outcomes and parents' own goals for their children within their particular ecological setting (see further discussion in Chapter 12).

Before turning to changes in overall intervention philosophy, one other approach to intervention will be mentioned. In Chapters 2 and 3, mention was made of day-to-day practical problems and of the wider links the family of the handicapped child may (or may not) have in their community. If intervention is to take account of the wider ecological framework within which the family operates, then a logical consequence is to consider how to help family members to improve and maintain social support networks. One basic strategy is for professionals to seek to involve extended family members in intervention programmes (Gabel and Kotsch, 1981). Furthermore there have recently been a number of descriptions of group workshops for parents of handicapped children which aim to increase interpersonal problem-solving skills (Intagliata and Doyle, 1984; Schilling et al., 1984). Intagliata and Doyle ran a group for ten weekly meetings, as a supplement to other services. At first parents tended to focus on the child as their only problem, and showed evidence of having developed more efficient strategies for solving problems to do with the handicapped child than for other problems. Gradually the parents learned strategies for dealing with problems such as unhelpful relatives, i.e. 'ordinary' sources of stress in their lives. The parents were reported to have appreciated an intervention of which the content focussed on them, rather than always having the focus on their handicapped child.

A brief summary can be made of the above discussion of early intervention programmes with parents, in terms of the points of analysis used in previous chapters.

Firstly, many interventions assume from the start that parents' handling of their handicapped children must change, i.e. they assume _deviance_ or _deficiency_ without first observing parents and children together at length and discussing with parents their goals for their children. (Interestingly, Hayden (1979) seems to regard most parents as of suspect competence: "While non-handicapped young children _may_ make acceptable progress without early educational interventions, handicapped or at risk children do not" (p.510, emphasis in the original).) Interventions are usually described in terms of standard structure or content rather than in terms of flexible modes of response to _individual_ families. Partly this will be explainable as the requirements of brevity for publication; but also it seems to imply a _clinical focus_ on families of handicapped children as a group for whom one model or one package will be the answer. Many interventions lack a _time_ perspective: either they are short-term and arrangements for long-term support (or research follow-up) of parents are not made clear; or they are long-term (e.g. home-based) but the changing nature of parents' and children's needs are not made central to their explicit model (e.g. parents' and children's needs around the time of transition to school). Most interventions fail to take account of the family ecology, i.e. they do not include _fathers_ and other care-takers, and they do not consider the possible effects of intervention on the family system. In addition, they may fail to make contact with other formal and informal networks of support available to the family, and they may take no account of the _cultural_ appropriateness of the intervention offered (for example, the role of parents in the play of the child, in that family's culture, may differ from the assumptions of the intervention model).

Finally, most intervention is conceived in terms of the parent affecting the child with her or his behaviour. The reciprocal nature of interaction frequently forms no part of the model, except as advice about 'child behaviour problems'. There are, however, theoretical difficulties in moving from interaction research to intervention strategies, and these have been discussed above. On the other hand, a lack of perspective about the child's interactional environment may have severely limited the applicability and maintenance of other interventions, and may account for the rather equivocal results obtained. In addition to other people's behaviour, their perceptions and attitudes are also a part of the child's environment. Parents' ideas about their children and about helping them have rarely been discussed in advance of intervention, and even more rarely have they influenced the nature of the intervention. (Parents' behaviour and philosophy are two aspects of parental characteristics to be reviewed in the following chapter.)

These points in analysis are to some extent reflected in the current philosophy which seems to influence parental involvement, that of professionals working with parents as equal partners.

Philosophy

The philosophy underpinning interventions with parents has undergone great change over the past fifteen years, as has been implied by the review of changes in the structure and particularly of the content of intervention. The move by professionals to working with parents instead of (or as well as) directly with the child was described in 1971 thus:

> "...it is not the task of the therapist to assume the full burden of 'treatment' and, in the process, allow the parents to relinquish their responsibility but it is the therapist's task to help the parent directly to be more effective in carrying out a parent's moral, ethical and legal obligation to care for his child." (Graziano, 1971, p.365)

The professional philosophy of the time was to train parents to carry out programmes designed by the experts in child care and mental handicap. Rationales given stressed the economy of such a move, given the lack of trained professionals, and looked for generalization and maintenance of learning, and prevention of future problems. Occasionally, it was mentioned that many parents wanted specific, practical guidance so that they could help their children (Cunningham, 1975). Gradually, however, it seemed that parents' reactions to intervention programmes, and ideas about their children, were listened to more and more by professionals. As an extreme development of this trend, parents would be described as the true 'experts' on their own children, and with very little training and/or with occasional support, could be expected to carry out sustained, high quality teaching of their children.

> "In fact, some professionals have been so busy teaching parents to be teachers, psychologists, and psychiatrists, not to mention research workers, physiotherapists and speech therapists, that there may not be enough time for parents to be parents." (Mittler, 1978, p.246)

As a partial resolution of these two extremes, there has recently been much discussion of the concept of 'partnership with parents' and a rethinking of previous assumptions about parent involvement (e.g. Buckley, 1981; Foster et al., 1981; Turnbull and Turnbull, 1982; Mittler and McConachie, 1983). 'Partnership' seems to imply equality of parents with professionals in defining intervention strategies and goals, recognising the different strengths each side brings to the partnership and what knowledge and perspectives each side lacks. Each handicapped child, and each family, is unique, and stereotyped expectations need to be questioned continually. The achievement of a partnership relationship thus relies on establishing good communication, sharing information and skills, and also sharing feelings openly, whether those feelings are of doubt and worry, or of satisfaction (Mittler and Mittler, 1982). Cunningham (1983b) has stressed the concept of parents as 'consumers' of a service, i.e. that professionals can and should offer ideas and knowledge, but that ultimately it is parents' responsibility to choose the approaches which suit them, at their own pace.

Without this respect for parents' unique role and responsibility, intervention may have unforeseen negative effects, for example, feelings of powerlessness and dependence on the advice of professionals (Farber and Lewis, 1975; Hess, 1980). The possible effects of learned helplessness have already been mentioned (Chapter 6). The other area of unforeseen effects discussed above has been the lack of awareness of effects within the family system, such as fathers potentially feeling estranged when mothers are the sole focus of intervention, or teaching not being carried out because of unacknowledged worries about balance of attention to the other children in the family, to mention just two possibilities (Foster et al., 1981).

A third problem for parents is the pressure to be involved, and the feelings of guilt and incompetence if they wish to opt out. At times intervention may seem part of the 'burden of care' rather than part of the solution. Parents sometimes need a break, or to have less intense demands made on them (Mittler, 1978; Buckley, 1981). Professionals may have applied too limited a psychological perspective to complex, real-life problems, and not been aware of the existing structures and influences in the home. The child's need for structured teaching has to be weighed against other needs (Buckley, 1984; Skrtic, Summers, Brotherson and Turnbull, 1984; Dessent, 1985). There is also a point of view which reasserts parents' rights to live their lives as they wish (for example, for women to be able to look for employment). They may feel that having worked hard in parents' associations to set up good facilities for handicapped children, or to have their children integrated into ordinary education, they wish now to choose how much to be involved.

> "In essence, the parents' responsibility for training of new abilities has now been transferred to professionals. The parents' task is to provide the best possible environment in a socially intact family, in which the handicapped child can best use his or her new abilities." (Lund and Pelling, in McConachie, 1983, p.213)

This transfer of responsibility back to professionals may seem like 'coming full circle'. The ideal would be to retain a whole spectrum of options, so that services for families of young mentally handicapped children can be characterized by maximum flexibility to individual changing circumstances and needs.

NOTE

1. The review of literature will thus not cover other issues in parent-training such as measurement of outcome, methods of teaching, child characteristics, etc. These have been reviewed recently by several authors (Baker, 1984; Howlin, 1984; Clements, 1985; Cunningham, 1985).

Chapter Eleven

PROGRAMME VARIABLES AND PARENT CHARACTERISTICS

In the previous chapter, a brief description has been given of current approaches to parent involvement in the education of their young mentally handicapped children, with more extended discussion of the philosophical framework and content of intervention. When research evidence is sought which might offer guidance to future developments, it is sadly lacking. For example, there seems to have been only one study which effectively compared two approaches to parent involvement which differed radically in content (Tavormina, 1975). The extent to which parents have been seen simply as vehicles for professionals' programmes of child education is reflected clearly in the lack of available research into parents' characteristics and their relation to programme success and to various types and amount of intervention (Molloy, 1980a,b).

HOW MUCH INTERVENTION?

Among the issues discussed in Chapter 10 was the question of the extent to which intervention is, or should be, aimed at producing a different kind of interaction between parent and handicapped child from that which they already have or from that considered 'optimal' for parents and non-handicapped children. A separate but related issue is the question of how much intervention is required.

Research has looked at four separate areas:

1) the extent of planned generalization of learning;
2) the need for training in principles as well as practice;

3) the amount of contact between parents and professionals;
4) the need for and efficacy of particular training techniques.

Generalization

The extent to which parents and children generalize newly acquired behaviours beyond the situation of the initial learning has been an explicit concern of behaviour modification based training. One part of the rationale for home-teaching services was precisely avoidance of the expected problem of transfer of learning from a clinic or laboratory setting to home. However, the issue is wider, encompassing maintenance of effects, generalization across all the settings in which the individuals are active, generalization to other similar behaviours or tasks, generalization to other people with whom the child interacts, and even to the interaction between parents and siblings (Forehand and Atkeson, 1977). Evidence on all these counts has been patchy in research into the effectiveness of parent training, and Forehand and Atkeson suggest that the more rigorous the method of assessment, the less positive the results. Their observations derived primarily from studies of parents of children with behaviour problems. However, they are usually taken as applying equally to interventions with parents of handicapped children (e.g. Molloy, 1980a; Parker and Mitchell, 1980).

On the issue of maintenance, it is commonly observed by authors that many parents did not continue with structured teaching sessions beyond the period of intervention (e.g. Callias and Carr, 1975; Beveridge, 1982; Firth, 1982; Gardner, 1983). Baker, Heifetz and Murphy (1980) found that only 44 per cent of parents followed up continued "a useful degree of regular teaching" (p.35). But they also found what they described as a high level of incidental teaching (86 per cent), i.e. behavioural teaching reported as consistently carried out in the daily routine. This way of utilizing their learning may be easier for parents to maintain in the long run, and is advocated as possibly the way to train parents in the first place (Cunningham, 1975; Mittler, 1975; Ramey et al., 1980; Baker and Clark, 1983; Salzburg and Villani, 1983). However, one major problem with this suggestion is the difficulty of reliably monitoring the use of teaching strategies spread 'opportunistically' throughout the day.

On the issue of generalization across settings, mention has already been made in the previous section of the difficulties parents may have given the wider impact of intervention in the total family dynamics (Berger and Foster, 1976; Patterson and Fleischman, 1979). Thirdly, generalization of skills between family members has rarely been considered, even though most interventions have involved only the mother, and consistency of handling is of vital importance to mentally handicapped children. Adubato, Adams and Budd (1981) reported a single-case study in which the mother of a six year old severely mentally handicapped boy successfully passed on her training to his father with no assistance. Both parents maintained their skills at follow-up, and generalized their teaching to new behaviours. Similar reports exist for the training by parents of siblings as 'co-therapists' (Laviguer, 1976; Miller and Cantwell, 1976). Essential skills for parents to use in supporting each other's efforts have been outlined by Kelley, Embry and Baer (1979). These were derived for work with children with behaviour problems but seem to have applicability in the case of managing the behaviour of mentally handicapped children. They include - attending positively to each other in front of the child, reporting the other's disobeyed instructions only once, providing appropriate reinforcement to the child for the other's instructions, and encouraging the other's appropriate and consistent use of child management skills.

An important consideration for future research would be the identification of which training arrangements and techniques most enable parents to generalize skills and child progress (Wehman, Abramson and Norman, 1977; Parker and Mitchell, 1980). For example, Gardner (1983) has discussed the benefits in terms of maintenance of parents' teaching of cooperation on programmes with teachers, where the school has an objectives-based curriculum. Salzburg and Villani (1983) adopted a procedure whereby parents received feedback at school on audiotapes made at home as part of teaching expressive language. With careful structuring of reinforcement and opportunity for learning, good generalization of learning between home and school can be demonstrated (Zifferblatt, Burton, Horner and White, 1977). Certainly, many authors suggest that generalization procedures should be carefully planned as an integral part of the intervention.

Principles

Whatever the theoretical base of the content of intervention with parents, divergence is evident between those authors who advocate teaching parents principles and those who maintain that practice is of paramount importance. For example, perhaps the majority of early parent training in behaviour modification included either didactic sessions on the underlying principles, or manuals for parents (Yule, 1975). However, many case studies suggested that practical teaching techniques were the most effective in terms of behaviour change (e.g. Johnson and Brown, 1969; Christopherson, Arnold, Hill and Quilitch, 1972), particularly for less-well-educated parents (O'Dell, 1974).

A number of studies have directly compared the effectiveness of training with and without theoretical background. For example, Koegel, Glahn and Nieminen (1978) found parents were able to generalize teaching (of their autistic children) to various tasks when taught principles, whereas videotape or live demonstrations on one specific task enabled parents only to teach what they had seen (c.f. Glogower and Sloop, 1976; McMahon, Forehand and Griest, 1981). Cunningham and Jeffree's (1975) explicit aim in their workshops was that "parents would internalise a teaching model" (p.407). That is, parents would achieve a level of skill in applying principles and concepts such that they would react 'intuitively' to their mentally handicapped child and maximise potential learning situations. Starting from a rather different theoretical background, Moxley-Hegaert and Serbin (1983) also obtained results suggesting the efficacy of training parents in principles. In this case, they gave parents a short course in 'developmental change' to enable parents to recognize small steps in their children's progress, thereby apparently motivating them to continue with teaching.

However, two rather careful research studies of this question, involving parents of handicapped children, have come to an opposite conclusion. Hudson (1982) compared three ten-session workshop training procedures: a 'specific focus' group in which each mother planned and revised a task relevant to her child; a 'specific focus plus principles' group in which the first half of each group session was spent in a lecture on some principle of behaviour modification; and a 'specific focus plus controlled learning environment' group which the children also attended so that modelling and feedback for appropriate teaching could be incorporated. In addition there was a waiting-list control. Assessment included knowledge of principles, generalization to teaching a second task, skill application in a videotaped situation, the number of home tasks completed and child development rate. Hudson concluded that the specific teaching of behavioural principles did not appear to contribute at all to training outcomes, but that the use of modelling and role-playing appeared beneficial. The parents were very satisfied with whichever type of training they had received. O'Dell, Flynn and Benlolo (1977) compared a pre-training on principles, with a placebo pre-training and no pre-training, before a six session practical workshop. The authors not only found that the didactic training did not enhance the acquisition of teaching skills, they also suggested that the pre-training might have inhibited home implementation of teaching through making parents more likely simply to talk about solving problems. Additional evaluation of training formats also showed the superiority of practical monitoring of parents' skills in comparison with parents reading a manual, each procedure being in addition to watching a videotape (O'Dell, Mahoney, Horton, and Turner, 1979). With parents of non-handicapped children, videotape modelling plus guided practice has been shown superior in the learning of time-out skills in comparison with written instruction or lecture instruction. However, for such a discrete technique, modelling alone may be sufficient (Nay, 1975).

Thus, where short-term workshops are the intervention structure adopted, it seems as if practical training approaches may be of most benefit to parents and to children. For home-visiting interventions distinctions will be harder to make between theoretical discussion and practical training within the intervention style of the home-visitor. Cunningham (1984) has made the point that home-visitors are likely to alter their style in any case, depending for example on the match between their own educational level and that of the parents.

Amount of contact

Research interventions have looked at several aspects of the question of how much contact is required, or most beneficial, between parent and intervener. For example, how frequent should home visits be?

It seems that children who are visited more often (once a week, once a fortnight) do better in the short term on developmental assessments, but that this effect evens out in the long run in comparison with less frequently visited children (Sandow and Clarke, 1978; Sandow, 1980; Sandow et al., 1981; Cunningham, 1985). The Sandow study found that the children visited every two months made greater progress in the second year of the study than the children visited very two weeks, surpassing the latter's gains on average. However, the difference disappeared after three years. They attribute the effect to the greater confidence of the mothers visited less often in their autonomous ability to help their children progress. They recommend initial frequent visiting, with a consistent gradual decline in frequency thereafter (though in fact their research design did not allow this conclusion). Sloper et al. (1983) found that parents preferred a two-weekly contact when their children were aged up to two years. They did, however, prefer a more flexible, less intensive type of programme from when the child was about 18 months, as the children began to have more varied activity of their own, and to resist direct teaching. Cunningham (1985) also found no lasting effect of how early or late a Down's syndrome infant's home-visiting programme started; that is, whether the programme began at six weeks or at nine months made no difference to developmental level at two years of age. Bromwich (1981) stresses the need for regular contact, however infrequent. For a number of families, a lapse in the home-visiting (e.g. because things were going smoothly) then militated against being able to intervene helpfully and quickly when problems arose. Decisions about when to stop intervention are made through research constraints, outside factors such as starting school, or clinical judgement, rather than there being any clear criteria available for guidance (Yule, 1975).

The most thorough study of how much contact parents require in order to successfully teach their mentally handicapped children has been the READ project (Heifetz, 1977a,b). The aim essentially was to make a comprehensive evaluation of a series of ten self-instructional manuals for parents to teach their children self-help, language and play skills and to manage behaviour problems. Four groups of volunteer parents were contrasted with a control: those who received manuals only, manuals plus weekly phone contact, manuals plus a biweekly training group with other parents, and manuals plus training group plus home visits. The results have been well documented, and a selection are presented in summary form below (see Table 1).

Table 1 Summary of READ project results, presented as rank order of means for each group.

	MO	MP	MG	MGV	C
improvement in knowledge of behavioural principles:					
- mothers	1*	4	3*	2*	5
- fathers	5	3	2	1*	4
improvement in self-help skills	1*	3*	2*	4*	5
additional areas programmed during training	4	3	2	1	-
follow-through on teaching after 14 months	4	1	2	3	-
continued use of manuals after 14 months	4	(a)	1	(a)	-

MO = manuals only
MP = manuals and phone
MG = manuals and groups
MGV = manuals, groups and visits
C = waiting-list control.

* Significantly greater than control group, at least $p < .05$.
(a) Data not given in Baker et al. (1980) paper.

The research team found that the 'manuals only' group of mothers were able to acquire behavioural knowledge and to change their children's self-help behaviour as much as or more than parents receiving the other formats. However they did less daily teaching, generalized their teaching less to other skill areas, and expressed less confidence in their teaching ability than parents who had had contact with trainers (Heifetz, 1977b). At one year follow-up they used the manuals little, less than the other groups did, and were doing less continued teaching (Baker, 1977; Baker et al., 1980). Fathers made gains only in the training format of greatest contact with the training team. No comparison was made of couples who were both trained versus families where one parent only took part. Also no in-home observation was made of parents' use of teaching skills. However, the research does seem to suggest that already informed and motivated parents are able to make good independent use of a minimal amount of professional contact, i.e. assessments plus self-instructional manuals. Other groups are likely to need greater support and follow-up in order to make significant changes. For example, unselected parents whose children attended the same school for severely mentally handicapped children failed to generalize teaching skills from a school-based course to home without additional home-visiting by the course team (Gardner, 1983). Thus, there are individual parent/training format interactions which require future research (Molloy, 1980a), and which will be discussed further below.

Amount of advice

Finally on the question of 'how much intervention', several researchers have considered how, within any given intervention structure, advice should be delivered. A related but contrasting question is to what extent can parents generate effective teaching strategies independently. For example, it has been found that parents can comparatively quickly grasp principles of reinforcement but that the principles of shaping and task analysis are much 'newer' and more difficult (Yule, 1975; Beveridge et al., 1982). Consequently, training parents in the systematic presentation of task materials is found to produce greater performance scores in their children than training parents in giving positive feedback for correct responses (Filler, 1976).

Three other studies have evaluated parents' effectiveness when given only a clear target, or suitable toys, or both, without additional training. In a home programme with low-income mothers and their two to four year old children, no superiority was found for the full intervention group children in terms of IQ gains, over the group who had received simply toys and books from time to time, at two year follow-up (even though an effect was found in terms of mothers' interaction style) (Madden, O'Hara and Levenstein, 1984). These children may have other sources of independent learning, or learn from a whole range of possible maternal interaction styles. However, a study of young mentally handicapped children suggested that various spontaneous teaching styles of parents are differentially effective. Nine parents of seven Down's syndrome children (mean age five years) were given appropriate toys and a language objective of encouraging the child to progress from single-word to two-word utterances with verbs. Specific targets were chosen for each child. Three children made marked progress in two weeks, and their parents were found to be modelling the target words as statements, whereas the less successful parents were using the target words in questions or commands (e.g. "Where has it gone?" to elicit "gone"). When specifically instructed in modelling, the unsuccessful parents then were able to elicit the target words from their children (Cheseldine, 1977; Cheseldine and McConkey, 1979). Thus, for some parents a very minimal level of help in structuring is sufficient for them to generate successful teaching strategies. These individual differences may be missed by most interventions, particularly group studies. Bidder, Hewitt and Gray (1983) compared the use of activity charts (Portage materials), target setting (i.e. without detailed instructions, but with initial practice) and verbal suggestion (no practice) on home visits to parents of young mentally handicapped children. They found the greatest percentage successful completion of the week's task for activity charts, but the success rate was still 78 per cent for verbal suggestion alone. However, parents expressed preference for the activity charts even though the home visits then took much longer.

Thus, in considering 'how much intervention?' the question cannot be divorced from a question of individual parent characteristics, such as their own teaching style and their confidence in their own competence. As Berger and Foster (1976) put it:

> "It would seem useful, therefore, for researchers to investigate client and family variables which would help professionals quickly distinguish between parents who need only to be given training and access to resources from parents who will not use techniques in which they have been trained and who will not seek access to resources they have been told about. If this can be accomplished, further research can focus on delineating the conditions which will maximize our chances of tailoring our treatment options to the particular needs and styles of the family with which we are working." (p.15)

INDIVIDUAL PARENT DIFFERENCES

Since at least 1967, reviewers of interventions with parents of mentally handicapped children have been criticising the lack of adequate evaluation (compare e.g. Ramsey, 1967, with Hornby and Singh, 1983). There have been repeated calls for attention to individual parent and family characteristics which might affect success of outcome or by which outcome should be measured (e.g. O'Dell, 1974; Yule, 1975; Griffin, 1979; Molloy, 1979, 1980a,b; Berry and Wood, 1981; Simeonsson, Cooper and Scheiner, 1982; Hornby and Singh, 1983; Reader, 1984; Clements, 1985; Cunningham, 1985). In this section, those parent characteristics which have been investigated will be reviewed; in the following section, the measurement of parents' teaching style and skills will be considered.

Demographic variables

Generally reviews have suggested that socio-economic status (SES) and educational level of parents are related to training success only when reliance is placed on verbal, didactic methods of training (e.g. O'Dell, 1974). Thus, for example, Salzinger, Feldman and Portnoy (1970) did find a relationship, while Mira (1970) did not. The more recent manuals plus workshop study of Heifetz and Baker did find a relationship for SES indices and short-term outcome, in terms of parents' proficiency at the end of training (Baker et al., 1981; Clark and Baker,

1983). These indices were not related to how much continued teaching parents did during follow-up (Clark, Baker and Heifetz, 1982). However, in studies of poor immigrant mothers, little increase was found in actual teaching at home (Baker et al., 1984). Of long-term, home intervention studies, Brassell (1977) found that 25 per cent of the variance in mental development rate was predicted by a cluster of SES variables. However, Sandow et al. (1981) found no such relationship. Cunningham (1984) found a relationship with parental education (and no separate social class effect) after the age of two years, which became increasingly significant. He suggested that the effect parallels that found in non-handicapped children's development, rather than it being indicative of differential success of the intervention. Thus there is no strong suggestion in these studies that the methods used in interventions are strongly differentially suited to one socio-economic grouping, i.e. less educated parents are able to make use successfully of the training offered. However, there are various ways in which the training can be organised which may increase the representation and the success of lower SES families in the intervention. Baker et al. (1984) suggest, on the basis of numerous group workshop formats, that transport and child-care arrangements should be made, that parents should be given incentives for taking part, that didactic presentations should be minimised, and active involvement of parents as observers and teachers be maximised, and that progress from one aspect of the content to the next should be based on demonstrated competence.

One demographic indicator which does affect success strongly is whether the parent is caring for the child on her or his own. For example, Baker et al. (1981) found single parents more likely to drop out of the workshop, showed lower proficiency in teaching at the end of training, and were much less likely to carry on with teaching during follow-up. Baker et al. suggest ways of supporting single parents more thoroughly, for example, through school-based training with more supervised cooperation with teachers (Brightman, Ambrose and Baker, 1980). One group programme designed specifically for single mothers found it helpful to arrange an additional session for individuals, in order to catch up if a group session was missed (Feldman, Manella and Varni, 1983). An alternative strategy is to attempt to intervene with the single parent's support networks so that they can do more to back up the parent's management of their handicapped child (Foster et al., 1981).

Fathers

Generally mothers have been the main target of intervention designed to help parents teach their children. However, several recent home-visiting or individual intervention studies mention either that some fathers were the primary care-giver, or that several fathers were reported by mothers to be significantly involved in teaching (McConachie, 1974; Jeffree et al., 1977; McConkey et al., 1979; Sandow, 1980; Bromwich, 1981; Sebba, 1982; Moxley-Haegert and Serbin, 1983; Sloper et al., 1983). Some researchers have made evening and weekend visits to promote the involvement of fathers (e.g. Bromwich, 1981). In the case of Asian families living in Britain, fathers may choose to be the main link for the family with the intervention team (Sebba, 1982).

Workshops have involved a much higher proportion of fathers, being held primarily in the evenings (e.g. Cunningham and Jeffree, 1975; Saunders et al., 1975; Heifetz, 1977b; Attwood, 1978; Harris et al., 1981; Katz and Kenig, 1981; McConkey et al., 1982). Mothers may report difficulty in conveying to fathers the content of the workshops where the latter have not attended (Hattersley and Tennant, 1981; Firth, 1982). In some families, the parents feel that the father is generally more successful with the child, and yet he may not be the one involved in the intervention programme (Jeffree et al., 1977). Fifty-six per cent of mothers in another study (Tavormina, Hampson and Luscomb, 1976) commented on the desirability of fathers' involvement in intervention, but many felt there should be separate groups for fathers which could incorporate discussion of feelings. Groups for fathers are not a new idea - one of the earliest reports of group training for parents of mentally handicapped children was in fact for fathers (Lindsley, 1966). Groups which involve both parents have been judged very successful in terms of commitment, and child progress; but a number of new issues may be very evident and need to be acknowledged in the discussion, such as marital conflict (Hattersley, 1979).

The lack of transfer of skills from a trained parent to the other parent has been illustrated in one study of middle-class parents of young handicapped children. Both parents' attitudes, knowledge and interaction skills with the child were assessed, but then only the mothers were trained. There was some indication of adverse effects of the intervention. That is, as children progressed, mothers expressed more positive attitudes but fathers tended to express more negative attitudes about the child and family (Sandler et al., 1983). The authors suggested that the intervention may have acted to unbalance the total family system in a potentially harmful direction (c.f. Townsend and Flanagan, 1976). Changes in knowledge and skills were found for mothers, but no significant collateral changes had taken place for fathers at the end of the three-month intervention.

As yet, there does not seem to be any study of parents of handicapped children in which couple training has been compared with training only one parent. In the case of children with behaviour problems, one study found a particular benefit of couple training at follow-up in terms of maintained improvements in child behaviour (Webster-Stratton, 1985), and one study found no beneficial effects (Martin, 1977). However, both studies had a number of limitations; for example, Webster-Stratton was comparing two-parent families with single parents, thus confounding the effect of couple training with higher income level and the general involvement of two parents with the child. Metzl (1980) investigated training of couples in an infant stimulation programme involving parents of 60 non-handicapped infants. In terms of developmental scores and parent-interaction scores, trained parents were superior to untrained, and jointly-trained parents to mothers trained on their own. "It appeared that the more alert and responsive the baby, the more the father became interested in continued interaction." (p.585) Though studies of fathers of handicapped children do not suggest that they are less attuned to their children than mothers (in contrast to findings for fathers of non-handicapped children, see Chapter 8), it may be that intervention at a very early stage would be beneficial in promoting fathers' confidence that they can interpret unclear responses of their handicapped infants.

Only Heifetz (1977a,b) seems to have related the variable of parental sex to success in training. As was mentioned above, fathers required more contact with the training team than mothers did in order to improve significantly on the Behavioral

Vignettes Test, a measure of the application of behavioural knowledge. As the desirability of taking account of all family members in intervention is increasingly acknowledged, future research should elucidate if and when particular supportive strategies are required.

Motivation and philosophy

The first issue in terms of parents' motivation is whether they choose to participate in the offered intervention or not. Usually very little is known about those who choose not to join. Yet they may constitute a significant proportion of the potential population for the intervention. For example, 40 per cent of parents of preschool mentally handicapped children in one urban area did not want to take part in a University-based individualized intervention (Jeffree et al., 1977). Firth (1982) invited families with a mentally handicapped child to join parent workshops, but only 46 per cent accepted and attended.

Two workshop studies have followed up non-volunteers, to give an indication of their characteristics and views. Baker et al. (1981) offered a workshop to parents of children who attended a school for mentally handicapped children. Those who joined had more severely handicapped children, with more behaviour problems. The parents tended to have been involved in other school activities, and were of higher socio-economic status than those who did not join. In contrast, socio-economic status did not distinguish the two groups in the other study, a video-based workshop on helping children learn through play (McConkey and McEvoy, 1984). The variables which best discriminated volunteers from non-volunteers were attitudinal ones, and responses to questions about family interaction (see Chapter 5).

Once parents have actually become involved in an intervention programme, there will still be differences in motivation among them. Drop-out rates are rarely reported, but may be high (Wright et al., 1984; Cunningham, 1985). For example, a number of authors suggest that parents of more severely or multiply handicapped children find it difficult to sustain teaching or accept very slow progress (e.g. Saunders et al., 1975), and may prefer a day-care programme for their children to a home-visiting service (Wishart et al., 1980).

Several early studies used varying strategies

to 'encourage' parents' continuity in programmes, e.g. requiring parents to have filled in record sheets (Mira, 1970) or giving tokens exchangeable for money (Peine and Munro, 1970, cited in Johnson and Katz, 1973). More commonly, there is dependence on parents being reinforced by seeing their child progress. Shearer (1976) provides examples of how to enhance this presumed reinforcement for parents whose motivation flags. Rosenberg (1977) identified a variable which he defined as 'commitment', which was a significant predictor both of child's development rate and of mothers' teaching skills after training. 'Commitment' summarised the decision by family members to facilitate the learning and development of the handicapped child, and to work toward attainment of particular goals. This may be similar in character to the prediction of success in teaching derived from scores on the Parent As A Teacher inventory, described in Chapter 5 (Strom et al., 1981). Baker et al. (1981) measured parents' expectations about teaching and about the workshop programme. They found no relationship with outcome for parents' expectations of success in the programme, expectation of their proficiency in teaching nor perception of their responsibility for teaching. However, expectation of problems in teaching was predictive of lower post-training proficiency and of less follow-through in teaching at home. It is unclear whether 'expectation of problems' refers to reality constraints on teaching, lack of confidence or lack of commitment to the idea of teaching.

These observations on motivation intimately involve consideration of parents' own philosophy of child development (Loevinger, 1959). If it does not match that of the intervention programme, then parents may appear 'unmotivated'. Several authors have mentioned a proportion of parents who are ill at ease with the behaviour modification approach (15-20 per cent, Baker, 1977; Holmes et al., 1982), or who espouse a different philosophy of education, e.g. that achievement is a matter of luck (Tizard, 1984). Parents may also differ from interveners in terms of their implicit philosophy of parenting. For example, they may not feel happy with the role of 'teacher', feeling it takes the fun out of playing with the child, or that it is the school's responsibility (Gregory, 1976; Baker, 1977; Buckley, 1981). The dimension of parental authoritarianism has been related to training outcome in a number of studies, though apparently mainly in studies of non-handicapped children (Cole and Morrow, 1976; Zegiob and Forehand, 1978). Cole and Morrow described various strategies for use in group interventions, to promote a shift in attitude of authoritarian parents. It is rare for studies to attempt to measure parents' philosophies and attitudes in child-rearing in advance of rather than following intervention.

There are also cultural assumptions bound up in the nature of parent-teaching interventions which may not be shared by all parents. Powell and Perkins (1984) identified four assumptions of the Portage approach which were potentially problematic in intervention with Asian parents living in Britain. That is, Portage seems to require that parents already believe that children develop through similar stages, and that teaching can accelerate development; also that parents understand that handicap can be ameliorated, and that they can be effective teachers. Some limited research suggests, for example, that the idea of parents teaching children to help them progress may be unfamiliar to many Asian parents. Also some cultural beliefs contradict the idea that handicap can or perhaps even should be ameliorated if, for example, the child is seen as 'God's child', or the handicap is thought to result from a curse.

More generally, there are great cultural variations in ideas about play. Many children have very few or no toys, which is only partly explained by poverty (e.g. Punjab : Ghuman, 1975; Zambia : Goldberg, 1977; Jamaica : Grantham-McGregor, Landman and Desai, 1983). These children may instead have many social contacts and outdoor activities in a close community of neighbours. Toys may not be seen primarily as having a broadly educational value, but rather to keep children busy (Bernstein and Young, 1967; Grantham-McGregor et al., 1983). Parental 'teaching' may imply to parents primarily drilling children in school-related subjects. The impact of such ideas, and of different patterns of play, have not been assessed in intervention studies.

The following section will consider the measurement of parents' teaching skills as an outcome measure. However, one study has treated parents' interaction styles as an independent characteristic, on the basis of which appropriate adjustments can be made to the intervention programme. Beveridge (1982) used a free-play situation to measure the proportion of interaction sequences initiated by the parent or by the child.

From this she designated parents as 'more directive' or 'less directive'. Following a balanced design experimental study to establish the effectiveness of differential programming, she adopted the procedure of introducing parents first to teaching techniques closer to their natural style (e.g. prompting with more directive parents, positioning with less directive parents) before introducing less obviously 'familiar' techniques. This is a rare example of experimental evidence about interaction being used in planning flexibility of programme content. Flexibility is often advocated, but not related to available knowledge about parents' characteristics.

MEASUREMENT OF PARENTS' TEACHING

Two areas will be briefly reviewed in this section, the quality and the quantity of parents' teaching following intervention.

Recording

How much teaching parents do during and following an intervention programme has been measured in two basic ways, asking parents and counting records of sessions. However, often the teaching activity is assumed. Ludlow and Allen (1979) expected that parents carried on with teaching 'seven days a week', and Watson and Bassinger (1974) claimed that when

> "the mother had all programs going, she would be spending two to three hours a day in intensive training. In addition, she maintained newly acquired behavioral skills, 24 hours a day." (p.7)

This was after six to eight weeks of daily visiting at home, and mothers were expected to keep full records. A quote from one mother involved in the study of Cunningham, Aumonier and Sloper (1982) has a greater ring of truth: "I found I did a lot with K.... after each visit and just before the next one but in between I got a bit lazy" (p.14).

Some studies asked parents to record the number and length of the sessions they carried out with their child daily (e.g. Bidder et al., 1975; Revill and Blunden, 1979). Beveridge (1985) asked parents to record the child's success and their own use of prompts, etc. Parents filled in an average of three records a week, though they verbally reported doing more sessions. Records may be more likely to be kept when the session-length advised is around ten minutes, as in the Beveridge and Bidder et al. studies. In studies using the Portage materials, records are an integral part of the teaching directions, and are very simplified. Given that record-keeping is found burdensome by many parents, Sandler et al. (1983) compared record-keeping with no record-keeping, to see whether there was any difference in outcome for parent or child. No difference was found in terms of children's skills, but mothers did give more positive feedback for correct responses in observed interaction when they had been trained in record-keeping. The authors suggested that record-keeping may have heightened mothers' awareness of the quality of children's responses. More research of this nature is needed in order to judge the long-term importance of record-keeping. An inventive additional measure of teaching completed was reported by Moxley-Hegaert and Serbin (1983). They issued parents with large sheets of paper and blow-bubbles for use in their stimulation exercises, and measured the amount used up in a month. This measure correlated well with the number of sessions recorded, though not with the number reported.

It is important to note that record-keeping may presuppose a particular structure for parents' teaching, i.e. a specially structured session on an individual basis with the child. To adapt teaching formats to parents' preferences and to natural interaction opportunities with the child would require a different kind of parental record-keeping to be devised. Parents' existing opportunities for teaching interactions in the daily routine have not apparently received attention, except by Howlin et al. (1973). However, they have not presented data relating this information to the success of intervention, for example, whether parents with certain overall patterns of daily interaction with the child have more difficulty than others in carrying out teaching programmes.

Thus, some studies have been concerned to demonstrate that parents' behaviour reflects the interveners' intentions, i.e. that parents do carry out teaching with their mentally handicapped child. In addition, many studies have attempted to show that the detail of their training is subsequently reflected in the quality of parents' teaching skills. Potentially such detailed observation will identify those parents who have not responded to intervention; it may also enable identification of those parents whose skills were of such a level as to obviate the necessity for detailed advice on interaction and teaching technique. However, the prevailing group analyses of studies tend to obscure such distinctions.

Researchers seem to have adopted one of two differing approaches to the measurement of parents' behaviour: a 'skill-acquisition' approach, or an 'interactional' approach wherein the parents' behaviour is judged in sequence with the child's behaviour. Studies which are based on behaviour modification principles have evidenced both approaches. Measurement of skills will be reviewed first, and has been undertaken in three basic settings: role-play simulation, a structured situation in clinic or laboratory, and a structured situation at home.

Measurement of teaching skills

Role-play simulation has been used by researchers in order to introduce a degree of standardisation into the assessment procedure (O'Dell et al., 1977; O'Dell et al., 1979; Sibisi and Yule, 1982; Thorley and Yule, 1982; Cowart, Iwata and Poynter, 1984). One method is to ask the parent to role-play with a stooge (e.g. an adult playing a child - Thorley and Yule, 1982). In this case, the parent was rated on ten categories of behaviour in a role play of teaching new skills (and different categories for increasing desirable behaviour, and dealing with temper tantrums). Another method is to have parents react to filmed sequences of child behaviour, i.e. defining, counting and graphing behaviours, doing a task analysis, and indicating when ignoring and reinforcement should be used (O'Dell et al., 1977). Although such methods allow comparison between parents, their artificiality may affect parents differentially and leave out assessment of the child and situational variables which may be crucial in determining parents' implementation of the techniques.

Observation of parents and children in structured settings in a laboratory is the most frequently used method. It allows a degree of standardisation, but is somewhat less artificial than a role-play. Parents are observed in free play with the child, or more usually provided with some materials and asked to teach the child. The teaching goal may be unspecified, or may be related to previous assessment. For example, the parent may be asked to teach one target within and one target just beyond the child's assessed performance (Weitz, 1982). Instruments used in this way have included the Training Proficiency Scale (Gardner, Brust and Watson, 1970) adapted for use with parents (Brightman, Baker, Clark and Ambrose, 1982; Hudson, 1982), the Maternal Teaching Style Assessment Scale (Robinson and Filler, 1971; Filler, 1976; Filler and Bricker, 1976), the Behaviour Assessment Form for Learning Evaluation (Kiernan and Riddick, 1973) adapted for use with parents (Beveridge, 1982) and other such categorisations (Koegel et al., 1978; Weitz, 1982; Cowart et al., 1984; Hornby and Singh, 1984). The number of categories ranges from five up to 40, and thus are usually scored from videotape. One dilemma has been how to score the difference between use of a technique and whether it was needed at that point (Weitz, 1982). Another issue has been whether to simply code 'instruction' or whether to categorise the level of cognitive complexity of the demand made (McGillicuddy-DeLisi, 1982). However, the difficulty in using reliably a large number of subordinate categories has been noted by Hogg, Foxen and McBrien (1981). Parents at the start of training have been judged generally to use too many verbal directions, and too little physical guidance, demonstration and feedback (Filler and Bricker, 1976), and training programmes have been designed to modify this.

Several studies use simply one assessment session before and after training. This has led to criticism (e.g. Farrell, 1982) that change may primarily reflect parents' greater familiarity with being filmed in such a situation. Weitz (1982) filmed parents three times before training, twice in a laboratory and once at home, the second laboratory testing being after a five week gap. He found no significant differences in parents' use of teaching techniques between home and laboratory, and no differences across the waiting period (but large changes post-training) (c.f. Tavormina, 1975, for a two month waiting period).

What is not examined in these studies is generalization to the home where the emotional climate may be very different, e.g. the child more or less manageable. Flanagan, Adams and Forehand (1979) found no correlation between a simulation situation and in-home observation of parents' skills in using time-out. This suggests that there is no real substitute for observing parents' teaching in situ (Gardner, 1983; Breiner and Beck, 1984). Another use of on-the-spot observation may be to share with parents areas of high and low scoring in order to work on problem areas (Watson and Bassinger, 1974, using the Training Proficiency Scale). The Portage materials include a Parental Behavior Inventory (Boyd, Stauber and Bluma, 1977) including rating of ten hierarchies of skills, which can be used similarly.

Observation in the home is not, however, a panacea as an observer's presence can change a parent-child interaction considerably (Zegiob and Forehand, 1978). There have been some reported attempts to observe unobtrusively, though rarely with handicapped children. Cheseldine (1977) provided parents with a tape-recorder to use in recording their language-teaching sessions at home. However, studies of interaction in families of children with behaviour problems have overcome the difficulty of parents being aware of being recorded by using automatic audio tape recording (Bernal, Gibson, Williams and Pesses, 1971) or a radio-transmitter (Johnson, Christensen and Bellamy, 1976). The transmitter was switched on at times which parents had identified as most problematic, and also at random times. After treatment procedures, child behaviour improved on average at identified times, but not at random times. Some thought might be given to having parents observe or film each other teaching, or observing the parent teaching in a situation where the observer can be less obtrusive, e.g. in a playgroup or toy library. Techniques of measurement of teaching effectiveness in the home have made relatively little progress, even though its necessity was pointed out at least 15 years ago (Terdal and Buell, 1969).

Measurement of interactional skills

Although the measurement scales reviewed in the previous section frequently include categories for the child's behaviour, or define certain parent categories in relation to the preceding child behaviour, they do not treat the parent-child interaction as an interrelated whole. Obviously interaction-focussed interventions have done so; but a number of behaviour modification based interventions with mentally handicapped children have collected this kind of data also, as it does in fact reflect the behavioural model.

One way of simplifying the complexity of observed behaviour chains has been to formulate them in a response-class matrix. For example, Mash and Terdal (1973) observed a free-play situation before and after intervention, and two coders simultaneously recorded antecedent and consequent behaviours as they applied to both mother and child. Results were then presented as increases or decreases in various child or mother responses in sequences of two or three behaviours. Thus it was possible to interpret more accurately the appropriateness, for example, of a rise in maternal positive feedback. Tavormina (1975) made similar observations of free-play, and also of mothers requiring children to put the toys away (i.e. 'command-play'). Following group intervention, changes during free play were not significant, but interactional changes in command-play improved significantly. McConkey et al. (1979) related children's use of words to parents' antecedent and consequent language use, and were able to show how an increase in statements, versus questions or demands, was related to child progress (c.f. Whitehurst, Novak and Zorn, 1972).

A number of more complex and comprehensive ratings of parent-child interaction have been developed, which can be interpreted in terms of parental teaching skills. Usually they are used in evaluating videotape of short structured teaching sessions, and they may use the concept of a 'behavioural clause' (Caldwell, 1969) in order to break up the flow of events into segments for analysis. Examples of such rating schemes are those of Mitchell, D.R. (1976, 1980), Gaussen (1979), Russo and Owens (1982), Clezy (1984), the Maternal Interactive Behavior (MIB) record (Levenstein, 1970; Madden, Levenstein and Levenstein, 1976) and the Maternal Teaching Style Instrument (MTSI) (Sandler, Dokecki, Stewart, Britton and Horton, 1973; Gray and Ruttle, 1980). The scheme developed by Mitchell was used by Emerson et al. (1981) in evaluating workshops for parents. However, they found no significant changes. As the method measures sequences of behaviour in a one-to-one teaching situation, and their eight week workshop covered a variety of topics primarily through discussion and viewing of videotapes, the lack of focussed change is perhaps not surprising. Significant changes have been found with both the MIB and the MTSI in the course of two-year home-visiting interventions with low-income mothers and toddlers, and for the MTSI with mothers of handicapped preschool children following a workshop intervention, but only on two out of eleven categories (Sandler et al., 1983).

Finally, studies of intervention focussed on interaction have sometimes made use of molar, qualitative ratings, such as the Home Observation for the Measurement of the Environment (HOME) (Bradley and Caldwell, 1976), the Parent Behavior Progression (PBP) (Bromwich, 1981) or Kogan's Interpersonal Behavior Constructs (IBC) (Kogan and Gordon, 1975). These ratings reflect the affective quality of interaction as well as its value in terms of cognitive stimulation. They have been developed to give ways of discussing with parents the nature of their interactions with the child (PBP: Bromwich, 1981; Affleck et al., 1982; HOME: Brassell, 1977) but can also be used as measures of outcome (PBP: Allen, Affleck, McQueeney and McGrade, 1982; IBC: Kogan et al., 1974). They have the advantage of being relatively quick and efficient measures of the quality of everyday home interaction. Interestingly, as ratings become more qualitative, professionals may be less likely to share information fully with parents. This may be a result of the embarrassment felt in making value judgements about another person's parenting; however, Bromwich (1981) argues rather convincingly against sharing Parent Behavior Progression information on the grounds that parents may then try to do everything contained in the rating and lose the spontaneity of their natural style.

CONCLUSION

This final section of the literature review has attempted two rather different things. Firstly, Chapter 10 surveyed current practice in parent involvement and discussed the content and philosophy of such intervention. Links have also been made with aspects of a detailed conceptual framework for parental involvement, the development of which was a primary aim of the review of literature. The consideration of current practice in this light suggested many issues on which services could be criticised. For example, workshop training of parents in teaching techniques would seem to ignore the family system and ecology. Home-based programmes may, in effect, be similar by intervening with one parent only and by potentially creating a lengthy dependency of the parent on the home-visitor. Within any type of service structure, the content of intervention may have a restricted focus on child developmental progress and on parent skill acquisition, thereby ignoring the existing interaction patterns of parent and child, the range of family needs and longer-term family goals. However, it was argued that changing the focus of intervention to interaction and interrelationships is not a simple matter, and at this early stage in research involves issues of how judgements are to be made about what is or is not beneficial for any particular mentally handicapped child. For example, how are independence of exploration and increased structure of learning to be balanced for the handicapped child? How are enhanced parental responsiveness and fulfilment of the needs of all the family members to be balanced?

Both in terms of the content, and particularly in terms of the philosophy of parent involvement, there are great difficulties in pulling together ideas which have developed mostly through experience, expediency and political reflection, with a conceptual analysis drawn from several areas of psychological research. 'Partnership with parents' arose as a response to practice (e.g. Mittler and Mittler, 1982); theoretical justification, for example, in terms of the interactive basis of child development, would seem largely to be post hoc.

The purpose of Chapter 11 was to review research into some variables affecting the success of intervention. The relative lack of material concerning parental variables, and their relationship to the content of intervention, has shown up how radical is a change of focus in service and research on to parents, that is, their day-to-day situation, behaviour, skills, philosophy, goals, and so on. Certainly there have been a variety of attempts to measure parents' teaching skills, but the consequent links with how to amend intervention strategy are not always clear. For example, individual differences in behaviour change have not been related back in analysis to other parent variables, nor to whether or how parents taught their child before intervention. The final chapter will summarise themes raised in the review of literature and from this basis will suggest some directions for future research and intervention.

Chapter Twelve

IMPLICATIONS FOR RESEARCH AND PRACTICE

In the concluding chapter, it is intended to summarise themes and information which have emerged from the broad review of literature. This is not simply so that the reader may avoid the detailed slog of Chapters 1 to 11, but is intended to take matters a step further, in attempting to suggest how lessons may be drawn in order to inform future research and practice. This is necessarily a speculative exercise. However the purpose of the book was to take a broader look at available literature than might usually be done, and to use the opportunity to examine questions about how professionals attempt to help parents of young mentally handicapped children from a basis of more than day to day expediency.

FRAMEWORK FOR RESEARCH AND INTERVENTION

The future evaluation of teaching interventions needs to be founded on a clear philosophy of goals and processes. That is why the aim of the book was to draw together a coherent conceptual structure for intervention, and for further research to inform intervention. Appropriate measures to use in research should logically follow from the philosophy.

The philosophy developed in the preceding chapters is founded on a recognition of the child's world as a network of interlocking systems. The child's interaction with the environment takes place not only at the level of the home, and interaction with parents and siblings, but is impinged on by broader family activities and expectations, the neighbourhood the family lives in, the services provided (or not) by the community for children and families, society's current and past attitudes toward mental handicap, etc. etc. Indeed, the handicapped infant him or herself can usefully be conceptualised for assessment as a network of systems, more or less organised - physiological, motor, regulatory, attentional, etc. - which affect readiness for and reaction to the environment including interaction with parents (Als, Lester, Tronick and Brazelton, 1982). Although there may be some general similarities between mentally handicapped children, the processes within each system and network will vary with the age level, developmental skills, sensory impairments of the child plus several care-giver factors plus many cultural factors (such as assumptions about the goals and methods of child-rearing). Thus, intervention must be carried out in the awareness of its potential impact on this interlocking network; how by concentrating on one part such as the mother teaching the child to stack cubes, many possibly unforeseen effects (positive or negative) will ensue. It is important that teaching interventions advance beyond the stage of being a 'mindless technology' (Berger, 1979) and at least monitor their broader impact (c.f. Milne, 1985, who found training nurses in behavioural methods led to a <u>decrease</u> in number and appropriateness of interactions with long-stay psychiatric patients). For example, the intervention would need to take account of interactional factors between mother and child, and to consider how to facilitate the active role of the infant in interaction. Skills-teaching interventions may show

> "...a preoccupation for reinforcement, a minimizing of the importance of selecting relevant learning goals and an over-reliance on prompting techniques which can inhibit the child's spontaneous behaviour." (McConkey et al., 1982, p.346)

Instead it is proposed that intervention be guided by the goal of promoting the mutual adaptiveness of child and environment; that is

> "... when the properties of the environment and its expectations and demands are in accord with the organism's own capacities, motivations and style of behaving. When this consonance between organism and environment is present,

> optimal development in a progressive direction is possible." (Thomas, 1981, p.603)

This implies looking at outcome in terms of long-term developmental progress, but not necessarily at any particular short-term milestone. Each child and family system is unique, and atypical patterns of development and atypical styles of achieving it may be adaptive in that case (Walker and Crawley, 1983). The goal of child-environment adaptiveness also implies measuring outcome in terms of satisfactory family functioning (satisfying to the family). To push hard for one particular developmental goal may be a meaningless (and perhaps non-maintained) accomplishment if strain on the family has taken an unwarranted toll.

If this degree of flexibility of thinking about intervention with individual children and families is to be pursued, it implies conducting intervention in a research spirit. The conceptual guidelines for analysis of research studies developed from the review of literature may be used in structuring such intervention and its evaluation. That analysis can be summed up in these terms:

- questioning assumptions of deviance;
- assuming change over time;
- studying the family as a system;
- considering other systems in the child's ecology;
- evaluating multimodally.

Interventions, and research related to intervention, would thus centrally consider individual differences in themselves, looking at systems on their own merits and not simply with reference to some assumed or ill-defined 'normality'. For example, the lack of some behaviour in the parent of a handicapped infant should be interpreted within the frame of reference of that dyad, and the demands of their environment. The parent may be adapting in a way which will prove to be positive, if the child is lacking in a particular sensory modality, or is overreactive to external stimuli. Walker (1982) gives an example of such an intervention, being based first on careful observation of a mother and her non-interactive severely mentally and physically disabled two year old child. Using videotape, mother and intervener noted that two mother behaviours - moving her face close to the child's, and imitating his few vocalisations - were associated with greater frequency of child vocalisations. Increasing these two behaviours in a gentle way increased overall and contingent vocalisation. And, it might have been added, probably also increased parental pleasure and involvement, and altered parents' perceptions about teaching the child, etc. It is important also to consider changing patterns in different settings and over time - for example, variability in a child's behaviour may be more indicative of adaptiveness and coping strategies than stability is (Brazelton, 1981). Also, children will need different kinds of responses from their parents as their skills increase and interests change. For example, physical contact seems not so necessary to a (physically able) child after six months of age, and may be restrictive of the child's need to explore and reach (Wachs and Gruen, 1982). Parents' needs from an intervention will change - at first it may be how to help the child directly, later how to deal with siblings' reactions or whether to have another child, and later still how to prepare for the child going to school. Fathers', siblings' and grandparents' interaction with and reactions to the child all impinge directly and indirectly on the child and the mother. Intervention may need to consider how to include them. For example, grandparents may never have been asked directly if they want to know more about the child's disability. Increased information and a chance to talk may have great positive benefit for the child and the immediate family. Thus, from such a philosophy of intervention, guided by the goal of child-environment adaptiveness, necessarily follows the need for broad strategies and multiple measures of evaluation.

Descriptive variables

A great deal more fundamental descriptive research is needed. Consideration of the research literature leads to suggestions of several parent and child characteristics which it would seem of importance to study further. Certainly in terms of broader ecological variables, the list is extensive. Published studies have attested the relevance to various outcome measures of assessing marital relationships (and also the variable of single parenthood) (e.g. Friedrich, 1979; Baker and Clark, 1983), the quality of the home environment (e.g. Nihira, Mink and Meyers, 1981), the family as a system (e.g. Turnbull et al., 1982), and parental stress (e.g. Burden, 1980; Beckman, 1983). As discussed in Chapter 6, the last is a multifaceted variable and difficult to interpret if assessed simplistically. It does not tend to bear a direct relationship with demographic indicators (e.g. Bradshaw and Lawton, 1978), being mediated by individual parents' perceptions of events, and coping strategies. Looked at in a comprehensive way (e.g. with the Questionnaire on Resources and Stress), this kind of ecological analysis of parental adjustment underlines the contention in this review of literature that multiple variables operate upon parents and the ways in which they interact with their children. Friedrich et al. (1983) identified four main factors in the Questionnaire on Resources and Stress: Parent and family problems, Pessimism, Child characteristics, and Physical incapacitation. To follow these factor groupings loosely, this might suggest that future research should take account not only of parents' perceptions of themselves and the child but also of how these relate to marital satisfaction and everyday social and economic problems; and not only of obvious variables to do with the child's handicap (such as degree of physical problems) but also interactional characteristics of the child. In addition, it would seem necessary to study the family's home life not solely in terms of 'problems', but to look at how proposed interventions might fit in with or alter current family patterns, particularly of child-care (McConachie, 1982).

One child characteristic which has repeatedly been suggested in research as a powerful discriminator, both directly and also as mediated by parental reaction is that of child sex (e.g. Mink et al., 1983). That is, certain family patterns of interaction and home environment have been found more likely with mentally handicapped boys as opposed to girls, and vice versa. Precisely how this might come about is understood only in a fragmentary way - for example, Down's syndrome girls have been shown more able generally than boys over time (e.g. Carr, 1985; Cunningham, Glenn, Wilkinson and Sloper, 1985), but how this is translated through parents' perceptions into differing patterns of family harmony is a matter more of speculation than having been answered by research. A similar point could be made in relation to aetiology, i.e. that Down's syndrome children may have differing effects on families from children of other aetiologies (e.g. Mink et al., 1983, who found Down's syndrome children having relatively a positive effect on home patterns). Thus, in future research sampling considerations would be important, with the possibility being maintained of comparing groupings on child sex and aetiology.

Another class of variables suggested as important by the literature review is parent-child interaction. Published studies of interaction between parents and their handicapped children were found to be severely limited in number and quality. Most used observational methods which limit the generalizability of the findings. At least two main problems need to be tackled in the future. Firstly, the methods for describing the observed interaction often emphasise parental behaviour out of context, and child compliance with parent's directions. Where children give hard-to-interpret cues, it is necessarily easier to focus on parents' than on children's initiations. However, the ways in which parents respond to child initiations, by exploring their intention and supporting their execution, are theoretically likely to be of key relevance for child development, for handicapped as well as non-handicapped children (e.g. Mogford, 1979a; Jones, 1980). If observers have difficulty in interpreting children's cues, then by making parents part of the research team and involving them in categorisation, they may find out what it is important to study in the case of individual children. Several studies have shown that parents' perceptions of child interactional characteristics such as irritability or liveliness are key variables (Affleck et al., 1982; Beckman, 1983). Secondly, observation of interaction has been confined almost exclusively to dyadic situations. Particularly when father-child interaction is being considered, having the mother there too may be a far more usual setting, and one in which parental similarities and differences may be clearer, and more validly observed than in structured dyadic settings. However, the questions of how, where and when to observe are difficult to answer. Different times of day have differing properties; for example, if observation is carried out after fathers in dual-role families come home, mothers may well 'take a back seat' not only as a rule but more especially for the 'benefit' of the researcher. Teaching-type interactions may show the father relatively more at a loss with the child than would be the case in more relaxed interactional settings such as on an outing to the park.

In the current state of knowledge what is primarily needed is many more observational, descriptive studies, in a variety of settings, with children of a variety of ages, where findings are interpreted carefully in relation to known patterns of change in interaction of parents and non-handicapped children. For example, summing up parents' interactional style in terms of 'directiveness' may be useful, but only if it is done in relation to the context of children's behaviour (Crawley and Spiker, 1983) so that its appropriateness can be properly judged. If parents of handicapped children are found more physically intrusive than parents of non-handicapped children the same age or developmental age, it may be that the child is appropriately being helped with physical prompting to achieve goals, and that the same parents would generally in a few weeks be intervening much less frequently as children's competence increased (McConkey and Martin, 1984). Thus, the studies need also to be longitudinal.

Requirements for research into interaction

Parent-child interaction research with non-handicapped children has provided a picture of what seem to be facilitative interactional strategies for mothers and young children (e.g. Clarke-Stewart, 1973; Rutter, 1985). But these are very limited. They assume particular definitions of child competence which may not be appropriate for many cultural settings beyond the white middle-class, American, dual-role families in which the research was conducted (Gray and Wandersman, 1980; Ogbu, 1981). For example, they do not consider sufficiently the difference between creative behaviour and task-achievement. Most certainly, the models of competence and the processes by which child competence are to be promoted may not be appropriate to be taken over wholesale in the case of disabled children. Secondly, the research has been conducted within a limited definition of parenting, with a very restricted understanding of parents' and children's emotional (rather than cognitive) development. How might the adaptiveness of a handicapped child's developing anger be interpreted by the parent? 'Fathering' has hardly been considered as a separate entity; the study of interaction between fathers and handicapped children has only just begun. What is needed from this research is more than correlational studies. Past studies, in which only a relatively small part of the variance in child development was accounted for by patterns of mother-child interaction, have been taken as providing a 'positive interaction model' to use in intervention. Yet, the design of these studies has not allowed important questions to be answered such as: how do unsatisfactory interactions develop?, and how may they be ameliorated? Once a more comprehensive body of descriptive studies of children and parents at home is available, including handicapped children and their parents, then it will be possible to develop and to test hypotheses about which patterns are effective in promoting development, with children of differing kinds of characteristics. Only at that point will research really be able to inform intervention, so that effort can be directed toward discovering how to maintain and shape such interaction patterns for maximum mutual adaptiveness of child and environment. Similarly, many more descriptive studies are needed at broader ecological levels, looking at different strategies which families use in order to cope with a handicapped child, and attempting to trace how they might have arisen. This will require complex, multivariate descriptive analysis, based on obvious and more subtle measures of the child, the family and their social networks, in various areas of functioning - and balanced by qualitative methods which illuminate analytical answers for individuals (Byrne and Cunningham, 1985). Once more descriptive information is available it will then be possible to test hypotheses concerning how effective various coping strategies are for families, and the community resources which are needed to support them.

These are long-term, rather utopian, implications for research into handicapped children which will inform service intervention. Fundamental to the philosophy is the perceived danger of premature judgement of a particular pattern or part of a family's system as 'bad' in itself, without regard to long-term adaptiveness. However, is it possible to make judgements about where to intervene in the short term?

IMPLICATIONS FOR PRACTICE

In discussing implications of the research literature for professional practice, it is important to be aware of the real situation with which families of young mentally handicapped children are faced. That is, services are few and do not by any means cover the country comprehensively, speaking both geographically and in terms of their scope and variety. Many parents are offered a teaching-type intervention with their young child, but many are not. Secondly, there are ideological and practical constraints on collaboration between parents and professionals. In Chapter 10, the changing philosophy behind intervention was described, moving toward the ideal of partnership between parents and professionals, each contributing from their own knowledge and skills toward a programme for the benefit of the child. However, problems which may come in the way of this type of movement include professionals' lack of confidence in their own skills, lack of training in working with parents and feeling that their professional training and position is being undermined (Wolfendale, 1985). Parents may find intervention an imposition on their time and an intrusion into family life - for them, 'partnership' will imply a mutual decision on no action at that time. These issues cannot be addressed here, with the exception of some comments on professional training. But solving the problems regarding further implementation of what is already known to be helpful to children and parents is crucial.

The practice of intervention is inevitably guided as much by common-sense and guesswork as by research evidence - there is little firm evidence available to guide the hundreds of administrative and clinical decisions which have to be made in implementing a programme. And, in the most critical view, it has recently been suggested that even the available evidence of behaviour change in children and parents with group intervention is "unconvincing" (Hornby and Singh, 1983). Others are more sanguine about positive effects demonstrated by a range of programme models, but stress the number of questions which remain to be answered.

> "Long-term benefits are uncertain; although initial child changes are generally maintained, it is unclear how much parents use procedures they have learned for new interventions. Not all parents benefit equally, but there is little basis for predicting which families will benefit in a particular program." (Baker, 1984, p.364)

It would also be informative to attempt to ask parents who drop out of intervention programmes why; that is, not simply to measure their levels of depression (c.f. McMahon, Forehand, Griest and Wells, 1981), to note that they are single parents (c.f. Baker and Clark, 1983), and so on, but to ask for their perceptions of the programme and its problems for them.

In the previous section it was suggested that implications for research and for practice are not really separate issues - that intervention needs to be undertaken with a research orientation. Equally intervention can inform research questions, not least through intensive prospective case studies (replicated with different children), to build up information in a broad-based way about children and families. A number of suggestions for the practice of intervention will now be outlined drawing on the conceptual framework for intervention developed and on the research literature reviewed.

Interaction

The first suggestion is that intervention should initially concentrate on parent-child interaction, before specific skill-teaching is introduced. In the literature review, some intervention programmes taking an 'interactional approach' were criticised for seeming to direct parents toward a particular 'beneficial parenting style' (Lamb, 1980). (As such programmes appear so far to be implemented in North America, and the writer has not observed them directly, this perception is based solely on written evidence and commentary and may be inaccurate.) While maintaining caution about deciding that a particular style of interaction between parent and handicapped child is 'inappropriate', just because it might deviate from an expected norm for parents and non-handicapped children, it does seem clinically possible to use information from the literature to guide intervention. For example, intervention seems to be appropriate where a child's interactional activity is limited or passive, or where the parent and child 'clash' in interaction, in the sense both of continual simultaneous action with differing intentions, and of generating emotional conflict. What can guide intervention, particularly with parents and very young children, is not a particular model pattern of interaction, but rather examination of the principles on which interaction between parent and child seems to develop. These principles include: reciprocity and synchronicity, i.e. that parent and infant frequently carry out similar actions, taking turns; cyclical chaining of interaction, i.e. that there is rhythmical repetition of sequences of activity; and variation in modality, speed, intensity and length of cycles. Thus, though handicapped infants give fewer cues, which are harder for parents to understand (e.g. Jones, 1977; Emde, Katz and Thorpe, 1978; Walker, 1982; Yogman, 1982), intervention can be directed at helping parents to observe more closely (c.f. Mogford, 1979a; Bromwich, 1981), not only the child but also themselves. Having noted the rate and pattern of their mutual activity, the parent can then be helped to decide how to experiment with altering interaction according to the principles outlined above. The experimental manipulations described by Field (1977b) and by Berger and Cunningham (1981a) are an example along these lines, but the mothers were asked only to 'imitate' which is less specific than what is being suggested here. For example, a parent might be making isolated, vigorous attempts to stimulate an inactive child, interspersed with long intervals of no attention. This type of pattern might be altered in the direction of approaches by the parent becoming more frequent, gentler and looking for any reaction to which the parent might respond by imitation and then pausing to allow time for a reciprocal response. If a parent is attempting turn-taking, but is being prevented, for example, by a child's habit of rapid repeated vocalisation (Jones, 1977), then imitation may still be attempted but with variations on the theme, perhaps moving into other modalities to look for cues which may more easily be utilised in flexible interaction. If parents have developed a rather stereotyped habit of repetition of the same games, then variation along a number of different lines may be introduced, to insert surprise into the interaction. The principles described above have been most often observed to underlie the development of interaction in terms of gaze and vocalisation; however, Brazelton, Tronick, Adamson, Als and Wise (1975) have suggested that they may be more general, and may contribute to establishing the foundations of social and cognitive development if expressed in other channels such as touch and kinaesthetics. This suggestion if supported would have helpful implications for handicapped children impaired in one or more modalities.

Implications

These suggestions do imply that parents of handicapped children not only have to do 'ordinary' things with their child, but also can meet their child's special needs even more by going beyond what ordinary parenting would involve. They do have to 'try harder'; research results have suggested that parents of handicapped children may do so by tending to dominate the interaction and to give commands, at a faster rate (e.g. Cardoso-Martins and Mervis, 1985; McConachie and Mitchell, 1985). Certainly the children in such studies are generally older and more independently skilled than the infants for whom apparently helpful principles of interaction have been being discussed above, and thus a very active style on the part of the parents may (in terms of mutual enjoyment and long-term outcome) have been appropriate. But it seems at least worth observing interaction with such children more closely, in a variety of settings, and to experiment with parents on allowing the child to make more initiations. Moss and Hogg's (1983) study of the development of manipulative skills suggested that once an initial level of competence is reached, children tend to develop further by exploring the possibilities of a task rather than necessarily perfecting the 'correct' way of doing something. Establishing with parents through observation and experiment what children's own style of problem-solving may be, would seem a useful foundation from which then to proceed to skill-teaching.

Research on interaction between fathers and handicapped children tended to suggest little difference from the patterns of interaction between mothers and the children. However, small samples may have obscured differences. A larger study did suggest some differences in parallel with findings of research on fathers and non-handicapped children, i.e. that fathers might not be as well attuned to the changing detail of interaction as mothers (McConachie and Mitchell, 1985). This study also suggested that fathers who were more participant in their children's care were more responsive in interaction, but these tended to be fathers whose children were more able, perhaps easier to understand (McConachie, 1982, 1986). The implications of this pattern of results would seem to be that fathers might particularly benefit from intervention which helped them focus on their interaction with the child, observe more clearly what the child is doing, and shift focus as the child does. If fathers are comparatively less attuned to interaction with a non-speaking child, who needs help in accomplishing actions and whose play may still be at a rather repetitive and exploratory rather than constructive level, then observation (particularly if videotape is available for detailed study) may help them to see more clearly the child's intentions and lead to strategies whereby they and the child can sustain mutual attention for longer. It should be noted that the intervention should not necessarily be directed at promoting similarity of style between mothers and fathers. Clarke-Stewart's (1980) findings suggested that development might be promoted best through couples having similar attitudes about the child, but differing in the content of interaction, so that children experienced variety and challenge. Clarke-Stewart's work was with non-handicapped children and their parents; it may be that mentally handicapped children would instead gain more from similarity and consistency. This is a matter for further study.

Can intervention at the level of parent-child interaction be seen as too much intrusion in the parents' primary responsibility for child-rearing? Does it run too high a risk of fostering dependency of the parent on the professional, undermining parents' confidence in their independent ability to solve problems, making them feel inadequate and helpless (Gray and Wandersman, 1980; Wright et al., 1984)? The answer seems twofold. Firstly, it is perhaps important that a direct approach to intervening in interaction be short-term, and particularly that it be undertaken as a problem-solving experiment with parents, and not one in which interveners attempt to impose their own values about interaction. Parents are the ones who know most about how their children react. Also, interveners' values are likely to be culturally limited. For example, Baumrind (1972) found that black American mothers classified as rejecting by white norms had daughters who were satisfactorily developing competence. Secondly, this approach is perhaps best as part of very early intervention, when parents are floundering, unsure of what to do with a baby suddenly defined as mentally handicapped (Cunningham, 1983b). It is at this point that professionals can perhaps best impart the twin ideas of parents trusting their own instincts, acting in normal ways, plus also adopting some special measures. Parents of mentally handicapped children do need ideally to be able to judge when their child is ready to move on a stage; sensitivity in interaction includes not only responding to the child, but also giving appropriate challenge. But to maintain the long-term focus of intervention on interaction may be to distort the parent-child relationship. It is a heavy burden on parents to be responsible for responding and anticipating at the same time, and any adverse impact may well be magnified by the vulnerability of families. Early intervention should therefore crucially seek to boost parents' feelings of control over their own lives and upbringing of the child, while helping parents to focus positively on what the child can do and on how they can facilitate all-round development through interaction. Parent enjoyment of the child is likely to be a key factor in adaptive interaction (Bromwich, 1981).

Parents teaching

Many intervention programmes with preschool, handicapped children choose teaching tasks for children according to developmental progress charts. Apart from their value in enabling intervention staff to proceed on the basis of rather short specific training, charts may also be reassuring to parents in providing guidelines over a considerable period of time on 'what to do next'.

However, there are some further points which might be taken into consideration. Parents have a variety of ideas on what will most help their child and on what situations are relevant for teaching (e.g. McConkey and McEvoy, 1984; McConachie, 1986). Also parents have a variety of teaching/play styles. Fathers are less likely than mothers to choose 'intellectual' or toy-related play activities, and tend to have a more engaging, active style of play (Clarke-Stewart, 1978). This seems to imply that adopting a 'packaged' approach in choosing teaching tasks and methods may not be as appropriate as basing teaching on what parents are already doing and feel confident with. Thus if a mother feels that bathtime is a situation highly relevant for teaching, the intervener could take her perception seriously, observe bathtime interactions, discuss with the mother what she and the child are doing, and use this information in deciding on, for example, language goals or object manipulation goals to be pursued in this and other teaching contexts. If a father is currently highly involved with the child but describes his activity more in terms of the child's growing independence than in terms of teaching, then these may also be the terms which the intervener might use. A teaching task focussed on parental involvement in play with jigsaws might seem less relevant to this parent than the child learning to put away cutlery in different drawer sections when father dries the washing-up. If a father is currently comparatively little involved with the child, the intervener may wish to explore the potential of the father's engaging style of play, perhaps at the time when the father comes home from work. If the intervention involves specific language goals in a structured teaching situation with the mother, then it can be explored explicitly with the couple how these goals might best be translated into less structured, playful situations. (Boisterous play, and promotion of understanding of the preposition "under", comes readily to mind.)

The approach of capitalising on what parents already do, and extending it, includes the realisation that whatever the rhetoric about 'equality of care' between mothers and fathers, it is simply not becoming a reality. As far as can be determined from retrospective research (given problems with research method), fathers have in the past forty years always thought they were more child-centred than their own fathers. Yet their documented activity in child-care is not generally greater, except perhaps at specific points in time when family circumstances may necessitate their 'taking-over' to some extent. Given shorter working hours, present-day fathers may in effect do proportionately less (Lewis, 1984). It therefore seems realistic that intervention, rather than aiming in an unsubtle way to shift more of the 'unshared care' on to fathers, should accept family roles as they are. Intervention can, however, draw on fathers' obvious caring about their child, feelings of responsibility, and willingness to play so as to make the time that fathers and children spend together mutually fruitful. It should also be noted here that the research basis on which to make any recommendation about intervention with fathers is woefully thin. In particular, ideas about father-child interaction have almost all been gathered in 'artificial' structured teaching situations. (The study by Stoneman and Brody (1984) is a notable exception.) It may be, for example, that fathers' sensitivity and success in interaction may be quite different in informal, familiar situations.

The above discussion of teaching-oriented intervention has focussed on mothers and fathers. However, other members of the family may be involved in playing with and caring for the child. Whether or not to involve those other family members in detailed consideration of the goals and methods of teaching is a matter for each individual family. Certainly it may be helpful for intervention to be extended to them short-term, with the goal of making more productive and harmonious the time already spent together (c.f. Weinrott, 1974). Another consideration is exploration of the meanings of 'teaching', 'learning' and 'parenting' with parents, before deciding on a particular form of intervention. Some parents may not be in accord with the assumptions underlying intervention for cultural reasons (e.g. Powell and Perkins, 1984). This does not in any way preclude intervention. Partnership would imply working with parents to discover their goals, problems and assumptions, and offering intervention in flexible forms to meet them.

Broader goals of intervention

The role of teacher is only one of the many which parents assume. The philosophy of intervention which has been outlined suggests considerations of teaching the child should not be allowed to obscure other needs which the family may have - reduction of multiple pressures on them, making service networks respond efficiently, giving advice about respite care availability, responding to siblings' or elderly grandparents' needs, help with transport or babysitting, etc. What is suggested here is not that an intervention programme must offer everything, which might swamp the family, so that every day is taken up with being a 'special' family. Rather, the intervention staff should be aware of what a family's needs might be, and ask from time to time what parents want (not "need", as this might imply they are not coping, Wilkin, 1979). If parents are kept informed of what opportunities are available, then they can choose in their own time.

The coping resources which may be available to a family include:

- physical health and emotional stability;
- past experience in problem-solving, such as seeking out information and support;
- the supportiveness and size of their social network;

- financial resources;
- their values and beliefs.
  (Cunningham and Davis, 1985a)

In the first place, these are aspects of the family ecology which it is of relevance to monitor, in order to observe possible wider effects of intervention, and to enable evaluation of coping strategies as more or less effective in the long run. Secondly, it may in the short term be as important for intervention to be directed towards enabling mothers to look after their own physical health as to consider the child directly. And it may be as important to facilitate parents of handicapped children meeting each other for mutual support as to focus direct services on the child.

At all points, it is important to be aware of parents of handicapped children as differing individuals. For some parents, meeting other parents may bring to mind all kinds of questions about their child which they have not previously considered, thus initially raising rather than relieving anxiety. The research literature has indicated that single parents in particular have difficulty in coping, and in maintaining involvement in teaching interventions. Therefore, particular consideration may need to be given to how to maximise support for them; for example, if the local authority has a policy of appointing community-based care assistants then also to involve the one who is attached to the family for some hours each day in the teaching intervention. Of major importance in the philosophy of partnership is the issue of parents' right to opt out of involvement with professionals at any particular time. Greater services should not bring with them greater pressures on parents (Turnbull and Turnbull, 1982).

As and if interventions routinely broaden the scope of their evaluation measures, new methods of data collection will have to be developed. This is particularly the case for family members other than the mother. Most research studies have gathered information indirectly on fathers and on siblings. Yet a direct approach may show up rather different results, as was the case for studies of siblings; when they have been interviewed directly, generally fewer harmful effects and more positive benefits of living with a handicapped child are evidenced (see Chapters 2 and 4). Measuring children's attitudes and interviewing them directly poses quite different methodological problems from interviewing adults.

For example, it has been shown that the terms in which children describe other people change over time from mostly concrete descriptions of appearance, social role and kinship around the age of seven years, to descriptions in terms of behaviour and personality predominating by the age of 13 (Brierly, 1967). Thus, the concepts which the child is being asked to grasp and report on must not be too complex. There is, however, another aspect to consider. Siblings' understanding of each other can frequently be shown to be more sophisticated than would otherwise be expected (Dunn, 1984). In particular, siblings may be able to discuss their brothers and sisters in more elaborate, sophisticated ways when they are discussing <u>disliked</u> qualities, and this applies even to siblings as young as six years (Bigner, 1974). In interviewing siblings of handicapped children, a variety of factors require consideration; any apparent greater complexity of negative feelings would need careful interpretation. In addition, it may be very important to distinguish between actions and feelings with siblings (McConachie and Domb, 1983). For example, fighting and jealousy may not be linked for siblings, but may be interpreted in this way by parents. Finally, questions of siblings' reactivity to being observed may have to be explored as a quite separate question to parents' reactivity.

When it comes to interviewing fathers, again there are important differences from interviewing mothers. The gender role implications of discussing care of children are quite different, and fathers may not be at all fluent at talking about their ideas about their children. Taking 'fathering' seriously does not mean simply asking men the same questions as the mothers were asked. An additional question to be explored is what difference a male versus a female researcher might have upon the data collected (O'Brien and McKee, 1982).

The devoting of family and professional time and effort to measuring broader aspects of the ecology of the family will be an intervention in itself. The professional staff are indicating that they perceive these broader aspects as important. If the measurement is presented as part of a joint exploratory strategy, then professionals will be able to show that they respect and want to learn from family members' broader interests, concerns and opinions, thus potentially strengthening parents' confidence in their own pattern of coping.

Training of professional staff
Very few professional staff receive direct training in working with parents of mentally handicapped children (Atkin and Bastiani, 1984), although more pre-service and in-service courses may include some discussion of the topic, perhaps with some parents themselves. In-service training is needed in the area of skills (such as communicating clearly with parents, and running meetings in attractive, involving ways). It is needed also in the area of attitudes, for example, making teachers more aware of how they themselves feel as parents in relation to contacts with their own children's schools, and of the fact that ideas about 'good parenting' are essentially relative and thus of the ways in which their ideas have evolved from their own experiences and differ from other people's (Cox and Cattell, 1985). Broad-based training materials have only recently begun to be available (e.g. McConkey, 1985).

Thus, most professionals have a training in a particular field working directly with their client group, and only gradually find out by trial and error how most effectively to impart their skills to parents. As pointed out by Hornby and Murray (1983) one of the main benefits accruing from running parent workshops may be the in-service training it provides for support professionals in the attitudes and skills necessary for further work with parents of handicapped children. Likewise, carrying out an ecologically wide range of measures with parents is likely to be as much of a learning experience for the professionals as it is for the parents, opening their eyes to the totality of the situation with which parents cope.

The conceptual framework which has been put forward for intervention with families of young mentally handicapped children poses something of a dilemma in its implementation. The skills, attitudes, knowledge and energy required to be aware of and to attempt to meet in some way the varying needs of a whole family in the context of their community inevitably raises the question of whether this role can be accomplished by one person. Many studies of families of mentally handicapped children have concluded that what parents want most is to deal with a 'key person', who can coordinate all the information and services in a coherent way, and to whom the family can always turn for advice (Warnock, 1978; Russell, 1983). Some preschool programmes interpret this as requiring a 'transdisciplinary' approach, i.e. that professional workers will have to expand their skills and function effectively out of their area of primary specialisation (e.g. Brynelsen, 1983). Other approaches stress the benefits of a multidisciplinary team, with the parents as full members of the team (e.g. Beveridge et al., 1982). In either case, a great deal of good back-up communication between professionals of different disciplines is called for. The training of professionals, particularly for the transdisciplinary model of working, will need to be carefully considered, examining their attitudes about parents as well as their skills in child development, fostering non-directive, cooperative and experimental approaches to working rather than following routine answers.

SUMMING UP

The basic standpoint taken in this chapter on the question of evaluation research is that it is not now sufficient for professional staff to say simply that an intervention programme has been successful for many parents. Firstly, what criterion of success is being used? If it is merely the number of record sheets filled in, it may disguise the extent to which a lot of extra pressure has been put on a parent; or the father has felt cut off from feeling competent in caring for his child; or parents have been encouraged to insist on the child always doing things the 'correct way', leaving little room for the child to explore possibilities and for the parents to be responsive to the child's initiations, etc.

Secondly, what about the families who drop out? Did they find the extra pressure too much, or the intervention philosophy of teaching alien? Professional workers have to understand more fully what they are suggesting parents undertake, and to be guided by them as much as vice versa. The aim should be to build in maximum flexibility, rather than new service structures, and respect for how and why parents already do what they do.

The research review was undertaken in order to survey a wide range of topics of relevance to the families of young mentally handicapped children, and in particular to describe individual differences among parents in ways which would be of relevance to improving intervention strategies, in the context of a coherent conceptual framework for such intervention. However, the question of how finally to apply knowledge of individual differences in practice cannot really be answered - it implies being able to make judgements about what is and is not currently appropriate in how parents and children live together. The current state of research findings in the field cannot inform such judgements. Therefore the way forward suggested is:

a) to describe in a structured way how families currently act and think on a number of levels, and to intervene on a rational basis where it seems justified (e.g. if the pressure for concentrated daily interaction with the child felt by parents seems unwarrantedly great). The important caveat would be to question making easy judgements about appropriateness on the basis of patterns in living with non-handicapped children.

b) to replicate such studies as there are, in similar and differing situations, with fathers as well as mothers involved, with children of differing characteristics, taking multiple measures so that interpretation is not confounded.

c) to conduct intervention in such a way that it informs research, and vice versa. Long-term interventions with families provide an opportunity to observe the process of development, and to generate and test longitudinally hypotheses about the factors in an individual child's social environment which influence development. From the basis of broadly conceived monitoring of family functioning, opportunity will then be created for group studies to evaluate comparatively the effectiveness of various options in intervention strategy in relation to particular family characteristics. This will be an important stage in advancement of knowledge about families and young mentally handicapped children, testing out current working assumptions as controlled research hypotheses, attempting to unravel causal paths in the interrelationships between various patterns of parent-child interaction and family coping in daily living. Such a basis of research knowledge to guide intervention seems achievable from the current ferment of ideas and activity in the field of childhood disablility. Informed flexibility in intervention strategies, within a framework of partnership between parents and professionals, seems a worthwhile goal in the promotion of positive child development and the mutual adaptiveness of children and the environments in which they live.

REFERENCES

Abramson, L.Y., Seligman, M.E.P. & Teasdale, J.D. (1979). Learned helplessness in humans - critique and reformulation. Journal of Abnormal Psychology, 87, 49-74

Adams, J.L., Campbell, F.A. & Ramey, C.T. (1984). Infants' home environments: a study of screening efficiency. American Journal of Mental Deficiency, 89, 133-139

Adubato, S.A., Adams, M.K. & Budd, K.S. (1981). Teaching a parent to train a spouse in child management techniques. Journal of Applied Behavior Analysis, 14, 193-205

Affleck, G., Allen, D.A., McGrade, B.J. & McQueeney, M. (1982). Home environments of developmentally disabled infants as a function of parent and infant characteristics. American Journal of Mental Deficiency, 86, 445-452

Affleck, G., Allen, D.A., McGrade, B.J. & McQueeney, M. (1984). Factors associated with parents' and professionals' perceptions of infants in an early intervention programme. Applied Research in Mental Retardation 5, 305-316

Affleck, G., McGrade, B.J., McQueeney, M. & Allen, D.A. (1982). Relationship-focussed early intervention in developmental disabilities. Exceptional Children, 49, 259-261

Ainsworth, M.D.S. & Bell, S.M. (1969). Some contemporary patterns of mother-infant interaction in the feeding situation. In A. Ambrose (ed.) Stimulation in Early Infancy. London: Academic Press. pp.133-170

Allen, D.A., Affleck, G., McQueeney, M. & McGrade, B.J. (1982). Validation of the Parent Behavior Progression in an early intervention program. Mental Retardation, 20 (4), 159-163

References

Als, H., Lester, B.M., Tronick, E.Z. & Brazelton, T.B. (1982). Manual for the Assessment of Preterm Infants' Behavior (APIB). In H.E. Fitzgerald, B.M. Lester & M.W. Yogman (eds) Theory and Research in Behavioral Pediatrics, vol.1. New York: Plenum Press. pp.65-132

Appell, M., Williams, C. & Fishell, K. (1964). Changes in attitudes of parents of retarded children effected through group counselling. American Journal of Mental Deficiency, 68, 807-812

Arco, C.M.B. & McCluskey, K.A. (1981). 'A change of pace': an investigation of the salience of maternal temporal style in mother-infant play. Child Development, 52, 941-949

Ashby, G., McGaw, B., Perry, R. & Grant, J. (1978). The Pre-School Correspondence Program: An Overview. Queensland: Department of Education

Atkin, J. & Bastiani, J. (1984). Preparing Teachers to Work with Parents: a Survey of Initial Training. University of Nottingham School of Education

Attwood, T. (1978). The Croydon workshop for parents of pre-school mentally handicapped children. Child: Care, Health and Development, 4, 79-97

Ayer, S. & Alaszewski, A. (1984). Community Care and the Mentally Handicapped. Beckenham: Croom Helm

Bakeman, R. & Brown, J.V. (1977). Behavioral dialogues: an approach to the assessment of mother-infant interaction. Child Development, 48, 195-203

Bakeman, R. & Brown, J.V. (1980). Early interaction: consequences for social and mental development at three years. Child Development, 51, 437-447

Baker, B.L. (1977). Support systems for the parent as therapist. In P. Mittler (ed.) Research to Practice in Mental Retardation, vol.1. Baltimore: University Park Press. pp.213-219

Baker, B.L. (1984). Intervention with families with young, severely handicapped children. In J. Blacher (ed.) Severely Handicapped Young Children and their Families. London: Academic Press. pp.319-375

Baker, B.L., Brightman, A.J., Heifetz, L.J. & Murphy, D.M. (1976). Steps to Independence Series (for parents of retarded children). Champaign, Illinois: Research Press

Baker, B.L. & Clark, D.B. (1983). The family setting: enhancing the retarded child's development through parent training. In K.T. Kernan, M.J. Begab & R.B. Edgerton (eds.)

Environments and Behavior. Baltimore: University Park Press

Baker, B.L., Clark, D.B. & Yasuda, P.M. (1981). Predictors of success in parent training. In P. Mittler (ed.) Frontiers of Knowledge in Mental Retardation, vol. 1. Baltimore: University Park Press. pp.281-291

Baker, B.L., Heifetz, L.J. & Murphy, D.M. (1980). Behavioral training for parents of mentally retarded children: one-year follow-up. American Journal of Mental Deficiency, 85 (1), 31-38

Baker, B.L., Prieto-Bayard, M. & McCurry, M. (1984). Lower socioeconomic status families and programs for training parents of retarded children. In J.M. Berg (ed.) Perspectives and Progress in Mental Retardation, vol.1. Baltimore: University Park Press. pp.459-468

Baldwin, S. (1977). Disabled Children: Counting the Costs. London: Disability Alliance

Baldwin, V.L., Fredericks, H.D.B. & Brodsky, G. (1973). Isn't It Time He Outgrew This? or A Training Program for Parents of Retarded Children. Springfield, Illinois: Charles C. Thomas

Ball, T.S., Coyne, A., Jarvis, R.M. & Pease, S.S. (1984). Parents of retarded children as teaching assistants for other parents. Education and Training of the Mentally Retarded, 19 (1), 64-69

Barna, S., Bidder, R.T., Gray, O.P., Clements, J. & Gardner, S. (1980). The progress of developmentally delayed pre-school children in home-teaching schemes. Child: Care, Health and Development, 6, 157-164

Barnard, K.E. (1981). An ecological approach to parent-child relations. In C.C. Brown (ed.) Infants at Risk: Assessment and Intervention. Pediatric Round Table, Vol. 5. Johnson and Johnson. pp.89-96

Barnard, K.E., Bee, H. & Hammond, M. (1984). Developmental changes in maternal interactions with term and preterm infants. Infant Behavior and Development, 7, 101-113

Barnett, R.C. & Baruch, G.K. (1978). The Competent Woman. New York: Irvington Publishers

Barsch, R.H. (1968). The Parent of the Handicapped Child. The Study of Child-Rearing Practices. Springfield, Illinois: Charles C. Thomas

Barton, K. & Ericksen, L.K. (1981). Differences between mothers and fathers in teaching style and child-rearing practices. Psychological

Reports, 49, 237-238

Baskett, L.M. & Johnson, S.M. (1982). The young child's interactions with parents versus siblings: a behavioral analysis. Child Development, 53, 643-650

Bates, E. (1971). The development of conversational skill in 2, 3 and 4 year olds. Unpublished paper, University of Chicago. (Cited in D.R. Mitchell (1980). Down's syndrome children in structured dyadic communication situations with their parents. In J. Hogg & P. Mittler (eds) Advances in Mental Handicap Research, vol.1. Chichester: Wiley.)

Bates, J.E. & Pettit, G.S. (1981). Adult individual differences as moderators of child effects. Journal of Abnormal Child Psychology, 9, 329-340

Battersby, S. (1982). A comparison of fathers' and mothers' speech to their young Down's syndrome children. Unpublished B.Sc. thesis, City of Manchester College of Education, Manchester

Baumrind, D. (1967). Child care practices anteceding three patterns of pre-school behavior. Genetic Psychology Monographs, 76, 43-88

Baumrind, D. (1971). Current patterns of parental authority. Developmental Psychology Monographs, 4, 1-103

Baumrind, D. (1972). An exploratory study of socialization effects on black children: some black-white comparisons. Child Development, 43, 261-267

Beail, N. (1985). Personal communication. (Psychology Department, St. Luke's Hospital, Huddersfield)

Beail, N. & McGuire, J. (1982). Fathers: Psychological Perspectives. London: Junction Books

Becker, W.C. & Krug, R.S. (1965). The parent attitude research instrument: a research review. Child Development, 36, 329-365

Beckman, P.J. (1983). Influence of selected child characteristics on stress in families of handicapped infants. American Journal of Mental Deficiency, 88, 150-156

Beckman, P.J. (1984). A transactional view of stress in families of handicapped children. In M. Lewis (ed.) Beyond the Dyad. New York: Plenum Press. pp.281-298

Bee, H.L., Barnard, K.E., Eyres, S.J., Gray, C.A., Hammond, M.A., Spietz, A.L., Snyder, C. & Clark, B. (1982). Prediction of IQ and language skill from perinatal status, child performance, family characteristics and mother-infant interaction. Child Development, 53, 1134-1156

Bee, H.L., Van Egeren, L.F., Streissguth, A.P., Nyman, B.A. & Leckie, M.S. (1969). Social class differences in maternal teaching strategies and speech patterns. Developmental Psychology, 1, 726-734

Bell, R.Q. (1964). The effect on the family of a limitation in coping ability in the child: a research approach and a finding. Merrill-Palmer Quarterly, 10, 129-142

Belsky, J. (1979). Mother-father-infant interaction: a naturalistic observational study. Developmental Psychology, 15, 601-607

Belsky, J. (1980). Mother-infant interaction at home and in the laboratory: a comparative study. Journal of Genetic Psychology, 137, 37-47

Belsky, J. (1981). Early human experience: a family perspective. Developmental Psychology, 17, 3-23

Belsky, J., Gilstrap, B. & Rovine, M. (1984). The Pennsylvania Infant and Family Development Project, I: Stability and change in mother-infant and father-infant interaction in a family setting at one, three and nine months. Child Development, 55, 692-705

Belsky, J., Goode, M.K. & Most, R.K. (1980). Maternal stimulation and infant exploratory competence: cross-sectional, correlational and experimental analyses. Child Development, 51, 1163-1178

Belsky, J., Robins, E. & Gamble, W. (1984). The determinants of parental competence: toward a contextual theory. In M. Lewis (ed.) Beyond the Dyad. New York: Plenum Press. pp.251-27

Bendall, S. (1985). National Portage survey: preliminary results. In B. Daly, J. Addington, S. Kerfoot & A. Sigston (eds) Portage: The Importance of Parents. Windsor: NFER Nelson

Bentovim, A. (1972a). Emotional disturbance of handicapped pre-school children and their families: attitudes to the child. British Medical Journal, 3, 579-581

Bentovim, A. (1972b). Handicapped pre-school children and their families; effects on child's early emotional development. British Medical Journal, 3, 634-637

Berger, J. (1980). Early development of social signalling, attentional and communicative behaviours in Down's syndrome and non-handicapped infants. Unpublished Ph.D.

thesis, Faculty of Education, University of Manchester
Berger, J. & Cunningham, C.C. (1981a). Early development of social interactions in Down's syndrome and non-handicapped infants. In Finland Speaks: the Report of the EASE 80 Conference, Helsinki, August
Berger, J. & Cunningham, C.C. (1981b). The development of eye contact between mothers and normal versus Down's syndrome infants. Developmental Psychology, 17, 678-689
Berger, J. & Cunningham, C.C. (1983). The development of early vocal behaviour and interactions in Down's syndrome and non-handicapped infant-mother pairs. Developmental Psychology, 19 (3), 322-331
Berger, J. & Cunningham, C.C. (1985). Aspects of early social smiling by infants with Down's syndrome. Child: Care, Health and Development, 12 (in press)
Berger, M. (1979). Behaviour modification in education and professional practice: the dangers of a mindless technology. Bulletin of the British Psychological Society, 32, 418-419
Berger, M. & Foster, M. (1976). Family-level interventions for retarded children: a multivariate approach to issues and strategies. Multivariate Experimental Clinical Research, 2 (1), 1-21
Berko-Gleason, J. (1975). Fathers and other strangers: men's speech to young children. In D. Dato (ed.) Developmental Psycholinguistics: Theory and Applications. Washington, D.C.: Georgetown University Press. pp.289-297
Berkowitz, B.P. & Graziano, A.M. (1972). Training parents as behaviour therapists: a review. Behaviour, Research and Therapy, 10, 297-317
Bernal, M.E., Gibson, D.M., Williams, D.E. & Pesses, D.I. (1971). A device for recording automatic audio tape recording. Journal of Applied Behavior Analysis, 4, 151-156
Bernstein, B. & Young, D. (1967). Social class differences in conceptions of the uses of toys. Sociology, 1, 131-140
Berry, I. & Wood, J. (1981). The evaluation of parent intervention with young handicapped children. Behavioural Psychotherapy, 9, 358-368
Beveridge, S. (1982). Parent-teaching work: the development of the parent-teaching course at Anson House. In S. Beveridge, R. Flanagan, H. McConachie & J. Sebba, Parental Involvement in

References

Anson House. Anson House Preschool Project Paper 3. Barkingside: Barnardo's. pp.45-54

Beveridge, S. (1985). *Parent Teaching Work*. Anson House Preschool Project View Publication 10. Barkingside: Barnardo's

Beveridge, S., Flanagan, R., McConachie, H. & Sebba, J. (1982). *Parental Involvement in Anson House*. Anson House Preschool Project Paper 3. Barkingside: Barnardo's

Bidder, R.T., Bryant, G. & Gray, O.P. (1975). Benefits to Down's syndrome children through training their mothers. *Archives of Disease in Childhood*, *50*, 383-386

Bidder, R.T., Hewitt, K.E. & Gray, O.P. (1983). Evaluation of teaching methods in a home-based training scheme for developmentally delayed pre-school children. *Child: Care, Health and Development*, *9*, 1-12

Bigner, J.A. (1974). A Wernerian developmental analysis of children's descriptions of siblings. *Child Development*, *45*, 317-323

Birenbaum, A. (1971). The mentally retarded child in the home and the family cycle. *Journal of Health and Social Behavior*, *12*, 55-65

Blacher, J. (1984a) *Severely Handicapped Young Children and Their Families: Research in Review*. Orlando, Florida: Academic Press

Blacher, J. (1984b). Sequential stages of parental adjustment to the birth of a child with handicaps: fact or artifact? *Mental Retardation*, *22*, 55-68

Blacher, J. & Meyers, C.E. (1983). A review of attachment formation and disorder of handicapped children. *American Journal of Mental Deficiency*, *87*, 359-371

Bluma, S., Shearer, M., Frohman, A. & Hilliard, J. (1976). *Portage Guide to Early Education*. Wisconsin: Cooperative Educational Service Agency 12

Blurton-Jones, N. (1980). Observing parent-child interaction at home. Paper given to the Fatherhood Research Group, Institute of Education, London

Boles, G. (1959). Personality factors in mothers of cerebral palsied children. *Genetic Psychology Monographs*, *59*, 159-218

Booth, T. (1978). From normal baby to handicapped child: unravelling the idea of subnormality in families of mentally handicapped children. *Sociology*, *12*, 203-221

Boston, S. (1981). *Will, My Son: The Life and Death*

of a Mongol Child. London: Pluto Press

Boucher, J. (1981). Parents as partners. Paper given to Extra Mural course, Faculty of Education, University of Manchester, November

Bowlby, J. (1951). Maternal Care and Mental Health. Geneva: World Health Organisation

Bowlby, J. (1969). Attachment and Loss, Vol.1: Attachment. New York: Basic Books

Boyce, W.T., Jensen, E.W., James, S.A. & Peacock, J.L. (1983). The Family Routines inventory: theoretical origins. Social Science and Medicine, 17, 193-200

Boyd, R.D., Stauber, K.A. & Bluma, S.M. (1977). Portage Parent Program: Instructor's Manual. Wisconsin: Cooperative Educational Service Agency 12

Bradley, R.H. & Caldwell, B.M. (1976). The relation of infants' home environment to mental test performance at fifty-four months: a follow-up study. Child Development, 47, 1172-1174

Bradley, R.H. & Caldwell, B.M. (1978). Screening the environment. American Journal of Orthopsychiatry, 48, 114-130

Bradley, R.H. & Caldwell, B.M. (1979). Home observation for measurement of the environment: a revision of the pre-school scale. American Journal of Mental Deficiency, 84 (3), 235-244

Bradley, R.H. & Caldwell, B.M. (1984). The HOME Inventory and family demographics. Developmental Psychology, 20, 315-320

Bradshaw, J. & Lawton, D. (1975). Tracing the Causes of Stress in Families with Handicapped Children. York: University of York Publication

Bradshaw, J. & Lawton, D. (1978). Tracing the causes of stress in families with handicapped children. British Journal of Social Work, 8, 181-192

Brassell, W.R. (1977). Intervention with handicapped infants: correlates of progress. Mental Retardation, 15 (4), 18-22

Brazelton, T.B. (1976). Case finding, screening, diagnosis and tracking: Discussant's comments. In T.D. Tjossem (ed.) Intervention Strategies for High Risk Infants and Young Children. Baltimore: University Park Press. pp.325-331

Brazelton, T.B. (1981). (Discussion of paper 'Predicting developmental outcome: resume and redirection' by R.B. McCall.) In C.C. Brown (ed.) Infants at Risk: Assessment and Intervention. Pediatric Round Table, Vol. 5. Johnson and Johnson. p.69

References

Brazelton, T.B., Tronick, E., Adamson, L., Als, H. & Wise, S. (1975). Early mother-infant reciprocity. In Parent-Infant Interaction. Ciba Foundation Symposium 33. Amsterdam: Associated Scientific Publishers

Breiner, J. & Beck, S. (1984). Parents as change agents in the management of their developmentally delayed children's compliant behaviors: a critical review. Applied Research in Mental Retardation, 5, 259-278

Breiner, J. & Forehand, R. (1982). Mother-child interactions: a comparison of a clinic-referred developmentally delayed group and two non-delayed groups. Applied Research in Mental Retardation, 3, 175-183

Breslau, N. (1982). Siblings of disabled children: birth order and age spacing effects. Journal of Abnormal Child Psychology, 10 (1), 85-96

Breslau, N., Weitzman, M. & Messenger, K. (1981). Psychologic functioning of siblings of disabled children. Pediatrics, 67, 344-353

Bricker, D.D. & Casuso, V. (1977). Family involvement: a critical component of early intervention. Unpublished manuscript, Debbie Institute, Mailman Centre for Child Development, University of Miami

Bricker, W.A. & Bricker, D.D. (1976). The infant, toddler, and pre-school research and intervention project. In T.D. Tjossem (ed.) Intervention Strategies for High Risk Infants and Young Children. Baltimore: University Park Press. pp.545-572

Brierley, D.W. (1967). The use of personality constructs by children of different ages. Unpublished Ph.D. thesis, University of Manchester

Bright, M.C. & Stockdale, D.F. (1984). Mothers', fathers', and preschool children's interactive behaviors in a play setting. Journal of Genetic Psychology, 144, 219-232

Brightman, R.P., Ambrose, S.A. & Baker, B.L. (1980). Parent-training: a school-based model for enhancing teaching performance. Child Behavior Therapy, 2 (3), 35-47

Brightman, R.P., Baker, B.L., Clark, D.B. & Ambrose, S.A. (1982). Effectiveness of alternative parent training formats. Journal of Behavior Therapy and Experimental Psychiatry, 13, 113-117

Bristol, M.M. (1982). Families at risk. In Carolina Institute for Research on Early Education for the Handicapped, Final Report. Chapel Hill: University of North Carolina

Brody, G.F. (1969). Maternal child-rearing attitudes and child behavior. Developmental Psychology, 1, 66

Bromwich, R.M. (1981). Working with Parents and Infants: An Interactional Approach. Baltimore: University Park Press

Bronfenbrenner, U. (1976). Is early intervention effective? Facts and principles of early intervention: a summary. In A.M. Clarke & A.D.B. Clarke (eds) Early Experience - Myth and Evidence. London: Open Books. pp.247-305

Bronfenbrenner, U. (1977). Toward an experimental ecology of human development. American Psychologist, 32, 513-531

Brooks-Gunn, J. & Lewis, M. (1984). Maternal responsivity in interactions with handicapped infants. Child Development, 55, 782-793

Brophy, J. (1970). Mothers as teachers of their own preschool children: the influence of socio-economic status and task structure on teaching specificity. Child Development, 41, 79-94

Brown, G.W. & Harris, T. (1978). The Social Origins of Depression: A Study of Psychiatric Disorder in Women. London: Tavistock

Brown, G.W. & Rutter, M. (1966). The measurement of family activities and relationships. Human Relations, 19, 241-263

Brown, R. (1974). One of Seven is Special: Home Training of a Retarded Child. London: National Society for Mentally Handicapped Children

Bruner, J. (1976). The nature and use of immaturity. In K. Connolly & J. Bruner (eds) The Growth of Competence. London: Academic Press

Brynelsen, D. (1983). Infant Development Programmes in British Columbia. In P. Mittler & H. McConachie (eds) Parents, Professionals and Mentally Handicapped People: Approaches to Partnership. Beckenham: Croom Helm/ Cambridge, MA: Brookline Books. pp.77-90

Bubolz, M.M. & Whiren, A.P. (1984). The family of the handicapped: an ecological model for policy and practice. Family Relations, 33, 5-12

Buckhalt, J.A., Rutherford, R.B. & Goldberg, K.E. (1978). Verbal and non-verbal interaction of mothers with their Down's syndrome and nonretarded infants. American Journal of Mental Deficiency, 82 (4), 337-343

Buckley, S. (1981). Parents as partners - are we

sometimes asking too much? Early Childhood, 2 (1), 15-16

Buckley, S. (1984). The influence of family variables on children's progress on Portage. In T. Dessent (ed.) What is Important about Portage?. Windsor: NFER-Nelson. pp.21-28

Buckley, S. (1985). Teaching parents to teach reading to teach language - A project with Down's syndrome children and their parents. In K. Topping & S. Wolfendale (eds) Parental Involvement in Children's Reading. Beckenham: Croom Helm/ New York: Nichols

Budoff, M. & Siperstein, G.N. (1978). Low-income children's attitudes toward mentally retarded children: effects of labeling and academic behavior. American Journal of Mental Deficiency, 82, 474-479

Buium, N., Rynders, J. & Turnure, J. (1974). Early maternal linguistic environment of normal and Down's syndrome language learning children. American Journal of Mental Deficiency, 79, 52-58

Burden, R.L. (1978). An approach to the evaluation of early intervention projects with mothers of severely handicapped children: the attiude dimension. Child: Care, Health and Development, 4 (3), 171-181

Burden, R.L. (1980). Measuring the effects of stress on the mothers of handicapped infants: must depression always follow? Child: Care, Health and Development, 6, 111-125

Burden, R.L. (1981). Some problems in assessing and meeting the needs of mothers of severely handicapped infants: with specific reference to the evaluation of early intervention projects. Unpublished Ph.D. thesis, University of Exeter

Burden, R.L. (1985). Can parental adjustment to handicap be measured? Dreams, hopes and reality. Educational and Child Psychology, 2 (1), 33-39

Butler, N., Gill, R., Pomeroy, D. & Fewtrell, J. (1978). Handicapped Children: Their Homes and Life Styles. University of Bristol, Department of Child Health

Byrne, E.A. & Cunningham, C.C. (1985) The effects of mentally handicapped children on families - a conceptual review. Journal of Child Psychology and Psychiatry, 26 (6), 847-864

References

Cain, L.F. & Levine, S. (1963). Effects of community and institutional school programs on trainable mentally retarded children. Research monograph, Council for Exceptional Children. (Summarised in D. Pilling (1973). The Handicapped Child: Research Review, vol. 3. London: Longman and National Children's Bureau.)

Caldwell, B.M. (1969). A new 'approach' to behavioral ecology. In J.P. Hill (ed.) Minnesota Symposia on Child Psychology, vol. 2 Minneapolis: University of Minnesota Press.

Caldwell, B.M. & Guze, S.B. (1960). A study of the adjustment of parents and siblings of institutionalised and non-institutionalised retarded children. American Journal of Mental Deficiency, 64, 845-861

Callias, M. & Carr, J. (1975). Behaviour modification programmes in a community setting. In C.C. Kiernan & F.P. Woodford (eds) Behaviour Modification with the Severely Retarded. IRMMH Study Group 8. Amsterdam: Associated Scientific Publishers. pp.147-173

Campbell, S.B. (1973). Mother-child interaction in reflective, impulsive and hyperactive children. Developmental Psychology, 8, 341-349

Candy, A. (1976). A Long Way to Manhood. London: National Society for Mentally Handicapped Children

Canino, F.J. & Reeve, R.E. (1980). General issues in working with parents of handicapped children. In R.R. Abidin (ed.) Parent Education and Intervention Handbook. Springfield, Illinois: Charles C. Thomas. pp.82-106

Cardoso-Martins, C. & Mervis, C.B. (1985). Maternal speech to prelinguistic children with Down syndrome. American Journal of Mental Deficiency, 89, 451-458

Carnegie United Kingdom Trust (1964). Handicapped Children and their Families. Dunfermline: Carnegie UK Trust

Carr, J. (1975). Young Children with Down's Syndrome: Their Development, Upbringing and Effect on their Families. London: Butterworths

Carr, J. (1985). Six weeks to twenty-one years old: a longitudinal study of children with Down's syndrome and their families. Paper presented to Association for Child Psychology and Psychiatry annual conference, Guy's Hospital, London, July

Carr, J. & Hewett, S. (1982). Children with Down's syndrome growing up: a preliminary report. Association for Child Psychology and Psychiatry

News, no. 10, 10-13

Cheseldine, S. (1977). Parent-child interaction and language facilitation with the mentally handicapped. Unpublished Ph.D. thesis, University of Manchester

Cheseldine, S. & McConkey, R. (1979). Parental speech to young Down's syndrome children: an intervention study. *American Journal of Mental Deficiency*, *83*, 612-620

Chetwynd, S.J. (1985). Factors contributing to stress on mothers caring for an intellectually handicapped child. *British Journal of Social Work*, *15*, 295-304

Chetwynd, S.J. & Hartnett, O. (1978). *The Sex Role System*. London: Routledge and Kegan Paul

Chibucos, T.R. & Kail, P.R. (1981). Longitudinal examination of father-infant interaction and infant-father attachment. *Merrill-Palmer Quarterly*, *27*, 81-97

Christensen, A., Phillips, S., Glasgow, R.E. & Johnson, S.M. (1983). Parental characteristics and interactional dysfunction in families with child behavior problems: a preliminary investigation. *Journal of Abnormal Child Psychology*, *11* (1), 153-165

Christopherson, S.R., Arnold, C.M., Hill, D.W. & Quilitch, H.R. (1972). The Home Point System: token reinforcement procedures for application by parents of children with behavior problems. *Journal of Applied Behavior Analysis*, *5*, 485-497

Clark, D.B. & Baker, B.L. (1983). Predicting outcome in parent training. *Journal of Consulting and Clinical Psychology*, *51*, 309-311

Clark, D.B., Baker, B.L. & Heifetz, L.J. (1982). Behavioral training for parents of mentally retarded children: prediction of outcome. *American Journal of Mental Deficiency*, *87*, 14-19

Clarke, A.M. & Clarke, A.D.B. (1976). *Early Experience: Myth and Evidence*. London: Open Books

Clarke-Stewart, K.A. (1973). Interactions between mothers and their young children: characteristics and consequences. *Monographs of the Society for Research in Child Development*, *38* (153), 1-109

Clarke-Stewart, K.A. (1977). *Child Care in the Family: A Review of Research and Some Propositions for Policy*. New York: Academic Press

References

Clarke-Stewart, K.A. (1978). And Daddy makes three: the father's impact on mother and young child. Child Development, 49 (2), 466-478

Clarke-Stewart, K.A. (1980). The father's contribution to children's cognitive and social development in early childhood. In F. Pedersen (ed.) The Father-Infant Relationship. New York: Praeger. pp.111-163

Clarke-Stewart, K.A. & Hevey, C. (1981). Longitudinal relations in repeated observations of mother-child interaction from 1 to 2-1/2 years. Developmental Psychology, 17, 127-145

Clarke-Stewart, K.A., VanderStoep, L.P. & Killian, G.A. (1979). Analysis and replication of mother-child relations at two years of age. Child Development, 50, 777-793

Clements, J. (1985). Update: Training parents of mentally handicapped children. Association for Child Psychology and Psychiatry Newsletter, 7 (4), 2-9

Clements, J., Evans, C., Jones, C., Osborne, K. & Upton, G. (1981). The Development and Evaluation of an Assessment-Linked Early Language Training Scheme for the Mentally Handicapped Child. Gwent Area Health Authority

Clements, J., Evans, C., Jones, C., Osborne, K. & Upton, G. (1982). Evaluation of a home-based language training programme with severely mentally handicapped children. Behaviour, Research and Therapy, 20, 243-249

Cleveland, D.W. & Miller, N. (1977). Attitudes and life commitments of older siblings of mentally retarded adults: an exploratory study. Mental Retardation, 15 (3), 38-41

Clezy, G. (1984). Interactive analysis. In D.J. Muller (ed.) Remediating Children's Language. Beckenham: Croom Helm/ San Diego: College Hill Press. pp.85-112

Cohen, N.L. & Tomlinson-Keasey, C. (1980). The effects of peers and mothers on toddlers' play. Child Development, 51 (3), 921-924

Cohler, B.J., Weiss, J.L. & Grunebaum, H.U. (1970). Child-care attitudes and emotional disturbance among mothers of young children. Genetic Psychology Monographs, 82, 3-47

Cole, C. & Morrow, W.R. (1976). Refractory parent behaviors in behavior modification training groups. Psychotherapy: Theory, Research and Practice, 13, 162-169

Coleman, M., Ganong, L. & Brown, G.E. (1981). Effects of multimedia instruction on mothers'

ability to teach cognitive skills to preschool children. _Journal of Social Psychology_, _115_ (1), 89-94
Collins, M. & Collins, D. (1976). _Kith and Kids_. London: Souvenir Press
Connolly, J.A. (1978). Intelligence levels of Down syndrome children. _American Journal of Mental Deficiency_, _83_, 193-196
Consortium on Developmental Continuity (1977). _The Persistence of Preschool Effects: A Long-Term Follow-Up of Fourteen Infant and Preschool Experiments_. Final report to U.S. Office of Human Development Services, Administration on Children, Youth and Families. Washington, D.C.: U.S. Government
Cook, J.J. (1963). Dimensional analysis of child-rearing attitudes of parents of handicapped children. _American Journal of Mental Deficiency_, _68_, 354-361
Cooke, K. & Lawton, D. (1984). Informal support for the carers of disabled children. _Child: Care, Health and Development_, _10_, 67-79
Cooke, K. & Lawton, D. (1985). Housing circumstances and standards of families with disabled children. _Child: Care, Health and Development_, _11_, 71-79
Cooper, E.S., Costello, A.J., Douglas, J.W.B., Ingleby, J.D. & Turner, R.K. (1974). Direct observation? _Bulletin of the British Psychological Society_, _27_, 3-7
Cooper, J. & McNeil, J. (1968). A study of house-proud housewives and their interaction with their children. _Journal of Child Psychology and Psychiatry_, _9_, 173-188
Cowart, J.D., Iwata, B.A. & Poynter, H. (1984). Generalization and maintenance in training parents of the mentally retarded. _Applied Research in Mental Retardation_, _5_, 233-244
Cox, A. (1975). The assessment of parental behaviour. _Journal of Child Psychology and Psychiatry_, _16_, 255-259
Cox, K.M. & Cattell, J. (1985). Parents: problems or partners? _Educational and Child Psychology_, _2_, 10-16
Cramblit, N.S. & Siegel, G.M. (1977). The verbal environment of a language-impaired child. _Journal of Speech and Hearing Disorders_, _42_, 474-482
Crawley, S.B. & Spiker, D. (1983). Mother-child interactions involving two-year-olds with Down syndrome: a look at individual differences.

Child Development, 54, 1312-1323

Crittenden, P.M. & Bonvillian, J.D. (1984). The relationship between maternal risk status and maternal sensitivity. American Journal of Orthopsychiatry, 54 (2), 250-262

Crnic, K.A., Friedrich, W.N. & Greenberg, M.T. (1983). Adaptation of families with mentally retarded children: a model of stress, coping and family ecology. American Journal of Mental Deficiency, 88, 125-138

Crnic, K.A., Greenberg, M.T., Ragozin, A.S., Robinson, N.M. & Basham, R.B. (1983). Effects of stress and social support on mothers and premature and full-term infants. Child Development, 54, 209-217

Crnic, K.A., Ragozin, A.S., Greenberg, M.T., Robinson, N.M. & Basham, R.B. (1983). Social interaction and developmental competence of preterm and full-term infants during the first year of life. Child Development, 54, 1199-1210

Crown, S. & Crisp, A.H. (1970). Manual of the Middlesex Hospital Questionnaire. Barnstaple: Psychologic Test Publications

Cummings, S.T. (1976). The impact of the child's deficiency on the father: a study of fathers of mentally retarded and of chronically ill children. American Journal of Orthopsychiatry, 46, 246-255

Cummings, S.T., Bailey, H.C. & Rie, H.E. (1966). Effects of the child's deficiency on the mother: a study of mothers of mentally retarded, chronically ill and neurotic children. American Journal of Orthopsychiatry, 36, 595-609

Cunningham, C.C. (1975). Parents as therapists and educators. In C.C. Kiernan & F.P. Woodford (eds) Behaviour Modification with the Severely Retarded. IRMMH Study Group 8. Amsterdam: Associated Scientific Publishers. pp.175-193

Cunningham, C.C. (1982). Down's Syndrome: An Introduction for Parents. London: Souvenir Press

Cunningham, C.C. (1983a). Early Development and its Facilitation in Infants with Down's Syndrome. Final Report to the Department of Health and Social Security. Manchester: Hester Adrian Research Centre

Cunningham, C.C. (1983b). Early support and intervention: the Hester Adrian Research Centre Infant Project. In P. Mittler & H. McConachie (eds) Parents, Professionals and Mentally

Handicapped People: Approaches to Partnership. Beckenham: Croom Helm/ Cambridge, MA: Brookline Books. pp.91-110

Cunningham, C.C. (1984). The long term effects of early intervention with Down's syndrome infants. Seminar to Hester Adrian Research Centre, University of Manchester, June

Cunningham, C.C. (1985). Training and education approaches for parents of children with special needs. British Journal of Medical Psychology, 58, 285-305

Cunningham, C.C., Aumonier, M.E. & Sloper, P. (1982). Health visitor support for families with Down's syndrome infants. Child: Care, Health and Development, 8, 1-9

Cunningham, C.C. & Davis, H. (1985a). Early parent counselling. In M. Craft, J. Bicknell & S. Hollins (eds) Mental Handicap. London: Balliere-Tindall. pp.162-176

Cunningham, C.C. & Davis, H. (1985b). Working with Parents: Frameworks for Collaboration. Milton Keynes: Open University Press

Cunningham, C.C., Glenn, S.M., Wilkinson, P. & Sloper, P. (1985). Mental ability, symbolic play and receptive and expressive language of young children with Down's syndrome. Journal of Child Psychology and Psychiatry, 26, 255-265

Cunningham, C.C. & Jeffree, D.M. (1975). The organization and structure of workshops for parents of mentally handicapped children. Bulletin of the British Psychological Society, 28, 405-411

Cunningham, C.C., Morgan, P.A. & McGucken, R.P. (1984). Down's syndrome: is dissatisfaction with disclosure of diagnosis inevitable? Developmental Medicine and Child Neurology, 26, 33-39

Cunningham, C.E., Rueler, E., Blackwell J. & Deck J. (1981). Behavioral and linguistic developments in the interactions of normal and retarded children with their mothers. Child Development, 52, 62-70

Davie, C.E., Hutt, S.J., Vincent, E. & Mason, M. (1984). The Young Child at Home. Windsor: NFER-Nelson

Davies, A.J. & Hathaway, B.K. (1982). Reciprocity in parent-child verbal interactions. Journal of Genetic Psychology, 140, 169-183

Davis, H. (1979). An exploration of possible relationships between construing and behaviour in mothers. Unpublished Ph.D. thesis,

University of London
Davis, H. (1983). Constructs of handicap: working with parents and children. Changes, 1 (2), 37-39
Davis, H. (1985). Personal communication. (The London Hospital, Whitechapel Road, London.)
Davis, H. & Cunningham, C.C. (1985). Mental handicap: people in context. In E. Button (ed.) Personal Construct Theory and Mental Health. Beckenham: Croom Helm/ Cambridge, MA: Brookline Books. pp.246-261
Davis, H. & Oliver, B. (1980). A comparison of aspects of the maternal speech environment of retarded and non-retarded children. Child: Care, Health and Development, 6 (3), 135-145
Denhoff, E. & Hyman, I. (1976). Parent programs for developmental management. In T.D. Tjossem (ed.) Intervention Strategies for High Risk Infants and Young Children. Baltimore: University Park Press. pp.381-466
Department of Employment (1975). Women and Work: A Review. London: HMSO
Department of Health and Social Security (1972). Health and Personal Social Services Statistics for England and Wales. London: HMSO
Dessent, T. (1985). Parentology - a critique. Educational and Child Psychology, 2, 48-52
Dickie, J.R. & Gerber, S.C. (1980). Training in social competence: the effect on mothers, fathers and infants. Child Development, 51, 1248-1251
Dingman, H.F., Eyman, R.D. & Windle, C.D. (1963). An investigation of some child-rearing attitudes of mothers with retarded children. American Journal of Mental Deficiency, 67, 899-908
Dixon, N. & Flanagan, R. (1984). Meeting the Social Work Needs of Families with Mentally Handicapped Children. Anson House Preschool Project Paper 4. Barkingside: Barnardo's
Dixon, S.D., LeVine, R.A., Richman, A. & Brazelton, T.B. (1984). Mother-child interaction around a teaching task: an African-American comparison. Child Development, 55, 1252-1264
Dobson, C.A. (1980). Parental perceptions of mentally handicapped children. Unpublished M.Sc. thesis, University of Leicester
Douglas, J.W.B., Lawson, A., Cooper, J.E., & Cooper, E. (1968). Family interaction and the activities of young children. Journal of Child Psychology and Psychiatry, 9, 157-171
Dowdney, L., Skuse, D., Rutter, M., Quinton, D. &

Mrazek, D. (1985). The nature and qualities of parenting provided by women raised in institutions. Journal of Child Psychology and Psychiatry, 25, 599-625

Drotar, D., Baskiewicz, A., Irvin, N., Kennell, J. & Klaus, M. (1975). The adaptation of parents to the birth of an infant with a congenital malformation: a hypothetical model. Pediatrics, 56, 710-717

Dunn, J. (1975). Consistency and change in styles of mothering. In Parent-Infant Interaction. Ciba Foundation Symposium 33. Amsterdam: Associated Scientific Publishers

Dunn, J. (1984). Sisters and Brothers. London: Fontana

Dunn, J. & Kendrick, C. (1980). The arrival of a sibling: changes in patterns of interaction between mother and first-born child. Journal of Child Psychology and Psychiatry, 21, 119-132

Dunn, J. & Kendrick, C. (1982). Siblings: Love, Envy and Understanding. Oxford: Blackwell

Dupont, A. (1980). A study concerning the time-related and other burdens when severely handicapped children are reared at home. Acta Psychiatrica Scandinavia, Supplement 285, 62, 249-257

Eckenrode, J. (1983). The mobilisation of social supports: some individual constraints. American Journal of Community Psychology, 11, 509-528

Eheart, B.K. (1982). Mother-child interactions with non-retarded and mentally retarded preschoolers. American Journal of Mental Deficiency, 87, 20-25

Eheart, B.K. & Ciccone, J. (1982). Special needs of low-income mothers of developmentally delayed children. American Journal of Mental Deficiency, 87, 26-33

Elkins, J. (1981). Personal communication. (University of Queensland.)

Ellington, S.D. (1984). Grandmothers of mentally handicapped children. Unpublished Research project, Certificate in Social Work with Handicapped Children and Young People and their Families. Extra Mural Department, Manchester University

Elliott, F.R. (1978). Occupational commitments and paternal deprivation. Child: Care, Health and Development, 4, 305-315

Emde, R., Katz, E. & Thorpe, J. (1978). Emotional expression in infancy: II. Early deviations in Down's syndrome. In M. Lewis & L. Rosenblum (eds) The Development of Affect. New York: Plenum Press

Emerson, P., Hood, E., Pitt, I., Palmer, S. & Sinclair, A. (1981). Workshops for parents of mentally handicapped children. Journal of the Association of Educational Psychologists, 5 (6), 33-38

Enwemeka, C.S. & Adeghe, N.U. (1983). Some family problems associated with the presence of a child with handicap in Nigeria. Child: Care, Health and Development, 8, 133-140

Epstein, A.S. & Evans, J. (1979). Parent-child interaction and children's learning. High/Scope Report, no. 4, 39-43

Equal Opportunities Commission (1982). Caring for the Elderly and Handicapped: Community Care Policies and Women's Lives. Manchester: Equal Opportunities Commission

Erickson, G. (1976). The concept of personal network in clinical practice. Family Process, 14, 487-498

Erickson, M.T. (1969). MMPI profiles of parents of young retarded children. American Journal of Mental Deficiency, 73 (5), 728-732

Escalona, S.K. (1973). Basic modes of social interaction: their emergence and patterning during the first two years of life. Merrill-Palmer Quarterly, 19 (3), 205-232

Fagot, B.I. (1974). Sex differences in toddlers' behavior and parental reaction. Developmental Psychology, 10 (4), 554-558

Farber, B. (1959). Effects of a severely mentally retarded child on family integration. Monographs of the Society for Research in Child Development, 24 (71)

Farber, B. (1960). Family organization and crisis: maintenance of integration in families with a severely mentally retarded child. Monographs of the Society for Research in Child Development, 25 (75)

Farber, B. (1975). Family adaptations to severely mentally retarded children. In M.J. Begab & S.A. Richardson (eds) The Mentally Retarded and Society: A Social Science Perspective. Baltimore: University Park Press

Farber, B. & Lewis, M. (1975). The symbolic use of parents: a sociological critique of educational practice. Journal of Research and Development in Education, 8, 34-43

Farran, D.W. & Haskins, R. (1980). Reciprocal influence in the social interactions of mothers and three-year-old children from different socioeconomic backgrounds. Child Development, 51, 780-791

Farrell, P. (1982). An evaluation of an EDY course in behaviour modification techniques for teachers and care staff in an ESN(s) school. Special Education: Forward Trends, 9, 21-25

Featherstone, H. (1980). A Difference in the Family: Life with a Disabled Child. London: Harper and Row

Feinman, S. & Lewis, M. (1984). Is there social life beyond the dyad? In M. Lewis (ed.) Beyond the Dyad. New York: Plenum Press. pp.13-41

Feldman, W.S., Manella, K.J. & Varni, J.W. (1983). A behavioural parent training programme for single mothers of physically handicapped children. Child: Care, Health and Development, 9, 157-168

Ferguson, N. & Watt, J. (1980). Professionals and the parents of mentally handicapped children. Bulletin of the British Psychological Society, 33, 59-60

Ferrara, D.M. (1979). Attitudes of parents of mentally retarded children toward normalization activities. American Journal of Mental Deficiency, 84 (2), 145-151

Ferrari, M. (1984). Chronic illness: psychosocial effects on siblings - I. Chronically ill boys. Journal of Child Psychology and Psychiatry, 25, 459-476

Field, T.M. (1977a). Maternal stimulation during infant feeding. Developmental Psychology, 13, 539-540

Field, T.M. (1977b). Effects of early separation, interactive deficits, and experimental manipulations on infant-mother face-to-face interaction. Child Development, 48, 763-771

Field, T.M. (1978). Interaction behaviors of primary versus secondary caretaker fathers. Developmental Psychology, 14, 183-184

Field, T.M. (1981). Fathers' interactions with their high-risk infants. Infant Mental Health Journal, 2, 249-256

Field, T.M. & Ignatoff, E. (1981). Videotaping effects on the behaviors of low-income mothers and their infants during floor play interactions. Journal of Applied Developmental Psychology, 2, 227-235

Field, T.M. & Pawlby, S. (1980). Early face-to-face interactions of British and American working- and middle-class mother-infant dyads. Child

Development, 51 (1), 250-253
Filler, J.W. (1976). Modifying maternal teaching style: effects of task arrangement on the match-to-sample performance of retarded pre-school age children. American Journal of Mental Deficiency, 80, 602-612
Filler, J.W. & Bricker, W.A. (1976). Teaching styles of mothers and the match-to-sample performance of their retarded pre-school age children. American Journal of Mental Deficiency, 80 (5), 504-571
Firth, H. (1982). The effectiveness of parent workshops in a mental handicap service. Child: Care, Health and Development, 8, 77-91
Flanagan, S., Adams, H.E. & Forehand, R. (1979). A comparison of four instructional techniques for teaching parents to use time-out. Behavior Therapy, 10, 94-102
Forehand, R. & Atkeson, M. (1977). Generality of treatment effect with parents as therapists: a review of assessment and implementation procedures. Behavior Therapy, 8, 575-593
Foster, M., Berger, M. & McLean, M. (1981). Rethinking a good idea: a reassessment of parent involvement. Topics in Early Childhood Special Education, 1 (3), 55-65
Fox, A.M. (1974). "They Get this Training, But They Don't Really Know How You Feel". London: Action Research for the Crippled Child
Frankel, M.T. & Rollins, H.A. (1983). Does mother know best? Mothers and fathers interacting with preschool sons and daughters. Developmental Psychology, 19, 694-702
Fransella, F. (1972). Personal Change and Reconstruction: Research and Treatment of Stuttering. London: Academic Press
Fransella, F. & Bannister, D. (1977). A Manual for Repertory Grid Technique. London: Academic Press
Friedrich, W.N. (1979). Predictors of the coping behavior of mothers of handicapped children. Journal of Consulting and Clinical Psychology, 47, 1140-1141
Friedrich, W.N. & Friedrich, W.L. (1981). Psychosocial assets of parents of handicapped and non-handicapped children. American Journal of Mental Deficiency, 85, 551-553
Friedrich, W.N., Greenberg, M.T. & Crnic, K. (1983). A short-form of the Questionnaire on Resources and Stress. American Journal of Mental Deficiency, 88 (1), 41-48

Fuchs, J. (1974). The impact of mentally handicapped children on family routine, with particular reference to siblings. Unpublished M.Ed. thesis, Institute of Education, London

Gabel, H. & Kotsch, L.S. (1981). Extended families and young handicapped children. Topics in Early Childhood Special Education, 1 (3), 29-35

Gallagher, J.J. (1982). Characteristics of successful parents of moderately/severely handicapped children. In Carolina Institute for Research on Early Education for the Handicapped, Final Report. Chapel Hill: University of North Carolina

Gallagher, J.J., Beckman, P. & Cross, A.H. (1983). Families of handicapped children: sources of stress and its amelioration. Exceptional Children, 50 (1), 10-19

Gallagher, J.J., Bristol, M.M., Cross, A.H. & Scharfman, W. (1983). Carolina Family Responsibilities Scale. Chapel Hill, North Carolina: Frank Porter Graham Child Development Center

Gallagher, J.J., Cross, A.H. & Scharfman, W. (1981). Parental adaptation to a young handicapped child: the father's role. Journal of the Division for Early Childhood, 3, 3-14

Gardner, J. (1983). School-based parent involvement: a psychologist's view. In P. Mittler & H. McConachie (eds) Parents, Professionals and Mentally Handicapped People: Approaches to Partnership. Beckenham: Croom Helm/ Cambridge, MA: Brookline Books. pp.166-175

Gardner, J.M., Brust, D.J. & Watson, L.S. (1970). A scale to measure skill in applying behavior modification techniques to the mentally retarded. American Journal of Mental Deficiency, 74, 633-636

Gardner, L.P. (1943). A survey of the attitudes and activities of fathers. Journal of Genetic Psychology, 63, 15-53

Gath, A. (1973). The school age siblings of mongol children. British Journal of Psychiatry, 123, 161-167

Gath, A. (1974). Sibling reactions to mental handicap: a comparison of the brothers and sisters of mongol children. Journal of Child Psychology and Psychiatry, 15, 187-198

Gath, A. (1978). Down's Syndrome and the Family: The Early Years. London: Academic Press

Gath, A. and Gumley, D. (1984). Down's syndrome and the family: follow-up of children first seen in

infancy. Developmental Medicine and Child Neurology, 26, 500-508
Gaussen, T. (1979). Analysing parent-child interactions in clinical practice: the development of a procedure and method of reporting. Child: Care, Health and Development, 5, 111-134
Ghuman, P.A.S. (1975). The Cultural Context of Thinking. Windsor: NFER-Nelson
Glendinning, C. (1983). Unshared Care: Parents and Their Disabled Children. London: Routledge and Kegan Paul
Glogower, F. & Sloop, E.W. (1976). Two strategies of group training of parents as effective behavior modifiers. Behavior Therapy, 7, 177-184
Glossop, C. & Castillo, M. (1982). Summary of present and future research into the Portage model. In R.J. Cameron (ed.) Working Together: Portage in the UK. Windsor: NFER-Nelson. pp.127-138
Gold, M.W. (1973). Research on the vocational habilitation of the retarded: the present, the future. In N.R. Ellis (ed.) International Review of Research in Mental Retardation, Vol. 6. New York: Academic Press. pp.97-147
Goldberg, S. (1977). Infant development and mother-infant interaction in urban Zambia. In P.H. Liederman, S.R. Tulkin & A. Rosenfeld (eds) Culture and Infancy. Variations in Human Experience. New York: Academic Press. pp.211-243
Golinkoff, R.M. & Ames, G.J. (1979). A comparison of fathers' and mothers' speech. Child Development, 50, 28-32
Graham, H. (1982). Perceptions of parenthood. Health Education Journal, 41 (4), 119-122
Graliker, B.V., Fishler, K. & Koch, R. (1962). Teenage reaction to a mentally retarded sibling. American Journal of Mental Deficiency, 66, 838-843
Grantham-McGregor, S., Landman, J. & Desai, P. (1983). Child rearing in poor urban Jamaica. Child: Care, Health and Development, 9, 57-71
Gray, S.W. & Ruttle, K. (1980). The family-oriented home visiting program: a longitudinal study. Genetic Psychology Monographs, 102, 299-316
Gray, S.W. & Wandersman, L.P. (1980). The methodology of home-based intervention studies: problems and promising strategies. Child Development, 51, 993-1009
Graziano, A.M. (1971). Behavior Therapy With

Children. Chicago: Aldine
Green, J. & Evans, R. (1982). Honeylands' role in the pre-school years: I. Developing a relationship. Child: Care, Health and Development, 8, 21-38
Green, J. & Evans, R. (1984). Honeylands' role in the pre-school years: II. Patterns of use; and III. Factors inhibiting use. Child: Care, Health and Development, 10, 81-98
Green, J.A., Gustafson, G.E. and West, M.J. (1980). Effects of infant development on mother-infant interactions. Child Development, 51, 199-207
Greenberg, N.H. (1971). A comparison of infant-mother interactional behaviour in infants with atypical behaviour and normal infants. In J. Hellmuth (ed.) Exceptional Infant, Vol. 2. London: Butterworths
Greene, E.G. (1971). A comparative study of perceptions of parents toward their mentally retarded children. Dissertation Abstracts International, 31, (7-A), 3372
Gregory, S. (1976). The Deaf Child and his Family. London: Allen and Unwin
Griffin, M.W. (1979). Training parents of retarded children as behaviour therapists: a review. Australian Journal of Mental Retardation, 5 (5), 18-27
Grossman, F.K. (1972). Brothers and Sisters of Retarded Children: An Exploratory Study. New York: Syracuse University Press
Gumz, E.J. & Gubrium, J.F. (1972). Comparative parental perceptions of a mentally retarded child. American Journal of Mental Deficiency, 77, 175-180
Gunn, P., Berry, P. & Andrews, R.J. (1982). Looking behaviour of Down's syndrome infants. American Journal of Mental Deficiency, 87, 344-347
Gunn, P., Clark, D. & Berry, P. (1980). Maternal speech during play with a Down's syndrome infant. Mental Retardation, 18 (1), 15-18
Guralnick, M.J. & Paul-Brown, D. (1980). Functional and discourse analyses of nonhandicapped preschool children's speech to handicapped children. American Journal of Mental Deficiency, 84, 444-454
Hall, F., Pawlby, S.J. & Wolkind, S. (1979). Early life experiences and later mothering behaviour: a study of mothers and their 20 week old babies. In D. Shaffer & J. Dunn (eds) The First Year of Life. Chichester: Wiley. pp.153-174
Hannam, C. (1980). Parents and Mentally Handicapped

Children, 2nd ed. London: Penguin
Harmon, D. & Kogan, K.L. (1980). Social class and mother-child interaction. Psychological Reports, 46, 1075-1084
Harper, D.C. (1984). Child behavior toward the parent: a factor analysis of mothers' reports of disabled children. Journal of Autism and Developmental Disorders, 14, 165-182
Harris, S.L., Handleman, J.S. & Palmer, C. (1985). Parents and grandparents view the autistic child. Journal of Autism and Developmental Disorders, 15, 127-137
Harris, S.L., Wolchik, S.A. & Weitz, S. (1981). The acquisition of language skills by autistic children: can parents do the job? Journal of Autism and Developmental Disorders, 11, 373-383
Hart, D. & Walters, J. (1981). A group work project with siblings of mentally handicapped children. Association for Child Psychology and Psychiatry News, no. 8, 6-9
Hartlage, L.C. & Green, J.B. (1972). The relation of parental attitudes to academic and social achievement in epileptic children. Epilepsia, 13, 21-25
Hatfield, J.S., Ferguson, L.R. & Alpert, R. (1967). Mother-child interaction and the socialisation process. Child Development, 38, 365-414
Hattersley, J. (1979). Long-term parent support groups. Paper presented to British Institute of Mental Handicap day conference, "Help and Self-Help for Parents", Leeds, June
Hattersley, J. & Tennant, L. (1981). Parent workshops in Worcestershire. In G. Pugh (ed.) Parents as Partners. London: National Children's Bureau. pp.76-84
Hayden, A.H. (1979). Handicapped children, birth to age 3. Exceptional Children, 45, 510-516
Heifetz, L.J. (1977a). Professional preciousness and the evolution of parent training strategies. In P. Mittler (ed.) Research to Practice in Mental Retardation, Vol.1. Care and Intervention. Baltimore: University Park Press. pp.205-212
Heifetz, L.J. (1977b). Behavioral training for parents of retarded children: alternative formats based on instructional manuals. American Journal of Mental Deficiency, 82, 194-203
Heifetz, L.J. (1980). From consumer to middleman: emerging roles for parents in the network of services for retarded children. In R.R. Abidin (ed.) Parent Education and Intervention

Handbook. Springfield, Illinois: Charles C. Thomas. pp.349-384

Henry, J. (1967). My life with families of psychotic children. In G. Handel (ed.) The Psychosocial Interior of the Family: A Source-Book for the Study of Whole Families. Chicago: Aldine

Hereford, C.F. (1963). Changing Parental Attitudes Through Group Discussion. Austin: University of Texas Press

Hess, R.D. (1980). Experts and amateurs: some unintended consequences of parent education. In M.D. Fantini & R. Cardenas (eds) Parenting in a Multicultural Society. New York: Longman

Hetherington, E.M., Cox, M. & Cox, R. (1976). Divorced fathers. Family Coordinator, 25 (4), 417-428

Hewett, S. (1970). The Family and the Handicapped Child: A Study of Cerebral Palsied Children in their Homes. London: Allen and Unwin

Hewett, S. (1972). The Need for Long Term Care. Institute for Research into Mental Retardation Occasional Papers, no. 3. London: Butterworths

Heyman, R., Shaw, M.P. & Harding, J. (1983). A personal construct theory approach to the socialization of nursing trainees in two British general hospitals. Journal of Advanced Nursing, 8, 59-67

Hilton, I. (1967). Differences in the behavior of mothers toward their first- and later-born children. Journal of Personality and Social Psychology, 7, 282-290

Hinde, R.A. (1979). Towards Understanding Relationships. European Monographs in Social Psychology, no. 18. London: Academic Press

Hladik, E.G. & Edwards, H.T. (1984). A comparative study of mother-father speech in the naturalistic home environment. Journal of Psycholinguistic Research, 13, 321-332

Hoffman, M.L. (1967). An interview method for obtaining descriptions of parent-child interaction. In G.R. Medinnus (ed.) Readings in the Psychology of Parent-Child Relations. New York: Wiley

Hogg, J. (ed.) (1979). The First Two Years. Anson House Preschool Project Paper 1. Barkingside: Barnardo's

Hogg, J., Foxen, T. & McBrien, J. (1981). Issues in the training and evaluation of behaviour modification skills for staff working with profoundly retarded multiply handicapped children. Behavioural Psychotherapy, 9, 345-357

Holly, L. (1982). Ideologies of parenthood: politics of fatherhood. Paper presented to Fatherhood Research Group meeting, Nottingham University, June

Holmes, N., Hemsley, R., Rickett, J. & Likierman, H. (1982). Parents as cotherapists: their perceptions of a home-based behavioral treatment for autistic children. Journal of Autism and Developmental Disorders, 12, 331-342

Holroyd, J. (1974). The questionnaire on resources and stress: an instrument to measure family response to a handicapped family member. Journal of Community Psychology, 2, 92-94

Holroyd, J. & McArthur, D. (1976). Mental retardation and stress on the parents: a contrast between Down's syndrome and childhood autism. American Journal of Mental Deficiency, 80, 431-436

Holt, K.S. (1958). The home care of severely retarded children. Pediatrics, 22 (4,1), 744-755

Hornby, G. & Jensen-Procter, G. (1984). Parental speech to language-delayed children: a home intervention study. British Journal of Disorders of Communication, 19, 97-103

Hornby, G. & Murray, R. (1983). Group programmes for parents of children with various handicaps. Child: Care, Health and Development, 9, 185-198

Hornby, G. & Singh, N.N. (1983). Group training for parents of mentally retarded children: a review and methodological analysis of behavioural studies. Child: Care, Health and Development, 9, 199-213

Hornby, G. & Singh, N.N. (1984). Behavioural group training with parents of mentally retarded children. Journal of Mental Deficiency Research, 28, 43-52

Howlin, P. (1984). Parents as therapists: a critical review. In D.J. Muller (ed.) Remediating Children's Language: Behavioural and Naturalistic Approaches. Beckenham: Croom Helm/ San Diego: College Hill Press. pp.197-230

Howlin, P. and Lask, J. (1985). The home- and school-based management of autism and pervasive developmental disorders. Seminar given to Department of Psychological Medicine, Hospital for Sick Children, Great Ormond Street, London, October.

Howlin, P., Marchant, R., Rutter, M., Berger, M., Hersov, L. & Yule, W. (1973). A home-based approach to the treatment of autistic children.

Journal of Autism and Childhood Schizophrenia, 3, 308-336

Hudson, A.M. (1982). Training parents of developmentally handicapped children: a component analysis. Behavior Therapy, 13, 325-333

Humphrey, M. (1977). Sex differences in attitude to parenthood. Human Relations, 30 (8), 737-749

Hunter, A.B.J. (1980). The Family and their Mentally Handicapped Child. Barkingside: Barnardo's

Intagliata, J. & Doyle, N. (1984). Enhancing social support for parents of developmentally disabled children: training in interpersonal problem solving skills. Mental Retardation, 22 (1), 4-11

Jacobs, B.S. & Moss, H.A. (1976). Birth order and sex of sibling as determinants of mother-infant interaction. Child Development, 47, 315-322

Jaehnig, W. (1974). Mentally handicapped children and their families. Unpublished Ph.D. thesis, University of Essex

Jaehnig, W. & Townsend, P. (1973). The Mentally Handicapped and their Families. Final Report to the Department of Health and Social Security. Department of Sociology, University of Essex

Jay, S. & Farran, D.C. (1981). The relative efficacy of predicting IQ from mother-child interactions using ratings versus behavioral count measures. Journal of Applied Developmental Psychology, 2, 165-177

Jeffree, D.M., McConkey, R. & Hewson, S. (1977). Parental Involvement in Facilitating the Development of Young Mentally Handicapped Children. Final Report to Department of Health and Social Security and Department of Education and Science. Hester Adrian Research Centre, University of Manchester

Jensen, E.W., James, S.A., Boyce, W.T. & Hartnett, S.A. (1983). The family routines inventory: development and validation. Social Science and Medicine, 17 (4), 201-211

Johnson, C.A. & Katz, R.C. (1973). Using parents as change agents for their children: a review. Journal of Child Psychology and Psychiatry, 14 (3), 181-200

Johnson, C.B. & Deitz, J.C. (1985). Time use of mothers with preschool children: a pilot study. American Journal of Occupational Therapy, 39, 578-583

Johnson, S. & Brown, R. (1969). Producing behaviour

change in parents of disturbed children. Journal of Child Psychology and Psychiatry, 10, 107-121

Johnson, S.M., Christensen, A. & Bellamy, G.T. (1976). Evaluation of family intervention through unobtrusive audio recordings: experiences in 'bugging' children. Journal of Applied Behavior Analysis, 9, 213-219

Jones, O.H.M. (1977). Mother-child communication with pre-linguistic Down's syndrome and normal infants. In H. Schaffer (ed.) Studies of Mother-Infant Interaction. New York: Academic Press

Jones, O.H.M. (1979). A comparative study of mother-child communication with Down's syndrome and normal infants. In D. Shaffer & J. Dunn (eds) The First Year of Life. Chichester: Wiley. pp.175-195

Jones, O.H.M. (1980). Prelinguistic communication skills in Down's syndrome and normal infants. In T.M. Field (ed.) High-Risk Infants and Children: Adult and Peer Interactions. New York: Academic Press. pp.205-225

Joosten, J. (1979). Accounting for changes in family life of families with spina bifida children. Zeitschrift fuer Kinderchirurgie, 28, 412-417

Judson, S.L. & Burden, R.L. (1980). Towards a tailored measure of parental attitudes: an approach to the evaluation of one aspect of intervention projects with parents of handicapped children. Child: Care, Health and Development, 6 (1), 47-56

Kagan, J. (1982). The emergence of self. Journal of Child Psychology and Psychiatry, 23 (4), 363-381

Kanner, L. (1953). Parents' feelings about retarded children. American Journal of Mental Deficiency, 57, 375-383

Karnes, M.B. (1977). Alternative models for delivering services to young handicapped children. In J.B. Jordan (ed.) Early Childhood Education for Exceptional Children. Virginia: Council for Exceptional Children.

Karnes, M.B., Hodgins, A.S. & Teska, J.A. (1969). The impact of at-home instruction by mothers on performance in the ameliorative preschool. In M.B. Karnes (ed.) Research and Development Program on Preschool Disadvantaged Children: Final Report. Washington, D.C.: U.S. Office of Education (Cited by T.D. Tjossem (1976). Early intervention: issues and approaches. In T.D.

Tjossem (ed.) Intervention Strategies for High Risk Infants and Young Children. Baltimore: University Park Press.)

Karnes, M.B. & Teska, J.A. (1980). Toward successful parent involvement in programs for handicapped children. In J.J. Gallagher (ed.) Parents and Families of Handicapped Children. New Directions for Exceptional Children, vol. 4. San Francisco: Jossey-Bass

Katz, S. & Kenig, D. (1981). Evaluation of the efficacy of a group-individual method of training parents as behavior modifiers for their moderately to severely mentally handicapped children. In P. Mittler (ed.) Frontiers of Knowledge in Mental Retardation, vol. 1. Baltimore: University Park Press

Kaufman, B.N. (1976). To Love Is to Be Happy With. London: Souvenir Press

Kavanaugh, R.D. & Jirkovsky, A.M. (1982). Parental speech to young children: a longitudinal analysis. Merrill-Palmer Quarterly, 28 (2), 297-311

Kaye, R. (1979). Evaluation, feeling and behaviour in teacher-pupil relations. Unpublished M.Sc. thesis, Faculty of Education, University of Manchester

Kazak, A.E. & Marvin, R.S. (1984). Differences, difficulties and adaptation: stress and social networks in families with a handicapped child. Family Relations, 33, 67-77

Kelley, M.L., Embry, L.N. & Baer, D.M. (1979). Skills for child management and family support: training parents for maintenance. Behavior Modification, 3, 373-396

Kelly, G.A. (1955). The Psychology of Personal Constructs, Vols. 1 & 2. New York: Norton

Kew, S. (1975). Handicap and Family Crisis: A Study of the Siblings of Handicapped Children. London: Pitman

Kiernan, C.C. (1978). Report of work on mental handicap completed in the Thomas Coram Research Unit between September 1973 and December 1976. Institute of Education, London

Kiernan, C.C. (1981). Analysis of Programmes for Teaching. Basingstoke: Globe Education

Kiernan, C.C. & Riddick, B. (1973). A Draft Programme for Training in Operant Techniques: Vol.1. Theoretical Units; Vol.2. Practical Units. London: Institute of Education

Klebanoff, L.B. (1959). Parental attitudes of mothers of schizophrenic, brain-injured and retarded, and normal children. American Journal of Orthopsychiatry, 29, 445-454

Koegel, R.L., Glahn, T.J. & Nieminen, G.S. (1978). Generalization of parent-training results. Journal of Applied Behavior Analysis, 11, 95-109

Kogan, K.L. (1980). Interaction systems between preschool handicapped or developmentally delayed children and their parents. In T.M. Field, S. Goldberg, D. Stern & A.N. Sostek (eds) High Risk Infants and Children: Adult and Peer Interactions. New York: Academic Press. pp.227-247

Kogan, K.L. & Gordon, B.N. (1975). Interpersonal behavior constructs: a revised approach to defining dyadic interaction styles. Psychological Reports, 36, 835-846

Kogan, K.L. & Tyler, N. (1973). Mother-child interaction in young physically handicapped children. American Journal of Mental Deficiency, 77, 492-497

Kogan, K.L., Tyler, N. & Turner, P. (1974). The process of interpersonal adaptation between mothers and their cerebral palsied children. Developmental Medicine and Child Neurology, 16, 518-527

Kogan, K.L., Wimberger, H.C. & Bobbitt, R.A. (1969). Analysis of mother-child interaction in young mental retardates. Child Development, 40, 799-812

Kotelchuk, M. (1976). The infant's relationship to the father: experimental evidence. In M.E. Lamb (ed.) The Role of the Father in Child Development. New York: Wiley

Kotler, T. & Chetwynd, J. (1980). Changes in family members during psychotherapy. Human Relations, 33, 101-110

Kushlick, A., Smith, J. & Gold, A. (1985). An intervention package to teach parents of severely retarded and severely non-compliant children and adults at home to teach their child new relevant skills. In B. Daly, S. Kerfoot, A. Sigston & J. Addington (eds) Portage: The Importance of Parents. Windsor: NFER-Nelson. pp.119-137

Kysela, G.M. & Marfo, K. (1983). Mother-child interactions and early intervention programmes for handicapped infants and young children. Educational Psychology, 3, 201-212

Lamb, M.E. (1976a). The Role of the Father in Child Development. New York: Wiley

Lamb, M.E. (1976b). The role of the father: an overview. In M.E. Lamb (ed.) The Role of the Father in Child Development. New York: Wiley

Lamb, M.E. (1976c). Twelve-month-olds and their parents: interaction in a laboratory playroom. Developmental Psychology, 12, 237-244

Lamb, M.E. (1977a). Father-infant and mother-infant interaction in the first year of life. Child Development, 48, 167-181

Lamb, M.E. (1977b). The development of mother-infant and father-infant attachments in the second year of life. Developmental Psychology, 13, 637-648

Lamb, M.E. (1980). What can 'research experts' tell parents about effective socialization? In M.D. Fantini & R. Cardenas (eds) Parenting in a Multicultural Society. New York: Longman

Lamb, M.E. (1981a). The Role of the Father in Child Development, 2nd ed. New York: Wiley

Lamb, M.E. (1981b). The development of father-infant relationships. In M.E. Lamb (ed.) The Role of the Father in Child Development, 2nd ed. New York: Wiley. pp.459-488

Lamb, M.E. (1983). Fathers of exceptional children. In M. Seligman (ed.) The Family with a Handicapped Child: Understanding and Treatment. Orlando, Florida: Grune and Stratton. pp.125-146

Lamb, M.E., Frodi, M., Hwang, C.P., & Frodi, A.M. (1983). Effects of paternal involvement on infant preferences for mothers and fathers. Child Development, 54, 450-458

Lamb, M.E., Frodi, A.M., Hwang, C.P., Frodi, M. & Steinberg, J. (1982a). Mother- and father-infant interaction involving play and holding in traditional and non-traditional Swedish families. Developmental Psychology, 18, 215-221

Lamb, M.E., Frodi, A.M., Hwang, C.P., Frodi, M. & Steinberg, J. (1982b). Effect of gender and caretaking role on parent-infant interaction. In R.N. Emde & R.J. Harmon (eds) The Development of Attachment and Affiliative Systems. New York: Plenum Press

Land, A. (1985). Portage - parents' views. Educational Psychology in Practice, 1 (3), 120-123

Landman, S.H. (1979). A study of the relationship between parental overprotectiveness and the achievement of selected life skills among mildly retarded adolescents. Dissertation

Abstracts International, 40, 5075-B

Laosa, L.M. (1980). Maternal teaching strategies in Chicano and Anglo-American families: the influence of culture and education on maternal behavior. Child Development, 51 (3), 759-765

Larsen, L.A. & Bricker, W.A. (1968). A manual for parents and teachers of severely and moderately retarded children. IMRID papers and reports, 5 (22). Nashville: George Peabody College

Lavelle, N. & Keogh, B. (1980). Expectations and attributions of parents of handicapped children. In J.J. Gallagher (ed.) Parents and Families of Handicapped Children. New Directions for Exceptional Children, vol. 4. San Francisco: Jossey Bass. pp.1-27

Laviguer, H. (1976). The use of siblings as an adjunct to the behavioral treatment of children in the home with parents as therapists. Behavior Therapy, 7, 602-613

Lazar, I. & Darlington, R. (1979). Lasting Effects After Preschool. Washington, D.C.: U.S. Department of Health, Education and Welfare. DHEW Publ. 79-30178 (summary DHEW 79-30179)

Leifer, J.S. & Lewis, M. (1984). Acquisition of conversational response skills by young Down syndrome and nonretarded young children. American Journal of Mental Deficiency, 88, 610-618

Levenstein, P. (1970). Cognitive growth in preschoolers through verbal interaction with mothers. American Journal of Orthopsychiatry, 40, 426-432

Levine, R.A. (1980). A cross-cultural perspective on parenting. In M.D. Fantini & R. Cardenas (eds) Parenting in a Multicultural Society. New York: Longman. pp.17-26

Levine, S. (1966). Sex role identification and parental perceptions of social competence. American Journal of Mental Deficiency, 70, 822-824

Levinson, R.M. & Starling, D.M. (1981). Retardation and the burden of stigma. Deviant Behavior, 2, 371-390

Lewis, C. (1984). Men's involvement in fatherhood: historical and gender issues. Paper presented to Developmental Section Conference, British Psychological Society, Lancaster, September

Lewis, M., Feiring, C. & Kotsonis, M. (1984). The social network of the young child. In M. Lewis (ed.) Beyond the Dyad. New York: Plenum Press. pp.129-160

Lewis, M., Feiring, C. & Weinraub, M. (1981). The father as a member of the child's social network. In M.E. Lamb (ed.) The Role of the Father in Child Development, 2nd ed. New York: Wiley. pp.259-294

Lewis, M. & Weinraub, M. (1976). The father's role in the child's social network. In M. Lamb (ed.) The Role of the Father in Child Development. New York: Wiley

Light, P. (1979). The Development of Social Sensitivity. Cambridge: Cambridge University Press

Lillie, D.L. (1974). Dimensions in parent programs; an overview. In J. Grim (ed.) Training Parents to Teach: Four Models. Washington, D.C.: Department of Health, Education and Welfare

Lindsley, O.R. (1966). An experiment with parents handling behavior at home. Johnstone Bulletin, 9, 27-36

Lloyd-Bostock, S. (1976). Parents' experiences of official help and guidance in caring for a mentally handicapped child. Child: Care, Health and Development, 2, 325-338

Loader, P. & Kinston, W. (1984). Families of obese children. Paper presented to the Association for Child Psychology and Psychiatry, London, October

Locke, H.J. & Wallace, K.M. (1959). Short marital adjustment and prediction tests: their reliability and validity. Marriage and Family Living, 21, 251-255

Loevinger, J. (1959). Patterns of parenthood as theories of learning. Journal of Abnormal and Social Psychology, 59, 148-150

Lombardino, L. & Mangan, N. (1983). Parents as language trainers: language programming with developmentally delayed children. Exceptional Children, 49, 358-361

Lonsdale, G. (1978). Family life with a handicapped child: the parents speak. Child: Care, Health and Development, 4, 99-120

Long, C.G. & Moore, J.R. (1979). Parental expectations for their epileptic children. Journal of Child Psychology and Psychiatry, 20, 299-312

Longo, D.C. & Bond, L. (1984). Families of the handicapped child: research and practice. Family Relations, 33, 57-65

Love, H.D. (1970). Parental Attitudes Toward Exceptional Children. Springfield, Illinois: Charles C. Thomas

References

Ludlow, J.R. & Allen, L.M. (1979). The effect of early intervention and preschool stimulus on the development of the Down's syndrome child. Journal of Mental Deficiency Research, 23, 29-44

Lynn, D.B. (1974). The Father: His Role in Child Development. Monterey, California: Brooks/Cole

Lytton, H. (1973). Three approaches to the study of parent-child interaction: ethological, interview and experimental. Journal of Child Psychology and Psychiatry, 14, 1-17

Lytton, H. (1976). The socialization of 2 year old boys: ecological findings. Journal of Child Psychology and Psychiatry, 17, 287-304

Lytton, H. (1980). Parent Child Interaction: The Socialization Process Observed in Twin and Singleton Families. New York: Plenum Press

Lytton, H., Conway, D. & Sauve, R. (1977). Home observation, interview and experiment. Journal of Personality and Social Psychology, 35, 7-107

MacDonald, J. (1982). Language through conversation: a communication model for language intervention. In S. Warren & J. Rogers-Warren (eds) Productive Language Teaching. Baltimore: University Park Press

MacKeith, R. (1973). The feelings and behaviour of parents of handicapped children. Developmental Medicine and Child Neurology, 15, 524-527

Madden, J., Levenstein, P. & Levenstein, S. (1976). Longitudinal IQ outcomes of the Mother-Child Home Program. Child Development, 47, 1015-1025

Madden, J., O'Hara, J. & Levenstein, P. (1984). Home again: effects of the Mother-Child Home Program on mother and child. Child Development, 55, 636-647

Mahoney, G. (1983). A developmental analysis of communication between mothers and infants with Down's syndrome. Topics in Early Childhood Special Education, 3, 63-76

Malkin, S.F., Freeman, R.D. & Hastings, J.D. (1976). Psychosocial problems of deaf children and their families: a comparative study. Audiology and Hearing Education, 2 (3), 21-29

Malone, M.J. & Guy, R.F. (1982). A comparison of mothers' and fathers' speech to their 3-year-old-sons. Journal of Psycholinguistic Research, 11, 599-608

Marfo, K. (1984). Interactions between mothers and their mentally retarded children: integration of research findings. Journal of Applied Developmental Psychology, 5, 45-69

References

Markova, I., Macdonald, K. & Forbes, C. (1980). Impact of haemophilia on child-rearing practices and parental cooperation. Journal of Child Psychology and Psychiatry, 21, 153-162

Marshall, N.R., Hegrenes, J.R. & Goldstein, S. (1973). Verbal interactions: mothers and their retarded children vs. mothers and their non-retarded children. American Journal of Mental Deficiency, 77 (4), 415-419

Martin, B. (1975). Parent-child relations. In F.D. Horowitz (ed.) Review of Child Development Research, vol. 4. Chicago: University of Chicago Press. pp.463-540

Martin, B. (1977). Brief family intervention: effectiveness and the importance of including the father. Journal of Consulting and Clinical Psychology, 45, 1002-1010

Mash, E.J. & Terdal, L. (1973). Modification of mother-child interactions: playing with children. Mental Retardation, 10, 44-49

Masur, E.F. & Berko-Gleason, J. (1980). Parent-child interaction and the acquisition of lexical information during play. Developmental Psychology, 16, 404-409

Maxwell-West, M. & Konner, M.J. (1976). The role of the father: an anthropological perspective. In M. Lamb (ed.) The Role of the Father in Child Development. New York: Wiley. pp.185-216

McCollum, J.A. (1984). Social interaction between parents and babies: validation of an intervention procedure. Child: Care, Health and Development, 10, 301-315

McConachie, H. (1974). Developing syntax in retarded children: two individual case studies with parents as therapists. Unpublished M.Phil. thesis, Institute of Psychiatry, London

McConachie, H. (1979). Mothers' and fathers' daily involvement with their handicapped children. Paper presented at Fifth Congress of the International Association for the Scientific Study of Mental Deficiency, Jerusalem, Israel

McConachie, H. (1982). Fathers of mentally handicapped children. In N. Beail & J. McGuire (eds) Fathers: Psychological Perspectives. London: Junction Books. pp.144-173

McConachie, H. (1983). Examples of partnership in Europe. In P. Mittler & H. McConachie (eds) Parents, Professionals and Mentally Handicapped People: Approaches to Partnership. Beckenham: Croom Helm/ Cambridge, MA: Brookline Books. pp.205-220

References

McConachie, H. (1985). How parents of young mentally handicapped children construe their role. In D. Bannister (ed.) Issues and Approaches in Personal Construct Theory. London: Academic Press. pp.105-126

McConachie, H. (1986). Involvement of parents in teaching their young mentally handicapped children. Unpublished Ph.D. thesis, Faculty of Education, University of Manchester

McConachie, H. & Domb, H. (1983). An interview study of 20 older brothers and sisters of mentally handicapped and non-handicapped children. Mental Handicap, 11, 64-66

McConachie, H. & Mitchell, D.R. (1985). Parents teaching their young mentally handicapped children. Journal of Child Psychology and Psychiatry, 26, 389-405

McConkey, R. (1985). Working With Parents: A Practical Guide for Teachers and Therapists. Beckenham: Croom Helm/ Cambridge, MA: Brookline Books

McConkey, R., Jeffree, D.M. & Hewson, S. (1979). Involving parents in extending the language development of their young mentally handicapped children. British Journal of Disorders of Communication, 14 (3), 203-218

McConkey, R. & Martin, H. (1983). Mothers' play with toys: a longitudinal study with Down's syndrome infants. Child: Care, Health and Development, 9, 215-226

McConkey, R. & Martin, H. (1984) A longitudinal study of mothers' speech to preverbal Down's syndrome infants. First Language, 5, (in press)

McConkey, R. & McEvoy, J. (1984). Parental involvement courses: contrasts between mothers who enrol and those who don't. In J.M. Berg (ed.) Perspectives and Progress in Mental Retardation, vol. 1. Baltimore: University Park Press. pp.435-442

McConkey, R., McEvoy, J. & Gallagher, F. (1982). Learning through play: the evaluation of a videocourse for parents of mentally handicapped children. Child: Care, Health and Development, 8, 345-359

McConkey, R. & O'Connor, M. (1982). A new approach to parental involvement in language intervention programmes. Child: Care, Health and Development, 8, 163-176

McCubbin, H.I., McCubbin, M.A., Patterson, J.M., Cauble, A.E., Wilson, L.R. & Warwick, W. (1983). CHIP - Coping Health Inventory for

Parents: an assessment of parental coping patterns in the care of the chronically ill child. Journal of Marriage and the Family, 45, 359-370
McEvoy, J. & McConkey, R. (1983). Play activities of mentally handicapped children at home and mothers' perceptions of play. International Journal of Rehabilitation Research, 6, 143-151
McGillicuddy-DeLisi, A.V. (1982). The relationship between parents' beliefs about development and family constellation, socioeconomic status and parents' teaching strategies. In L. Laosa & I. Sigel (eds) Families as Learning Environments for Children. New York: Plenum Press. pp.261-300
McGreal, C.E. (1981). The father's role in the socialization of his infant. Infant Mental Health Journal, 2, 216-225
McHale, S.M. & Huston, T.L. (1984). Men and women as parents: sex role orientations, employment and parental roles with infants. Child Development, 55, 1349-1361
McLaughlin, A., Morrissey, M., Empson, J.M. & Sever, J. (1981). Language performance of disadvantaged children at 30 months: interpersonal and other environmental influences. In W.P. Robinson (ed.) Communication in Development. London: Academic Press. pp.109-128
McMahon, R.J., Forehand, R. & Griest, D.L. (1981). Effects of knowledge of social learning principles on enhancing treatment outcome and generalization in a parent training program. Journal of Consulting and Clinical Psychology, 49, 526-532
McMahon, R.J. Forehand, R., Griest, D.L. & Wells, K.C. (1981). Who drops out of treatment during parent behavior training. Behavioral Counseling Quarterly, 1, 79-85
McMichael, J.K. (1971). Handicap: A Study of Physically Handicapped Children and their Families. London: Staples Press
Metzl, M.N. (1980). Teaching parents a strategy for enhancing infant development. Child Development, 51, 583-586
Miller, N. & Cantwell, D. (1976). Siblings as therapists: a behavioral approach. American Journal of Psychiatry, 133, 447-450
Mills, M., Puckering, C., Pound, A. & Cox, A. (1985). What is it about depressed mothers that influences their children's functioning? In

J.E. Stevenson (ed.) Recent Research in Developmental Psychopathology. Oxford: Pergamon Press. pp.11-18

Milne, D. (1985). An observational evaluation of the effects of nurse training in behaviour therapy on unstructured ward activities and interactions. British Journal of Clinical Psychology, 24, 149-158

Minde, K.K., Hackett, J.D., Killou, D. & Silver, S. (1972). How they grow up: 41 physically handicapped children and their families. American Journal of Psychiatry, 128, 1554-1560

Mink, I.T., Nihira, K. & Meyers, C.E. (1983). Taxonomy of family life styles: I. Homes with TMR children. American Journal of Mental Deficiency, 87, 484-497

Mira, M. (1970). Results of a behaviour modification training programme for parents and teachers. Behaviour, Research and Therapy, 8, 309-311

Mitchell, D.R. (1976). Mentally handicapped children in structured dyadic communication situations with their parents. Unpublished Ph.D. thesis, University of Manchester

Mitchell, D.R. (1977). Parent involvement in the health, education and welfare of their children. Address to the Eighth Annual Seminar in Special Education, Brisbane, August

Mitchell, D.R. (1980). Down's syndrome children in structured dyadic communication situations with their parents. In J. Hogg & P.J. Mittler (eds) Advances in Mental Handicap Research, vol.1. London: Wiley. pp.161-194

Mitchell, J. (1976). Parents' linguistic input to mentally handicapped children in a structured dyadic situation. Unpublished Diploma thesis, Department of Education, University of Manchester

Mitchell, W.M. (1980). Fathers of children with Down syndrome. Dissertation Abstracts International, 41, 360-361B

Mittler, P. (1975). (Discussion of paper 'Behaviour modification programmes in a community setting' by M. Callias & J. Carr.) In C.C. Kiernan & F.P. Woodford (eds) Behaviour Modification with the Severely Retarded. IRMMH Study Group 8. Amsterdam: Associated Scientific Publishers. p.172

Mittler, P. (1978). Choices in partnership between parents and professionals. Chairman's introductory paper to Plenary Session 3, "Choices in Partnership". 7th Congress,

International League of Societies for the Mentally Handicapped, Vienna, October. (Congress Proceedings)

Mittler, P. & McConachie, H. (1983). Parents, Professionals and Mentally Handicapped People: Approaches to Partnership. Beckenham: Croom Helm/ Cambridge, MA: Brookline Books

Mittler, P. & Mittler, H. (1982). Partnership with Parents. London: National Council for Special Education

Mittler, P. & Serpell, R. (1985). Services for persons with intellectual disability: an international perspective. In A.M. Clarke, A.D.B. Clarke & J.M. Berg (eds) Mental Deficiency: The Changing Outlook, 4th ed. London: Methuen

Miyake, K., Wakai, K., Tajima, N., Seki, M., Gotoh, M. & Usui, H. (1978). An eco-psychological study of parent-child relationship and child development. Reprinted from Annual Report, 1977-1978, Research and Clinical Center for Child Development, Faculty of Education, Hokkaido University, Sapporo, Japan

Mogford, K. (1973). Development, play and handicap. Unpublished paper, Child Development Research Unit, University of Nottingham

Mogford, K. (1976). Developing the play of young mentally handicapped children through the participation of parents: a rationale. REAP (Research Exchange and Practice in Mental Retardation), 2, 40-46

Mogford, K. (1979a). Interaction and communication between handicapped children and their parents: a study of remedial play. Unpublished Ph.D. thesis, University of Nottingham

Mogford, K. (1979b). A study of interaction and communication in remedial play. In E. Newson, J. Newson, J. Head & K. Mogford, Play in the Remediation of Handicap: Report on an Action Research Project, 1971-1976. University of Nottingham Toy Library. pp.72-79

Molloy, G.N. (1979). Training parents of retarded children as behaviour therapists: what we know: I. Mental Retardation Bulletin, 7 (3), 109-122

Molloy, G.N. (1980a). Wanted: some guidelines for investigating, reporting and evaluating parent training interventions. Australian Journal of Developmental Disabilities, 6 (2), 71-77

Molloy, G.N. (1980b). Training parents of retarded children as behaviour therapists: what we need to know: II. Mental Retardation Bulletin, 8

(1), 3-12

Moss, H.A. & Jones, S.J. (1977). Relations between maternal attitudes and maternal behavior as a function of social class. In P.H. Leiderman, S.R. Tulkin & A. Rosenfeld (eds) Culture and Infancy. London: Academic Press. pp.439-467

Moss, S.C. & Hogg, J. (1983). The development and integration of fine motor sequences in 12- to 18-month-old children: a test of the modular theory of motor skill acquisition. Genetic Psychology Monographs, 107, 145-187

Moustakas, C.E., Sigel, I.E. & Schalock, M.D. (1956). An objective method for the measurement and analysis of child-adult interaction. Child Development, 27, 109-134

Moxley-Haegert, L. & Serbin, L.A. (1983). Developmental education for parents of delayed infants: effects on parental motivation and children's development. Child Development, 54, 1324-1331

Murray, D.G. (1967). This is Stevie's Story. New York: Abingdon Press

Nash, R. (1973). Classrooms Observed. London: Routledge and Kegan Paul

Nay, W.R. (1975). A systematic comparison of instructional techniques for parents. Behavior Therapy, 6, 14-21

Nelson, K. (1973). Structure and strategy in learning to talk. Monographs of the Society for Research in Child Development, 38, (149)

Newson, E. (1979). Unreasonable care: the establishment of selfhood. Seminar given to the Department of Psychology, University of Manchester, May

Newson, E., Newson, J., Head, J. & Mogford, K. (1979). Play in the Remediation of Handicap: Report on an Action Research Project, 1971-1976. University of Nottingham Toy Library

Newson, J. (1978). Dialogue and development. In A. Lock (ed.) Action, Symbol and Gesture: The Emergence of Language. London: Academic Press

Newson, J. & Newson, E. (1968). Four Years Old in an Urban Community. Middlesex: Allen & Unwin

Nihira, K., Meyers, C.E. & Mink, I.T. (1980). Home environment, family adjustment, and the development of mentally retarded children. Applied Research in Mental Retardation, 1, 5-24

Nihira, K., Mink, I.T. & Meyers, C.E. (1981). Relationships between home environment and school adjustment of TMR children. American Journal of Mental Deficiency, 86, 8-15

Nihira, K., Mink, I.T. & Meyers, C.E. (1984). Salient dimensions of home environment relevant to child development. In N.R. Ellis & N.W. Bray (eds) International Review of Research in Mental Retardation, vol. 12. Orlando, Florida: Academic Press. pp.149-175

Oakley, A. (1974). The Sociology of Housework. London: Robertson

O'Brien, M. & McKee, L. (1982). Interviewing men: 'Taking gender seriously'. Paper presented to the British Sociological Association Annual Conference, 'Gender and Society', University of Manchester, April

O'Connor, N. & Hermelin, B. (1974). Specific deficits and coding strategies. In A.M. Clarke & A.D.B. Clarke (eds) Mental Deficiency: The Changing Outlook, 3rd ed. London: Methuen

O'Dell, S.L. (1974). Training parents in behavior modification: a review. Psychological Bulletin, 81, 418-433

O'Dell, S.L., Blackwell, L.J., Larsen, S.W. & Hogan, J.L. (1977). Competency based training for severely behaviorally handicapped children and their parents. Journal of Autism and Childhood Schizophrenia, 7, 231-242

O'Dell, S.L., Flynn, J. & Benlolo, L. (1977). A comparison of parent training techniques in child behavior modification. Journal of Behavior Therapy and Experimental Psychiatry, 8, 261-286

O'Dell, S.L., Mahoney, N.D., Horton, W.G. & Turner, P.E. (1979). Media-assisted parent training: alternate models. Behavior Therapy, 10, 103-110

Oeser, O.A. & Hammond, S.B. (1954). Social Structure and Personality in a City. London: Routledge and Kegan Paul

Ogbu, J.U. (1981). Origins of human competence: a cultural ecological perspective. Child Development, 52, 413-429

Okunade, A.O. (1981). Attitude of Yoruba of Western Nigeria to handicap in children. Child: Care, Health and Development, 7, 187-194

Olson, S.L., Bates, J.E. & Bayles, K. (1982). Maternal perceptions of infant and toddler behavior: a longitudinal construct validation study. Infant Behavior and Development, 5, 397-410

Olson, S.L., Bates, J.E. & Bayles, K. (1984). Mother-infant interaction and the development of individual differences in children's cognitive competence. Developmental Psychology,

20, 166-179

O'Reilly, J. (1977). The interplay between mothers and their children: a construct theory viewpoint. In D. Bannister (ed.) New Perspectives in Personal Construct Theory. London: Academic Press. pp.195-219

Osborn, A., Butler, N.R. & Morris, A.C. (1984). The Social Life of Britain's Five-Year-Olds. London: Routledge and Kegan Paul

Osborn, A. & Morris, T.C. (1979). The rationale for a composite index of social class and its evaluation. British Journal of Sociology, 30, 39-60

Osofsky, J.D. & O'Connell, E.J. (1972). Parent-child interaction: daughters' effects upon mothers' and fathers' behaviors. Developmental Psychology, 7, 157-168

Oswin, M. (1971). The Empty Hours: A Study of the Weekend Life of Handicapped Children in Institutions. London: Allen Lane

Oswin, M. (1978). Children Living in Long-Stay Hospitals. London: Heinemann

Pakizegi, B. (1978). The interaction of mothers and fathers with their sons. Child Development, 49, 479-482

Papousek, H. & Papousek, M. (1983). Biological basis of social interactions: implications of research for an understanding of behavioural deviance. Journal of Child Psychology and Psychiatry, 24, 117-129

Parke, R.D. (1978). Parent-infant interaction: progress, paradigms and problems. In G.P. Sackett (ed.) Observing Behavior, vol. 1. Baltimore: University Park Press. pp.69-94

Parke, R.D. (1979). Perspectives on father-infant interaction. In J.D. Osofsky (ed.) Handbook of Infant Development. New York: Wiley. pp.549-590

Parke, R.D., Hymel, S., Power, T.G. & Tinsley, B.R. (1980). Fathers and risk: a hospital-based model of intervention. In D.B. Sawin, R.C. Hawkins, L.O. Walker & J.H. Penticuff (eds) Psychosocial Risks in Infant-Environment Transactions. New York: Brunner-Mazel

Parke, R.D. & O'Leary, S.E. (1976). Father-mother-infant interaction in the newborn period: some findings, some observations and some unresolved issues. In K. Riegel & J. Meacham (eds) The Developing Individual in a Changing World, Vol. 2: Social and Environmental Issues. The Hague: Mouton

Parke, R. & Sawin, D. (1980). The family in early

infancy: social interactional and attitudinal analyses. In F. Pedersen (ed.) The Father-Infant Relationship: Observational Studies in the Family Setting. New York: Praeger

Parke, R.D. & Tinsley, B.R. (1981). The father's role in infancy: determinants of involvement in caregiving and play. In M.E. Lamb (ed.) The Role of the Father in Child Development, 2nd ed. New York: Wiley. pp.429-457

Parker, M. & Mitchell, D. (1980). Parents as Teachers of Their Handicapped Children: A Review. PATH project, University of Waikato, New Zealand

Parsons, T. & Bales, R. (1955). Family, Socialization, and Interaction Process. Glencoe, Illinois: Free Press

Patterson, G.R. & Fleischman, M. (1979). Maintenance of treatment effects: some considerations concerning family systems and follow-up data. Behavior Therapy, 10, 168-185

Patterson, G.R. & Reid, J.B. (1969). Reciprocity and coercion: two facets of social systems. Unpublished manuscript. Oregon Research Institute, University of Oregon

Pawlby, S.J. & Hall, F. (1980). Early interactions and later language development of children whose mothers come from disrupted families of origin. In T.M. Field (ed.) High-Risk Infants and Children: Adult and Peer Interactions. New York: Academic Press. pp.61-75

Peck, J.R. & Stephens, W.B. (1960). A study of the relationship between the attitudes and behavior of parents and that of their mentally defective child. American Journal of Mental Deficiency, 64, 839-843

Pedersen, F.A. (1981). Father influences viewed in a family context. In M.E. Lamb (ed.) The Role of the Father in Child Development, 2nd ed. New York: Wiley. pp.295-317

Pedersen, F.A., Anderson, B.J. & Cain, R.L. (1980). Parent-infant and husband-wife interactions observed at age five months. In F.A. Pedersen (ed.) The Father-Infant Relationship: Observational Studies in the Family Setting. New York: Praeger

Pedersen, F.A., Cain, R., Zaslow, M.J. & Anderson, B.J. (1982). Variation in infant experience associated with alternative family roles. In L.M. Laosa & I.E. Sigel (eds) The Family as a Learning Environment. New York: Plenum Press.

pp.203-222
Perkins, E.A., Taylor, P.D. & Capie, A.C.M. (1980). Helping the Retarded: A Systematic Behavioural Approach. Kidderminster: British Institute of Mental Handicap
Petersen, G.A. & Sherrod, K.B. (1982). Relationship of maternal language to language development and language delay of children. American Journal of Mental Deficiency, 86, 391-398
Phinney, J.S. & Feshbach, N.D. (1980). Non-directive and intrusive teaching styles of middle- and working-class English mothers. British Journal of Educational Psychology, 50, 2-9
Pilling, D. (1973). The Handicapped Child: Research Review, vol. 3. London: Longman and National Children's Bureau
Piper, M.C. & Ramsay, M.K. (1980). Effects of early home environment on the mental development of Down syndrome infants. American Journal of Mental Deficiency, 85, 39-44
Pitfield, M. & Oppenheim, A.N. (1964). Child-rearing attitudes of mothers of psychotic children. Journal of Child Psychology and Psychiatry, 5, 51-57
Pleck, J.H. (1985). Working Wives / Working Husbands. New Perspectives on the Family, vol. 5. London: Sage
Pokela, J. (1980). Predicting foster parent success: the applicability of the psychology of personal constructs. Unpublished Ph.D. dissertation, University of Massachusetts
Pound, A., Cox, A.D., Puckering, C. & Mills, M. (1985). The impact of maternal depression on young children. In J.E. Stevenson (ed.) Recent Research in Developmental Psychopathology. Oxford: Pergamon Press. pp.3-10
Powell, M. & Perkins, E. (1984). Asian families with a preschool handicapped child. Mental Handicap, 12, 50-52
Power, T.G. (1981). Sex-typing in infancy: the role of the father. Infant Mental Health Journal, 2, 226-240
Power, T.G. & Parke, R.D. (1982). Play as a context for early learning: lab and home analysis. In L.M. Laosa & I.E. Sigel (eds) The Family as a Learning Environment. New York: Plenum Press
Price, P. (1984). A study of mother-child verbal interaction strategies with mothers of young developmentally delayed children. In J.M. Berg (ed.) Perspectives and Progress in Mental Retardation, vol.1. Baltimore: University Park

Press. pp.189-199

Price-Bonham, S. & Addison, S. (1978). Families and mentally retarded children: emphasis on the father. _Family Coordinator_, _27_ (3), 221-230

Puckering, C. & Mills, M. (1982). Maternal depression, mutual enjoyment and cognition in two year olds. Paper given to British Psychological Society, London conference, December

Pumroy, D.K. (1966). Maryland Parent Attitude Survey: a research instrument with social desirability controlled. _Journal of Psychology_, _64_, 73-78

Quinton, D., Rutter, M. & Rowlands, O. (1976). An evaluation of an interview assessment of marriage. _Psychological Medicine_, _6_, 577-586

Radin, N. (1973). Observed paternal behaviors as antecedents of intellectual functioning in young boys. _Developmental Psychology_, _8_, 369-376

Radin, N. (1976). The role of the father in cognitive, academic and intellectual development. In M.E. Lamb (ed.) _The Role of the Father in Child Development_. New York: Wiley. pp.237-276

Radin, N. & Russell, G. (1983). Increased father participation and child development outcomes. In M. Lamb and A. Sagi (eds) _Fatherhood and Family Policy_. Hillsdale, New Jersey: Erlbaum Associates (manuscript)

Ramey, C.T., Beckman-Bell, P. & Gowen, J.W. (1980). Infant characteristics and infant-caregiver interactions. In J.J. Gallagher (ed.) _Parents and Families of Handicapped Children_. New Directions for Exceptional Children, 4. San Francisco: Jossey-Bass

Ramey, C.T. & Campbell, F.A. (1984). Preventive education for high-risk children: cognitive consequences of the Carolina Abecedarian Project. _American Journal of Mental Deficiency_, _88_, 515-523

Ramey, C.T., Farran, D.C. & Campbell, F.A. (1979). Predicting IQ from mother-infant interactions. _Child Development_, _50_, 804-814

Ramsey, G.V. (1967). Review of group methods with parents of the mentally retarded. _American Journal of Mental Deficiency_, _71_, 857-863

Rapoport, R., Rapoport, R.N. & Strelitz, Z. (1977). _Fathers, Mothers and Others_. London: Routledge and Kegan Paul

Rayner, H. (1978). The Exeter home-visiting project: the psychologist as one of several therapists. Child: Care, Health and Development, 4 (1), 1-7
Reader, L. (1984). Review: pre-school intervention programmes. Child: Care, Health and Development, 10, 237-251
Rebelsky, F. & Hanks, C. (1971). Father's verbal interaction with infants in the first 3 months of life. Child Development, 42, 63-68
Revill, S. & Blunden, R. (1979). A home training service for pre-school developmentally handicapped children. Behaviour, Research and Therapy, 17, (3), 207-214
Ricci, C.L. (1970). Analysis of child-rearing attitudes of mothers of retarded, emotionally disturbed and normal children. American Journal of Mental Deficiency, 74, 756-761
Richman, N. (1974). The effects of housing on pre-school children and their mothers. Developmental Medicine and Child Neurology, 16, 53-58
Richman, N., Stevenson, J. & Graham, P. (1982). Pre School to School: A Behavioural Study. London: Academic Press
Robinson, C.C. & Filler, J.W. (1971). Maternal teaching style assessment scale. In D.D. Bricker and W.A. Bricker (eds) Toddler Research and Intervention Project Report: Year I. IMRID Behavioral Science Monograph no.20. Nashville: George Peabody College
Roesel, R. & Lawlis, G.F. (1983). Divorce in families of genetically handicapped/mentally retarded individuals. American Journal of Family Therapy, 11 (1), 45-50
Rogers-Warren, A.K., Warren, S.F. & Baer, D.M. (1983). Interactional basis of language learning. In K.T. Kernan, M.J. Begab & R.B. Edgerton (eds) Environments and Behavior. Baltimore: University Park Press. pp.239-266
Roith, A.I. (1963). The myth of parental attitudes. Journal of Mental Subnormality, 9, 51-54
Rondal, J.A. (1977). Maternal speech to normal and Down's syndrome children. In P. Mittler (ed.) Research to Practice in Mental Retardation, Vol. 2: Education and Training. Baltimore: University Park Press
Rondal, J.A. (1980). Fathers' and mothers' speech in early language development. Journal of Child Language, 7, 353-369
Rosenberg, S.A. (1977). Family and parent variables

affecting outcomes of a parent-mediated intervention. Unpublished Ph.D. dissertation, George Peabody College for Teachers, Kansas

Roskies, E. (1972). Abnormality and Normality: The Mothering of Thalidomide Children. Ithaca, New York: Cornell University Press

Ross, A.V. (1964). The Exceptional Child in the Family. New York: Grune and Stratton

Runkel, P.J. & Damrin, D.E. (1961). Effects of training and anxiety upon teachers' preference information about students. Journal of Educational Psychology, 52, 254-261

Russell, G. (1979a). Fathers! Incompetent or reluctant parents? Australia and New Zealand Journal of Sociology, 5 (1), 57-65

Russell, G. (1979b). The changing role of fathers. Paper presented to the Australian Psychology Society conference, Hobart

Russell, G. & Radin, N. (1983). Increased paternal participation: the father's perspective. In M.E. Lamb & A. Sagi (eds) Fatherhood and Family Policy. Hillsdale, New Jersey: Erlbaum Associates (manuscript)

Russell, G. & Russell, A. (1980). Mother-child and father-child relationships in middle childhood. Proposal submitted for research funding, Flinders University and Macquarie University, Australia

Russell, P. (1983). The parents' perspective of family needs and how to meet them. In P. Mittler & H. McConachie (eds) Parents, Professionals and Mentally Handicapped People: Approaches to Partnership. Beckenham: Croom Helm/ Cambridge, MA: Brookline Books. pp.47-61

Russo, J.B. & Owens, R.E. (1982). The development of an objective observation tool for parent-child interaction. Journal of Speech and Hearing Disorders, 47, 165-173

Rutter, M. (1985). Family and school influences on cognitive development. Journal of Child Psychology and Psychiatry, 26 (5), 683-704

Rutter, M., Tizard, J. & Whitmore, K. (1970). Education, Health and Behaviour. London: Longman

Ryle, A. & Breen, D. (1974). Change in the course of social work training: a repertory grid study. British Journal of Medical Psychology, 47, 139-147

Rynders, J.E., Spiker, D. & Horrobin, J.M. (1978). Underestimating the educability of Down syndrome children: examination of methodological problems in recent literature. American Journal of Mental Deficiency, 82, 440-448

Salzburg, C. & Villani, T. (1983). Speech training by parents of Down's syndrome toddlers: generalization across settings and instructional contexts. American Journal of Mental Deficiency, 87, 403-413

Salzinger, K., Feldman, R. & Portnoy, S. (1970). Training parents of brain-injured children in the use of operant conditioning procedures. Behavior Therapy, 1, 4-32

Sameroff, A.J. (1982). The environmental context of developmental disabilities. In D. Bricker (ed.) Handicapped and At Risk Infants: Research and Application. Baltimore: University Park Press

Sameroff, A.J. & Feil, L. (1984). Parental perspectives on development. In I.E. Sigel (ed.) Parental Belief Systems: The Psychological Consequences for Children. Hillsdale, New Jersey: Erlbaum Associates

Sandler, A., Coren, A., & Thurman, S.K. (1983). A training program for parents of handicapped preschool children: effects upon mother, father and child. Exceptional Children, 49 (4), 355-358

Sandler, H., Dokecki, P., Stewart, L., Britton, V. & Horton, D. (1973). The evaluation of a home-based educational program for preschoolers and their mothers. Journal of Community Psychology, 1, 372-375

Sandow, S.A. (1980). Home intervention with the young handicapped child and his family. Unpublished Ph.D. thesis, University of Hull

Sandow, S.A. & Clarke, A.D.B. (1978). Home intervention with parents of severely subnormal, pre-school children: an interim report. Child: Care, Health and Development, 4, 29-39

Sandow, S.A., Clarke, A.D.B., Cox, M.V. & Stewart, F.L. (1981). Home intervention with parents of severely subnormal pre-school children: a final report. Child: Care, Health and Development, 7, 135-144

Sapon, P.J. (1982). A comparison of mother-child and father-child relationships in young children with Down's syndrome. Dissertation Abstracts International, 43 (1-A), 71

Sarason, I.G., Levine, H.M., Basham, R.B. & Sarason, B.R. (1983). Assessing social support: the Social Support Questionnaire. Journal of

Personality and Social Psychology, 44, 127-139

Saunders, C.A., Jordan, R.R. & Kiernan, C.C. (1975). Parent-school collaboration. In C.C. Kiernan & F.P. Woodford (eds) Behaviour Modification with the Severely Retarded. IRMMH Study Group 8. Amsterdam: Associated Scientific Publishers. pp.195-211

Schaefer, E.S. (1982). Family networks and development of adaptive behaviour. In Carolina Institute for Research on Early Education for the Handicapped, Final Report. Chapel Hill: University of North Carolina

Schaefer, E.S., Bell, R.Q. & Bayley, N. (1959). Development of a maternal behavior research instrument. Journal of Genetic Psychology, 95, 83-104

Schaefer, N. (1979). Does She Know She's There?. London: Futura Publications

Schaffer, H.R. (1964). The too-cohesive family - a form of group pathology. International Journal of Social Psychiatry, 10, 266-275

Schaffer, H.R. (ed.) (1977a). Studies in Mother-Infant Interaction. London: Academic Press

Schaffer, H.R. (1977b). Mothering. London: Fontana

Schaffer, H.R. & Crook, C.K. (1980). Child compliance and maternal control techniques. Development Psychology, 16 (1), 54-61

Schaffer, H.R. & Emerson, P.E. (1964). The development of social attachments in infancy. Monographs of the Society for Research in Child Development, 29 (94)

Schilling, R.F., Gilchrist, L.D. & Schinke, S.P. (1984). Coping and social support in families of developmentally disabled children. Family Relations, 33, 47-54

Schludermann, S. & Schludermann, E. (1970). Conceptual frames of parental attitudes of fathers. The Journal of Psychology, 75, 193-204

Schreibman, L., O'Neill, R.E. & Koegel, R.L. (1983). Behavioral training for siblings of autistic children. Journal of Applied Behavior Analysis, 16, 129-138

Schwartz, C.G. (1970). Strategies and tactics of parents of mentally handicapped children. In N.R. Bernstein (ed.) Diminished People. Boston, Massachusetts: Little, Brown and Company. pp.73-105

Sebba, J. (1982). Parent-teaching work: working with parents of profoundly retarded and multiply handicapped children. In S. Beveridge,

R. Flanagan, H. McConachie and J. Sebba, Parental Involvement in Anson House. Anson House Preschool Project Paper 3. Barkingside: Barnardo's. pp.39-44
Sebina, D.B. & Kgosidintsi, A.D. (1981). Disability prevention and rehabilitation in Botswana. Assignment Children (Unicef), 53/54, 135-152
Seligman, M. (1983). Siblings of handicapped persons. In M. Seligman (ed.) The Family with a Handicapped Child. New York: Grune and Stratton. pp.147-174
Seligman, M.E.P. (1975). Helplessness: On Depression, Development and Death. San Francisco: Freeman
Shanas, E. (1973). Family-kin networks and aging in cross-cultural perspective. Journal of Marriage and the Family, 35, 505-511
Shearer, D.E. & Loftin, C.R. (1984). The Portage project: teaching parents to teach their preschool children in the home. In R.F. Dangel & R.A. Polston (eds) Parent Training. New York: Guilford Press
Shearer, D.E. & Shearer, M.S. (1976). The Portage project: a model for early childhood intevention. In T.D. Tjossem (ed.) Intervention Strategies for High Risk Infants and Young Children. Baltimore: University Park Press. pp.335-350
Shearer, M.S. (1976). A home-based training model. In D.E. Shearer (ed.) Portage Project Readings. Wisconsin: Cooperative Educational Service Agency 12
Shoben, E.J. (1949). The assessment of parental attitudes in relation to child adjustment. Genetic Psychology Monographs, 39, 101-148
Shotter, J. (1974). The development of personal powers. In M.P.M. Richards (ed.) The Integration of a Child into a Social World. Cambridge: Cambridge University Press. pp.215-244
Sibisi, Y.T. & Yule, W. (1982). Parent training in a small group: a pilot study. Child: Care, Health and Development, 8, 141-150
Simeonsson, R.J., Cooper, D.H. & Scheiner, A.P. (1982). A review and analysis of the effectiveness of early intervention programmes. Pediatrics, 69, 635-641
Simeonsson, R.J. & McHale, S.M. (1981). Review: research on handicapped children: sibling relationships. Child: Care, Health and Development, 7, 153-171

Siperstein, G.N. & Gottlieb, J. (1980). Parents' and teachers' attitudes toward mildly and severely retarded children. Mental Retardation, 16 (4), 321-322

Skinner, B.F. (1953). Science and Human Behavior. Toronto: Macmillan

Skrtic, T.M., Summers, J.A., Brotherson, M.J. & Turnbull, A.P. (1984). Severely handicapped children and their brothers and sisters. In J. Blacher (ed.) Severely Handicapped Young Children and their Families: Research in Review. New York: Academic Press. pp.215-246

Sloper, P. (1983). Personal communication. (Hester Adrian Research Centre, University of Manchester)

Sloper, P., Cunningham, C.C. & Arnljotsdottir, M. (1983). Parental reactions to early intervention with their Down's syndrome infants. Child: Care, Health and Development, 9 (6), 357-376

Slouth, N.M., Kogan, K.L. & Tyler, N.G. (1978). Derivation of parent norms for the Maryland Parent Attitude Survey: application to parents of developmentally delayed children. Psychological Reports, 42, 183-189

Smith, D.W. & Mullis, R.L. (1984). Analysis of parent-child dyads in verbal interactions. Journal of Genetic Psychology, 144, 293-294

Smith, J., Kushlick, A. & Glossop, C. (1977). The Wessex Portage Project: A Home Teaching Service for Families with a Pre-School Mentally Handicapped Child. Part 1: Report. Winchester: Health Care Evaluation Research Team

Smith, R., Filler, J., Bricker, W., Robinson, C. & Vincent-Smith, L. (1973). Evaluation of teaching style: a comparison of teachers and mothers. In D.D. Bricker & W.A. Bricker (eds) Infant, Toddler and Preschool Research and Intervention Project Report: Year 3. IMRID Behavioral Science Monograph no. 23. Nashville: George Peabody College

Smith, W.W. (1975). Judith: Teaching our Mongol Baby. London: National Society for Mentally Handicapped Children

Snow, M.E., Jacklin, C.N. & Maccoby, E.E. (1983). Sex-of-child differences in father-child interaction at one year of age. Child Development, 54, 227-232

Sommers, R.K., Furlong, A.K., Rhodes, F.E., Fichter, G.R., Bowser, D.C., Copetas, F.G. & Saunders, Z.G. (1964). Effects of maternal attitudes upon improvement in articulation when mothers are trained to assist in speech correction. Journal of Speech and Hearing Disorders, 29, 126-132

Sorce, J.F., Emde, R.N. & Frank, M. (1981). Maternal referencing in normal and Down's syndrome infants: a longitudinal analysis. In R.N. Emde & R.J. Harmon (eds) The Development of Attachment and Affiliative Systems. New York: Plenum Press

Spitz, R.A. (1945). Hospitalism: an inquiry into the genesis of psychiatric conditions in early childhood. Psychoanalytic Study of the Child, 1, 53-74

Staton, R.D. (1972). A comparison and evaluation of selected attitudes of mothers and fathers of mentally retarded children. Dissertation Abstracts International, 32, (12-A), 7106-7107

Stedman, D.J., Anastasiow, N.J., Dokecki, P.R., Gordon, I.J. & Parker, R.K. (1972). How Can Effective Early Intervention Programs Be Delivered to Potentially Retarded Children? ERIC report to U.S. Secretary to the Department of Health, Education and Welfare

Stevenson, J., Graham, P. & Dorner, S. (1978). Parental reactions to the birth of a handicapped child. British Journal of Psychiatry, 132, 105

Steward, M.S. and Steward, D.S. (1973). The observation of Anglo-, Mexican- and Chinese-American mothers teaching their young sons. Child Development, 44, 329-337

Stoneman, Z. & Brody, G.H. (1984). Research with families of severely handicapped children: theoretical and methodological considerations. In J. Blacher (ed.) Severely Handicapped Young Children and Their Families. Orlando, Florida: Academic Press. pp.179-214

Stoneman, Z., Brody, G.H. & Abbott, D. (1983). In-home observations of young Down syndrome children with their mothers and fathers. American Journal of Mental Deficiency, 87, 591-600

Streissguth, A.P. & Bee, H. (1972). Mother-child interactions and cognitive development in children. Young Children, 27, 154-173

Strom, R.D. (1982). The Parent as a Teacher Inventory. Chicago: Scolastic Testing Service Inc

Strom, R.D., Daniels, S., Wurster, S., Rees, R. & Goldman, R. (1984). A comparison of child rearing attitudes of parents of handicapped and non-handicapped children. Journal of Instructional Psychology, 11 (2), 89-103

Strom, R.D., Rees, R., Slaughter, H. & Wurster, S. (1981). Child-rearing expectations of families with atypical children. American Journal of Orthopsychiatry, 51 (2), 285-296

Strom, R.D., Wurster, S. & Rees, R.J. (1983). Parents as teachers of their exceptional children. Journal of Instructional Psychology, 10 (1), 21-39

Suelzle, M. & Keenan, V. (1981). Changes in family support networks over the life cycle of mentally retarded persons. American Journal of Mental Deficiency, 86 (3), 267-274

Tallman, I. (1965). Spousal role differentiation and socialization of severely retarded children. Journal of Marriage and the Family, 27, 37-42

Tavormina, J.B. (1975). The relative effectiveness of behavioral and reflective group counselling with parents of mentally retarded children. Journal of Consulting and Clinical Psychology, 43, 22-31

Tavormina, J.B., Boll, T.J., Dunn, N.J., Luscomb, R.L. & Taylor, J.R. (1981). Psychosocial effects on parents of raising a physically handicapped child. Journal of Abnormal Child Psychology, 9, 121-131

Tavormina, J.B., Hampson, R. & Luscomb, R.L. (1976). Participant evaluations of the effectiveness of their parent counseling groups. Mental Retardation, 14 (6), 8-9

Telford, C. & Sawrey, J. (1977). The Exceptional Child. Englewood Cliffs, New Jersey: Prentice-Hall

Tennant, L. & Hattersley, J. (1977). Working together: a progress report on parents' workshops. Apex, 5, 7-8

Terdal, L. & Buell, J. (1969). Parent-education in managing retarded children with behavior defects and inappropriate behaviors. Mental Retardation, 7, 10-13

Terdal, L., Jackson, R.H. & Garner, A.M. (1976). Mother-child interactions: a comparison between normal and developmentally delayed groups. In E.J. Mash, L.A. Hamerlynk & L.C. Handy (eds) Behavior Modification and Families. New York: Brunner-Mazel. pp.249-264

Tew, B.J. & Laurence, K.M. (1975). Some sources of stress found in mothers of spina bifida children. British Journal of Preventive and Social Medicine, 29, 27-30

Tew, B.J., Laurence, K.M., Payne, H. & Rawnsley, K. (1977). Marital stability following the birth of a child with spina bifida. British Journal of Psychiatry, 131, 79-82

Thoman, E.G., Becker, P.T. & Freese, M.P. (1978) Individual patterns of mother-infant interaction. In G.P. Sackett (ed.) Observing Behavior, vol. 1. Baltimore: University Park Press. pp.95-114

Thomas, A. (1981). Current trends in developmental theory. American Journal of Orthopsychiatry, 51, 580-609

Thomas, A. & Chess, S. (1977). Temperament and Development. New York: Brunner-Mazel

Thorburn, M.J. (1981). In Jamaica, community aides for disabled pre-school schildren. Assignment Children (Unicef), 53/54, 117-134

Thorley, G. & Yule, W. (1982). A role-play test of parent-child interaction. Behavioural Psychotherapy, 10, 146-161

Thurston, J.R. (1959). A procedure for evaluating parental attitudes toward the handicapped. American Journal of Mental Deficiency, 64, 148-155

Tinsley, B.R. & Parke, R.D. (1984). Grandparents as support and socialization agents. In M. Lewis (ed.) Beyond the Dyad. New York: Plenum Press. pp.161-194

Tizard, B. (1984). Parents, teachers and the infant school. Economic and Social Research Council Newsletter, 52 (June), 11-13

Tizard, J. & Grad, J.G. (1961). The Mentally Handicapped and Their Families. Maudsley Monographs, 7. London: Oxford University Press

Townsend, P.W. & Flanagan, J.L. (1976). Experimental preadmission program to encourage home care for severely and profoundly retarded children. American Journal of Mental Deficiency, 80 (5), 562-569

Trevarthen, C. (1981). Clinical significance of distressed and appealing responses of young infants to breakdown in communication. Seminar given to Hester Adrian Research Centre, University of Manchester, February

Trevino, F. (1979). Siblings of handicapped children: identifying those at risk. Social Casework - Journal of Contemporary Social Work, 60 (8), 488-493

Tronick, E., Als, H., Adamson, L., Wise, S. & Brazelton, T.B. (1978). The infant's response to entrapment between contradictory messages in face-to-face interaction. Journal of the American Academy of Child Psychiatrists, 17, 1-13

Turnbull, A.P., Brotherson, M.J. & Summers, J.A. (1982). The family's influence on the development of independence: rationale, design and methodology and conceptual framework. Paper presented at American Association on Mental Deficiency Annual Conference, Boston, June

Turnbull, A.P., Summers, J.A. & Brotherson, M.J. (1983). Working with families with disabled members: a family systems approach. Unpublished manual, University of Kansas

Turnbull, A.P. & Turnbull, H.R. (1982). Parent involvement in the education of handicapped children: a critique. Mental Retardation, 20 (3), 115-122

Turnbull, A.P. & Winton, P.J. (1984). Parent involvement policy and practice: current research and future perspectives. In J. Blacher (ed.) Severely Handicapped Young Children and Their Families: Research in Review. New York: Academic Press

Tyler, N.B., Kogan, K.L. & Turner, P. (1974). Interpersonal components of therapy with young cerebral palsied. American Journal of Occupational Therapy, 28, 395-400

Vadasy, P.F., Fewell, R.R., Meyer, D.J. & Schell, G. (1984). Siblings of handicapped children: a developmental perspective on family interactions. Family Relations, 33, 155-168

Van der Houten, J. (1968). Slant-Eyed Angel. Buckinghamshire: Colin Smythe

Vasquez, A.M. (1974). Race and culture variables in the acceptance-rejection attitudes of parents of mentally retarded children in the lower socioeconomic class. Dissertation Abstracts International, 34, 6774

Vicary, S. (1983). Mothers' construing of their handicapped children: developments over one year. Paper presented at the Annual Conference of Postgraduate Psychology, University of St. Andrews, April

Vicary, S. (1985a) Developments in mothers' construing of their mentally handicapped one-year-olds. In N. Beail (ed.) Repertory Grid Technique and Personal Constructs. Beckenham: Croom Helm/ Cambridge, MA: Brookline Books. pp.351-363

Vicary, S. (1985b). Observations of mothers interacting with their developmentally delayed one-year-olds. In B. Daly, S. Kerfoot, A. Sigston, & J. Addington (eds) Portage: The Importance of Parents. Windsor: NFER-Nelson

Vietze, P.M., Abernathy, S.R., Ashe, M.L. & Faulstitch, G. (1978). Contingent interaction between mothers and their developmentally delayed infants. In G.P. Sackett (ed.) Observing Behavior, vol. 1. Baltimore: University Park Press. pp.115-132

Vietze, P.M. & Anderson, B.J. (1981). Styles of parent-child interaction. In M.J. Begab, H.C. Haywood & H.L. Garber (eds) Psychosocial Influences in Retarded Performance, vol. 1. Baltimore: University Park Press. pp.255-283

Voysey, M. (1975). A Constant Burden. London: Routledge and Kegan Paul

Wachs, T.D. & Gruen, G.E. (1982). Early Experience and Human Development. New York: Plenum Press

Wahl, G., Johnson, S.M., Johansson, S. & Martin, S. (1974). An operant analysis of child-family interaction. Behavior Therapy, 5, 64-78

Waisbren, S.E. (1980). Parents' reactions after the birth of a developmentally disabled child. American Journal of Mental Deficiency, 24, 345-351

Walker, J.A. (1982). Social interactions of handicapped infants. In D. Bricker (ed.) Intervention with At Risk and Handicapped Infants. Baltimore: University Park Press. pp.217-232

Walker, J.A. & Crawley, S.B. (1983). Conceptual and methodological issues in studying the handicapped infant. In S.G. Garwood & R. Fewell (eds) Educating Handicapped Infants: Issues in Development and Intervention. Rockville, Maryland: Aspen Systems Corporation. pp.25-68

Warnock, H.M. (1978). Special Educational Needs. Report of the Committee of Enquiry into the Education of Handicapped Children and Young People. London: HMSO

Wastberg, I.C. (1985). The conditions of life for families with mentally retarded children in the age 11-14. Paper given at 7th IASSMD Congress, New Delhi, March

Watson, L.S. & Bassinger, J.F. (1974). Parent training technology: a potential service delivery system. Mental Retardation, 12 (5), 3-10

Watson, R.L. & Midlarsky, E. (1979). Reactions of mothers with mentally retarded children: a social perspective. Psychological Reports, 45,

309-310
Webster-Stratton, C. (1985). The effects of father-involvement in parent-training for conduct problem children. Journal of Child Psychology and Psychiatry, 26 (5), 801-810
Wedell-Monnig, J. & Lumley, J.M. (1980). Child deafness and mother-child interaction. Child Development, 51, 766-774
Wehman, P., Abramson, M. & Norman, C. (1977). Transfer of training in behavior modification programs: an evaluation review. Journal of Special Education, 11, 217-231
Weinrott, M. (1974). A training program in behavior modification for siblings of the retarded. American Journal of Orthopsychiatry, 44, 362-375
Weist, R. & Kruppe, B. (1977). Parent and sibling comprehension of children's speech. Journal of Psycholinguistic Research, 6, 49-58
Weist, R. & Stebbins, P. (1972). Adult perception of children's speech. Psychonomic Science Journal, 27, 359-360
Weitz, S.E. (1982). A code for assessing teaching skills of parents of developmentally disabled children. Journal of Autism and Developmental Disorders, 12, 13-24
Wetter, J. (1972). Parent attitudes toward learning disability. Exceptional Children, 38, 490-491
White, B.L., Kaban, B.T. & Attanucci, J.S. (1979). The Origins of Human Competence. Lexington: Lexington Books
White, B.L. & Watts, J.C. (1973). Experience and Environment, vol. 1. New York: Prentice-Hall
Whitehurst, G.J., Novak, G.J. & Zorn, G.A. (1972). Delayed speech studied in the home. Developmental Psychology, 7, 169-177
Wikler, L. (1979). A comment on families and mentally retarded children: emphasis on the father. Family Coordinator, 28, 421-424
Wikler, L., Wasow, M. & Hatfield, E. (1981). Chronic sorrow revisited: parent vs. professional depiction of the adjustment of parents of mentally handicapped children. American Journal of Orthopsychiatry, 51, 63-70
Wilkin, D. (1979). Caring for the Mentally Handicapped Child. London: Croom Helm
Wilkinson, L.C., Hiebert, E. & Rembold, K. (1981). Parents' and peers' communication to toddlers. Journal of Speech and Hearing Research, 24, 383-388
Wilks, J. & Wilks, E. (1974). Bernard: Bringing Up

Our Mongol Son. London: Routledge and Kegan Paul
Willems, E.P. (1977). Steps toward an ecobehavioral technology. In A. Rogers-Warren and S.F. Warren (eds) *Ecological Perspectives in Behavior Analysis*. Baltimore: University Park Press. pp.39-61
Wing, L. (1975). Practical counselling for families with severely mentally retarded children living at home. *REAP (Research Exchange and Practice in Mental Retardation)*, *1* (3), 113-127
Winton, P.J. & Turnbull, A.P. (1981). Parent involvement as viewed by parents of preschool handicapped children. *Topics in Early Childhood Special Education*, *1* (3), 11-19
Wishart, M.C., Bidder, R.T. & Gray, O.P. (1980). Parental responses to their developmentally delayed children and the South Glamorgan Home Advisory Service. *Child: Care, Health and Development*, *6*, 361-376
Wishart, M.C., Bidder, R.T. & Gray, O.P. (1981). Parents' report of family life with a developmentally delayed child. *Child: Care, Health and Development*, *7*, 267-279
Wolfendale, S. (1985). Parental involvement in children's development and education: an overview. *Educational and Child Psychology*, *2*, 3-9
Wolfensberger, W. (1967). Counselling the parents of the retarded. In A.A. Baumeister (ed.) *Mental Retardation: Appraisal, Education and Rehabilitation*. London: University of London Press. pp.329-400
Wolfensberger, W. & Kurtz, R.A. (1971). Measurement of parents' perceptions of their children's development. *Genetic Psychology Monographs*, *83*, 3-92
Wolfensberger, W. & Kurtz, R.A. (1974). Use of retardation-related diagnostic and descriptive labels by parents of retarded children. *Journal of Special Education*, *8* (2), 131-142
Woollacott, S., Graham, P. & Stevenson, J. (1978). A controlled evaluation of the therapeutic effectiveness of a psychiatric day centre for pre-school children. *British Journal of Psychiatry*, *132*, 349-355
Worchel, T.L. & Worchel, P. (1961). The parental concept of the mentally retarded child. *American Journal of Mental Deficiency*, *65*, 782-788
Worthington, A. (1982). *Coming to Terms with Mental*

Handicap. Huddersfield: Helena Press
Wright, J.S., Granger, R.D. & Sameroff, A.J. (1984). Parental acceptance and developmental handicap. In J. Blacher (ed.) Severely Handicapped Young Children and Their Families. London: Academic Press. pp.51-90
Yogman, M. (1982). Development of the father-infant relationship. In H. Fitzgerald, B. Lester & M.W. Yogman (eds) Theory and Research in Behavioral Pediatrics, vol. 1. New York: Plenum Press. pp.221-279
Yule, W. (1975). Teaching psychological principles to non-psychologists. Journal of the Association of Educational Psychologists, 10 (3), 1-12
Zegiob, L., Arnold, S. & Forehand, R. (1975). An examination of observer effects in parent-child interactions. Child Development, 46, 509-512
Zegiob, L. & Forehand, R. (1975). Maternal interactive behavior as a function of race, socioeconomic status, and sex of the child. Child Development, 46, 564-568
Zegiob, L. & Forehand, R. (1978). Parent-child interactions: observer effects and social class differences. Behavior Therapy, 9, 118-123
Zifferblatt, S.M., Burton, S.D., Horner, R. & White, T. (1977). Establishing generalization effects among autistic children. Journal of Autism and Childhood Schizophrenia, 7, 337-347
Zunich, M. (1961). A study of relationships between child rearing attitudes and maternal behavior. Journal of Experimental Education, 30, 231-241

INDEX